Praise for *An Arrow's A*

"This is a wonderful account of a nonpareil physician-scientist and, in recent decades, a creator of drug therapies and a lifesci macher. Carl Nathan illuminates his memoir with great storytelling and deeply considered reflections (regularly summed up in pithy 'life lessons') on how his person and his personal journey prepared, and propelled, him. Like Carl, I am a scientist whose asthma and serial pneumonias meant swapping a lot of childhood companionship for finding out young how rewarding adventures of the mind can be. *An Arrow's Arc* belongs on your bookshelf right next to *Surely You're Joking, Mr. Feynman!*"

—**Professor K. Barry Sharpless, PhD, Scripps Research Institute, two-time winner of the Nobel Prize in Chemistry**

"An epic and deeply personal journey by one of the great physician-scientists of our time."

—**Charles M. Rice, PhD, Rockefeller University, winner of the Nobel Prize in Physiology or Medicine**

"An extraordinary window into the life of an amazingly talented physician and wonderfully creative scientist."

—**Stanley B. Prusiner, MD, University of California, San Francisco, winner of the Nobel Prize in Physiology or Medicine**

"Anyone who believes that science and the arts are two non-intersecting worlds needs to read this powerful, deeply moving autobiography of a great physician-scientist. Carl Nathan is a poet as well as a biologist, a duality that is reflected in the lyrical way he presents his life, and life's work. It is one of the best examples I know of the often-overlooked fact that science, like art, is a form of self-expression."

—**Gregory A. Petsko, PhD, Harvard Medical School and Brigham & Women's Hospital, winner of the National Medal of Science**

"A thought-provoking story of the intersection of science, drug discovery, medicine, and humanity. A must read for those contemplating a career in biomedical research or for those seeking insight into the research enterprise. Nathan delivers an insightful appreciation of how discovery is shaped not only by a keen and inquisitive mind but by human experience and interactions."

—Jill O'Donnell-Tormey, PhD, Chief Executive Officer and
    Director of Scientific Affairs, Cancer Research Institute

"In this fascinating and beautifully-told autobiography, a great physician-scientist shares the story of his life. It is honest, emotional, and sometimes brutal, but his poet's sensibility makes it an unforgettable and moving book."

—Laurie H. Glimcher, MD, President and CEO
    of Dana-Farber Cancer Institute

"In this illuminating personal journey, Carl Nathan skillfully navigates the complex path of being both a physician-scientist and a healer, seamlessly merging the realms of clinical care and scientific discovery to benefit individuals and communities alike. Speaking with a calm, confident writer's voice, this world-leading medical researcher delves into the quest for inner harmony and societal contribution through rich anecdotes and invaluable lessons learned. This book is required reading for students of any age who are interested in the intersection of science and the human condition, as well as the broader betterment of humanity and the world."

—Kevin J. Tracey, MD, Feinstein Institutes for Medical
    Research

"An astonishing book, tracing the path of an eminent physician-scientist who is a moral, as well as scientific, force. The writing is beautiful, the structure wonderful—an impressionistic interweaving of stories and themes that mirrors the complexities of a life's journey in its narration, building to a lovely, satisfying whole. Nathan's bravery in self-examination paradoxically lays bare his profound humility and humaneness. Nabokov wrote, 'Beauty plus pity—that is the closest we can get to a definition of art.' Both are present in full measure. And more."

—Chris Karp, MD, Director, Discovery & Translational
    Sciences, Global Health, Bill & Melinda Gates Foundation

"Many of our most important medical breakthroughs are first discovered by specialized doctors known as physician-scientists, who spend years of training working in research laboratories. Sadly, most Americans have never met a physician-scientist or even know what we do daily. Few know about the struggles and hurdles we face to make important scientific discoveries as they apply to human health, a field sometimes known as translational medicine. The work is hard, and the remuneration is often modest. Carl Nathan is a world-class physician-scientist who has helped to pioneer several important treatments for infectious and inflammatory illnesses. He has also trained many others, either directly in his laboratory, or through his founding of an important MD-PhD program in New York City. Dr. Nathan's new book, *An Arrow's Arc*, is essential reading for those wishing to understand the complexities of translational medicine, and because he gives us the human side of what it means to undertake the daunting training required to become a successful physician-scientist."

—Peter Hotez, MD, PhD, Professor and Dean, National School of Tropical Medicine, Baylor College of Medicine

"A writer who makes life worth living. It is humane, original, inspiring, written with moral passion, and highly readable."

—Siamon Gordon, Emeritus Professor of Cellular Pathology, Sir William Dunn School of Pathology, University of Oxford

"*An Arrow's Arc* is a memoir that draws the reader in and continues to engage even after the last page. Carl Nathan shares his personal and professional story behind his remarkable achievements in science, medicine, complex discovery and collaborations, fueled by his love of family and humanity. A gifted writer, he shows us how even the shadows of our lives—loss, otherness, and more—can be woven with inspiration, purpose, and active hope."

—Elizabeth G. Christopherson, President and CEO, Rita Allen Foundation

An Arrow's Arc

An Arrow's Arc

Journey of a
Physician-Scientist

Carl Nathan, MD

PAUL DRY BOOKS
Philadelphia 2024

First Paul Dry Books Edition, 2024

Paul Dry Books, Inc.
Philadelphia, Pennsylvania
www.pauldrybooks.com

Cover image from:
> MacMicking, J. D., R. J. North, R. LaCourse, J. S. Mudgett, S. K. Shah and C. F. Nathan. Identification of nitric oxide synthase as a protective locus against tuberculosis. *Proc. Natl. Acad. Sci. USA*. 94:5243–5248, 1997. PMC24663
> Copyright (1997) National Academy of Sciences, U.S.A.

Printed in the United States of America

Library of Congress Control Number: 2023950715
ISBN: 978-1-58988-185-3

Whatever you do won't be enough . . .
Try anyway.

~ Barack Obama, *The Promised Land* ~

Acknowledgments

To the memories of Dorothy and Paul, and to Andy, Janet, Amy, Eric, Lu, Noah, Mai, Solomon, Nadine, nieces, nephews, grand-nieces, grand-nephews, and those we may yet be waiting for: If there is a greater privilege than to give love that is received with love, I have yet to know it. If there is a greater responsibility than intergenerational love, I have yet to embrace it. To Amy, special thanks for how you love, learn, and lead, and for your important contributions to this book.

My thanks to additional constructive critics and morale boosters Chris Karp, Liza Zapol, Jan Vilcek, editor Julia Sippel, and publisher Paul Dry. Julia's queries and Paul's guidance were invaluable.

Several passages are reprinted, with permission, from "A journey in science: promise, purpose, privilege," *Molecular Medicine*, volume 19, pages 305–319, 2013.

Contents

Preface

IF YOU STAND in one place long enough and still your thoughts, you can see that where you are is a shoreline. Before you is a lake, a reservoir of memory.

Who can resist picking up a small, flat stone and skipping it across the water? Where it lights and how many times before it sinks, you can't control. Do it again, and the stones will always touch down from near to far, but differently every time. There is a thrill as the stones defy gravity, postponing the inevitable, as we ourselves do each day, until we don't.

This is a book of stones' throws. Skipped lines mark jumps in time.

The memories are those from childhood that turned me toward medicine and science, and those from medicine and science that helped shape me in turn. They reflect growing up in the 1950s and '60s amidst demographic shifts, rising income inequality, and social upheaval; being excluded and included; experiencing anti-Semitism even as it seemed to be receding, while recognizing racism as unrelenting; choosing a career and choosing again; failing and adapting; practicing medicine, meeting key figures in the modern history of biomedical science and conducting research; and dealing with illness, grief, and death. I learned that the personal and professional, the inner and the outer, are as interdependent as our molecules, our cells, ourselves, and all living things.

Why has a key part of my journey become the telling of it? What does such a story mean to others? Details aside, what is there to learn that we don't already know? There are questions that are timeless, yet each of us, in our different times, can benefit by asking them—as much from the act as from the answers. I hope my doing so will encourage you to take the plunge.

From my lakeside perspective, these questions seem to rise from the water:

What does seeking acceptance look like? How much does it cost?

There are always options, often ones we haven't chosen. How do we choose among them?

We want to understand ourselves. How can we tell if we do? Can we still help others if we don't?

How do we hide what we do not understand?

What is possible to forgive?

Why does our immune system often let us down? Why is there no immunity from death?

What do we think about death? Why do we pretend we don't?

From what I have learned in medicine and science, I have come to see that we can understand death by understanding the constantly changing interdependence of living things.

And that to understand this is a gift worth sharing.

PART ONE
A Match

A Shove

EARLY IN THE spring of 1977, in the second year of my oncology fellowship at Yale, I received a written invitation from one of my patients. I accepted.

Mrs. C. put a lot into her last party—a lot of makeup to brighten her skin, a lot of morphine to dull her pain, and a lot of money to set bouquets about her New Haven home and freight her dining room table with drinks and delicacies. The guests were her family and long-time friends, together with her new set: her doctors and nurses.

She approached to bring me a glass of wine, put a hand on my chest, and shoved me against the wall. "I hear you've done research. Is that true?" I admitted I had—five summers in high school and college, a year and a bit more in medical school, two years at the National Cancer Institute (part of the National Institutes of Health). "Then promise me that's what you'll do. You doctors worked hard to help me, but you failed, didn't you? You failed a lot of us. Don't just keep doing what you do. Make it better."

I was nearing the end of the fellowship and had been invited to join the Yale faculty as an assistant professor. I had to decide whether to stay or leave. Mrs. C. would die in a few weeks, one of many to do so in my care, each of whom gave me far more than I could give them. Her demand didn't change my path; it made me realize that I had one.

This is the story of traveling one path in two worlds at once—outer and inner.

Where my journey has led in the outer world is an easier story to tell. I turned to biomedical research. What my colleagues and I found has influenced our understanding of disease and our ability to treat it. My work helped lead directly to the approval by the U.S. Food and Drug Administration (FDA) of a new drug, a protein called recombinant interferon-gamma (interferon-γ), for prevention of infection in a disorder called chronic granulomatous disease. I demonstrated the ability of this protein to treat lepromatous leprosy. Using interferon-gamma, I helped cure a patient with South American trypanosomiasis, also called Chagas disease, while others with whom I collaborated were able to show the benefits of using interferon-gamma to treat visceral leishmaniasis. Since those first studies, interferon-gamma has helped hundreds of patients to avoid or recover from infections with difficult-to-control bacteria and fungi.

Efforts are progressing in my lab to advance drugs against enzymes in the bacterium that causes tuberculosis, against an enzyme in the parasite that causes the most severe form of malaria, and against an enzyme that allows the body to attack itself in autoimmune diseases. By supplying basic knowledge, my lab's work indirectly helped others develop a diagnostic test for tuberculosis based on patients' cells' production of interferon-gamma, and helped still others earn FDA approval to treat certain lung diseases with an inhaled gas called nitric oxide. Inhaled nitric oxide is now being explored as a treatment for severe lung infections. Nitric oxide is produced in the body by an enzyme my lab discovered and characterized, called inducible nitric oxide synthase. Clinicians now often monitor the status of patients with asthma by detecting how much exhaled nitric oxide arises from this enzyme in their patients' lungs. Since then, others have found that inducible nitric oxide synthase impairs the immune system's ability to reject cancer cells, and an inhibitor of inducible nitric oxide synthase can help control advanced breast cancer.

I have participated in the development and operation of inter-sector, inter-institutional collaborations, lending support to still others who are developing multiple new drugs for tuberculosis and other infectious diseases. My colleagues and I discovered that Alzheimer's disease, the most common form of dementia, is accompanied by the expression of inducible nitric oxide synthase in neurons in the human brain, and that in mouse models of the disease, the enzyme contributes to disease progression. Working again with mouse models, we discovered that mutations causing frontotemporal dementia, the second most common form of dementia, can lead to an exaggerated inflammatory response in the brain. These two findings helped lead to a new view of neurodegenerative diseases as having a prominent inflammatory component. And so on.

It's the inner story that's harder to tell. In fact, it takes a book. That there is a Glossary at the end of this volume doesn't imply that this a science text. It's an effort to understand and illustrate what can draw a person into biomedical research, and how who they are affects the path they take there.

Death, Medicine, and Immunity: Early Rounds

IN APRIL, 1955, five days before my ninth birthday, my father, mother, older brother, younger sister, and I moved from Teaneck, New Jersey (population 33,772 in 1950), to Pound Ridge, New York (population 1,234 in 1950). The property's five acres included a pond, a hill, a "front" meadow behind the house (mowed several times a season), and a "back" meadow behind that (mowed every other year). Colonial settlers had marked the boundaries with stone walls. That way, they would neither lose their sheep nor break their plows (the rocks they dug from cleared land had to go somewhere). Next door, the neighbors' paddock housed a horse named Uncle Willie. Every evening, Uncle Willie lapped martinis from a bucket when the husband returned from the city and joined his wife and horse for cocktails. From the back meadow, I had access to dozens of acres of marsh, meadow, lake, and forest whose owners were unknown, unseen and uncomplaining.

The hill—elongate, craggy, edged with ledges, wooded—jutted up along one side of the front meadow and extended to the back meadow. That spring, the grassy apron of the hill nearest the house blazed with daffodils. Their trumpets blared; I followed. The hill became my first haunt and the symbol of my new world.

I imagined my life would take an arrow's arc, from the

flower-sprouting front slope high over the challenging rocks and forested crown to the unknown beyond. I wondered where the arrow would go. I pictured its descent not as a decline but as a reception. At the other end would be my older self. Young me would greet old me and ask how I had fared. Old me would supply the understanding of young me that young me lacked.

That first December in Pound Ridge, when I was nine and a half, on a day with no school, the air was as crisp as a Winesap from the neighbor's trees, the sky as blue as topaz. The past night's snowfall, smooth and blinding white, reached my knees each time I punched through the crust. I knew the hill well enough to pick my way down without falling from the ledges. As I high-stepped back toward the house, a sound rose in my chest like a whistling teapot. Breathing got hard, then harder. My chin itched furiously. The teapot gave way to a church organ. Then sound began to fade as my breath grew shallow.

I could walk no further. I lay on my back in the snow, closed my eyes against the sun and felt its warmth lull me while the cold melt beneath me seeped through my coat, pants and gloves.

An idea spread inside me as bright as the light on my face. I can die now. This is real. It will be peaceful.

But I don't have to. Not yet.

I rolled over, stood, staggered to the house. My mother called Dr. Krainin. He came with a glass ampoule of epinephrine and a glass hypodermic syringe with a steel needle. He cracked the ampoule, loaded the syringe, and injected the contents. Relief was almost instant. The asthma organ stopped piping. In the darkened bedroom, my mother's face became the sun.

I met a threat of death at the hands of my own immune system, which confuses cold, dry air for incipient infection. Trying to help, my immune system narrowed my airways and blocked them with microbe-trapping mucus.

And I met medicine—an injection from a bottle of a factory-made compound that mammals evolved the ability to make for themselves and release in the blood so their hearts would race and their airways widen in the face of danger.

Death, medicine, and immunity—round one.

Actually, as my mother told me, that was round two. Round one took place not my first December in Pound Ridge but my first December, when asthma began not from the cold outside our home but with a "cold" virus that damaged my airways, giving a foothold to bacteria, a stereotypical scenario that darkened many Decembers to come. As a blizzard swirled outside, bacteria capable of doubling their number every thirty minutes bred their own blizzard in my lungs, causing pneumonia. By the time the snow was blinding, the pneumonia was life-threatening. My father, whose job was writing materials for fund-raising campaigns for hospitals around the country, was away on one of his trips. Somehow, my mother got me to Columbia Presbyterian Hospital. I was admitted and injected, this time with penicillin. The nurse told my mother that if I had come a year earlier, I would have died. My immune system was not up to the task of saving me, unaided. Bacteria had outgunned it.

Penicillin was developed as a military asset during World War II when the U. S. government engaged chemical companies and academics in the Penicillin Project. By 1946, supplies had become adequate to begin to serve the civilian population.

The Penicillin Project was midwife to the birth of the

modern pharmaceutical industry, the National Institutes of Health, and government support of biomedical research. In later years, I would draw the historical connection between the Penicillin Project and its successor, the Tuberculosis Drug Accelerator, as I fought to resurrect, and also participated in, the development of antibiotics at a time when growing medical need coincided with pharmaceutical industry retreat.[1]

Death and medicine faced off often as I grew up. The immune system sometimes took one side, sometimes the other. With each bout of bronchitis from which I recovered on my own, I had immunity to thank. Each time pneumonia worsened, immunity let me down, and I needed antibiotics to pull me back. With each bout of asthma that made me doubt my ability to take a breath, immunity nearly did me in.

Many people have these experiences. Why did I feel it was my job to try to do something about it? Perhaps the story of "young me" helps answer this.

Going Alone

WHEN WE MOVED to Pound Ridge, my parents said I would stay in touch with my New Jersey friends. I only had two friends. After an awkward visit from one of them, I never saw either again.

Shortly after we moved, our neighbors on the side opposite Uncle Willie planted a long row of white pines on their side of the property line. The soft, pale green trees quickly grew tall and wide, shielding each home year-round from the sight of the other.

A boy my age lived on the other side of the pines. He was already driving a tractor, usually with a long stalk of timothy grass dangling from the corner of his mouth. He mowed our relatively smooth front meadow, his father the bumpier back one. I quickly learned to identify vulnerable young timothy stalks, take hold of the stem beneath the seed head, and slide the succulent shoot from its sheath. Walking about with a stalk between my teeth was a big step up from chewing gum. The boy next door was unimpressed. It took nearly a year before he was willing to speak to a newcomer who did not know how to drive a tractor.

The boy's father, an architect, regarded me with curiosity; his mother, a retired nurse, with compassion. The next spring, she invited me to a sleepover with their son. One Saturday evening he and I pitched a tent on their side of the pines and settled into sleeping bags. In time we let the night sounds worry about themselves. I was wakened at dawn by the three of them, dressed in fine clothes, shoes shined, standing outside the tent. "We're going to Mass," the mother said. "But I'm in pajamas," I said. The father's bushy brows shot up. "It's not for you," he said. Their car was already at the end of the driveway. They got back into it and drove away. I picked up my clothes, sneakers, and sleeping bag, walked barefoot through the cold, wet grass, and slipped through the pines. The boy and I did not play again.

Ten years after moving to Pound Ridge I was at last driving a tractor myself, a climb-up-to-the-seat Allis Chalmers. The summer after junior year at Harvard I mowed smooth lawns and rough meadows on an estate in Chappaqua near Hardscrabble Road. The road's name, once appropriate, must now amuse owners of the local estates. The head groundsman, formerly the overseer of a strawberry farm in Ireland, taught me how to pause the morning's work, retreat to the garage next to his cottage, and drink raw egg in Guinness stout. The fortification, he explained, was necessary before we undertook such labors as reseeding the lawns where the drunken owner was wont to drive his car after heavy rains. Thankfully, the owner and his family rarely stayed there; perhaps they favored one of their other homes. Most of the time, we kept the grounds beautiful, for the pleasure it gave us as much as the pay.

However, the groundsman let the lawns and shrubs go long when he knew the owner was on the way, lest the owner think he could skimp on hired help. On slowdown days we made ways to imitate work. One time, for example, the groundsman conceived the need to inspect a lightning-struck tree from the past night's storm. The tree stood in the woods across the road, not a hundred yards from the house, but the groundsman said we had to take the jeep. This required an excursion of half a mile up the road, through a gap in the stone wall, back through some fields and up to the forest. I drove. He sat on my right making sucking noises with his toothless gums and discoursing on the life of bees, the colors of the eggs of different birds, and the importance of matching cambiums when grafting a fruit tree scion to the stock. We came upon the masterly oak, bark and wood excised in thirty-foot strips straight up its sides, the air pungent with sap. Then off to prune, but just a few nips, where woods and meadows met at the property's edge. "You don't know what a mairn is, lad? A mairn is where your farmer puts up the fence, the dike or hedge as it may be, that marks his land from the adjining." The French cook, with nothing to do in the main house, was out for a walk. She spied us standing together like tethered horses, our pruning tools dangling like tails. "Why you not home with your wife, old man? Too old to keep her happy?" she cackled. At last the light went low and gold and we were done.

Throughout those days, the groundsman's many daughters summered in the pool. When I passed by, they screamed in faux fright over the slippage of the top of one or another's suits.

At summer's end I thought a fitting gift for the caretaker would be a collection of beers from around the world. He unwrapped each bottle with growing disgust, stared at me as if I were mad, popped an unscheduled Guinness, and waved me off.

As a nine- and ten-year-old immigrant to those sparsely populated parts, I had no one to play with save those I imagined. Gangs of us roamed the hill, ambushing, skirmishing, escaping narrowly, and rescuing captives. The side I was on generally came out ahead. Savoring victory, my gang and I congratulated ourselves on our teamwork. At night I recreated these epic contests as stories to help my pony-tailed sister drift to sleep. She loved Uncle Willie and, by extension, all horses, so I changed the good guys of my games into a team of horses led by a stallion named Borneo Jack and the bad guys into rustlers.

In retrospect, I see that my preference for teamwork began with loneliness. Loneliness also gave me wider freedom to have ideas, because there was no one present to dispute their worth (or no one awake enough to do so).

Once my ten-year-old self conquered the hill, the challenge was how to cross the marsh behind the back meadow. This watery expanse featured an archipelago of grassy hummocks, each wide enough to support one foot but too wobbly to support my weight for more than a moment. If I leapt onto one of them and made a quick enough decision where to spring next, I could cross the marsh without sinking up to my knees and filling my shoes with mud. Passage rewarded me with rambling rights around the two small lakes that fed the marsh and our pond, and beyond them, a hillside meadow dotted with cedars. From there, a barely discernible trail led into forest. Marsh-hopping required rapidly sizing up which second choice opened up the best third, fourth, and fifth choices. It was like playing chess without an opponent. Marsh-crossing trained me in what to do with a new idea: quickly leap to its implications and the implications of those implications, or quickly recognize it as a path to shoes filled with mud.

My introduction to the aspect of human nature that fears otherness began that first April with a just-turned-nine-year-old's bus rides to school. The gauntlet began with hoots, smacks, and shoves. My mother incited the mob by sending me off on the first day in a matching tweed jacket and cap. The cap went sailing with a slap that stung the back of my head. Not to be bullied, I put it on again. You can guess what that invited. But the bigger mistake was my own: I sat in an open seat without thinking why it was open. By sitting next to an older (uh-oh) girl (gasp) who was herself being shunned (as I learned later, she had a Czechoslovakian surname; she may even have come from Czechoslovakia), I found that otherness is not just considered a disease; it is a contagious one.

That the slapper was my seatmate brought another lesson: Those stung by disrespect tend to take it out on those lower on the ladder.

School brought more ways to be an "other." My third-grade teacher showed alarm that I knew no long division. Her alarm increased greatly when I could do it as soon as she explained how. A few weeks later she whisked me into a room where a woman I did not recognize began testing me. She placed a piece of paper before me with a large circle drawn on it and said, "Pretend this is a field and you've lost something small and valuable. Draw the path you would take to look for it." I drew a spiral beginning from the outer perimeter. "The distance between the arms of the spiral depends on how far I can see to either side and that depends on how tall the grass is," I said. The stranger's surprise matched that of the teacher. About a month later,

the principal plucked me from class and marched me into
the fourth-grade classroom. Now I was doubly branded an
outsider.

It got worse. At the end of fourth grade, the school gave
me fifth-grade textbooks to read over the summer and
enrolled me that fall in grade six. In this way, the older I
got, the younger I was, relative to my classmates, and the
more I was an outsider.

Other outsiders recognized me as one of them, but that
was not enough to bond. Economic disparity carves lanes
even for kids. At one extreme was Bob. His house had little
paint and no yard. Forest scratched the windows. He lived
with his father, who cut roadside growth in summer and
plowed snow in winter. To hide a stutter, Bob said little. He
offered me grape jelly on white bread. At the other extreme
was Steven. His burdens were an Arabic surname, the tint
of his skin, and his family's display of wealth. Steven's house
had many rooms. In one room, with a door to a fenced yard,
lived his father's cheetah. Steven got a large, raw steak from
the refrigerator, tossed it in the tub in one of the bathrooms,
and led the cheetah in. The proud cat's indifference under-
cut its captor. Grape jelly and white bread, or raw steak.
Despite the offerings, we outsiders stayed in our lanes.

Sixth grade brought my first exposure to science. Mr.
Vulcano leaned against the lime-green cinderblock wall
near the door and dictated to us from a botany book. We
copied down what he said. "Monocotyledons . . ." I understood why he chose to stand for science. Sitting, he would
have fallen into physical as well as mental sleep. It was the
custodian who kept him awake. Seeing the teacher through
the wired glass pane in the classroom door, the custodian
would reach in and pretend to strike a match on Mr. Vulca-

no's head. He did the same thing to children in the hallways, too. The custodian was Indigenous. He was trying to tell us something. It would be years before I began to understand.

The sense of being an outsider by virtue of being younger than my peer group continued into young adulthood when I entered Harvard as a sophomore. I accepted the option of moving from the freshman dorm on Harvard Yard into Lowell House, a residence for upperclassmen (sic), when a room became vacant in a suite shared by three "men" from Choate (the prep school). They were not man enough to shake my offered hand or speak to me, though they were aware of my presence, since they slammed their doors or mine whenever I walked past one of their rooms to or from my own. I suspected another form of "otherness" at work. In 1922, Harvard's President Lowell had called for a quota on Jews, as did other college presidents at the time. Anti-Semitism had abated since then, but at different rates in different quarters, and not at all in some. I moved back to the Yard, relinquished Advanced Standing and declared myself a freshman. I only stopped feeling younger than my peers in 2020, when COVID-19 forced me to look at my video image during Zoom meetings.

Why did my family move from Teaneck, New Jersey, to Pound Ridge, New York? The move created a much longer commute to New York City for my father—half an hour to the railroad station, time to park his car and walk to the train, over an hour onboard, often longer when something broke down. Every second car on the New York, New Haven, and Hartford line at that time was a smoker. Walking through the smokers to find a seat or a spot to stand in a non-smoker left his clothing reeking of cigarettes. On the trip back, the bar car generated extra hazard from the other drivers on the roads for the drive home.

The answer may trace back to the Kiev pogrom of 1905. One of my mother's uncles survived by hiding under a barrel—which the exhausted mob of murderers sat on when they paused to rest. The father of one of my own uncles—the man who married my father's sister—stole a rowboat and set out down the Dnieper, hoping to reach the Black Sea. He found a British freighter and bribed a sailor to hide him until they got to Liverpool. Many days later, a pre-arranged signal on a moonless night let him slip onshore. Morning showed him the wonders of India. In time he became hairdresser to a maharajah. He earned enough to give his son, my Uncle Al, a western education in a school run by nuns. Similar inhospitality from Ukrainians drove my mother's parents to Woodburn, Oregon, a go-to destination for emigres from Ukraine and Russia. The next wave came in 1917, as Russian Orthodox believers fled the Bolsheviks. The ancestors on my father's side left, perhaps fled, Darmstadt, Germany, for Liverpool. I don't know why Liverpool was a destination of choice for ancestors on both sides, but at least one of them got there. From there they reached Berkeley, California.

My parents met at UC Berkeley, married at graduation, and continued their families' tradition of flight, reversing direction and settling in New York City. My arrival as a second child drove them to set up house in Teaneck, New Jersey. We lived one block from the elementary school but only a few blocks from each of three synagogues. For the Jews of Teaneck, my parents weren't Jewish enough. The remedy was an American classic: those who seek to escape the Old Country's continued constraints in the new country go farther out, seeking a place with fewer people. For most Pound Ridge residents, a Jewish-sounding name was too rare for concern. For others, it was too odd for comfort. It took years before I understood that and buried the thought, and years more before I retrieved the buried understanding.

Each reason to feel like an outsider was minor in the scheme of things—being a stranger in a new town at a young age; going from having playmates to having none; being advanced into peer groups progressively older than I; scoring school grades at the top of the charts, to the other students' displeasure; being poor amidst the rich; experiencing anti-Semitism in mild forms amidst reminders of its persistent menace and recurrent ferocity, while also being rejected by Jews for not actively practicing the religion. Eventually I embraced outsiderness itself, brought the attitude with me into medicine and science, and put it to use.

Death and Medicine:
Round and Round

OUR JUNIOR AND SENIOR high school brought together students from four towns. Those from each town were outsiders to the others, so at last my outsider brand made me an insider, and at last I had friends.

One friend's family was particularly welcoming. At my first sleepover at his house, set far back on a winding drive through a meadow, I didn't react when the father and mother signaled their acceptance of me by continuing their custom of parading naked as they prepared for bed and as they rose the next morning. To my relief, my friend, his sister, and I were exempted from the practice, at least while I was there. Having passed the test, I was invited to join the family's summer road trip up Route 1 to Cape Cod. Interstate 95 was not yet open. We shared a long, hot, sunny, dusty drive in a convertible.

Two events brought an end to my friendship with the son. The first was the father's coming to our house to see me himself. My friend seemed not to appreciate that I was an object of his father's attention. The man had close-cropped, early-graying hair and a military bearing, a counterpart to his wife's bended head and soft-spoken gentleness. He insisted on precision from his family but was vague about himself. His job involved long absences, but what he did and where he did it were off-limits. What he was eager to share were his back issues of *Science*. He left me a stack of them. I went through them. At one level, I understood nothing; at another, everything. Science was people in teams who shared ideas and tried to find out if they were right.

The day came for me to host a sleepover with the son. That afternoon he and I made our way to the far side of Uncle Willie's paddock. We scaled a stone wall surrounding a small, grassy cemetery whose occupants dated to the 1800s. Only one monument was taller than I. It marked the grave of Captain Miller. According to the engraving, he had returned victorious from the Mexican-American war. His monument was capped by a large concrete piece shaped like an urn.

Apparently, I found it unsatisfactory to be overshadowed. This turned out to be a lifetime drive and curse, a reaction, perhaps, to having been shunned.

To mount the monument, I wrapped my hands around the urn and pulled. Even in death, Captain Miller was adept at self-defense. The urn tumbled, splitting my scalp, bonging my skull, and dulling my wits. The combination of immobility and bloodshed convinced my friend that I was dead. He fled. Days later his mother learned from mine why he was refusing to speak or eat. When his mother told him I was alive, he recovered his ability to speak, but not to me.

In his flight he had opened a gate rather than leaping the wall. Blinded by blood, I crawled through the opening, into Route 104. The next vehicle to come was a multi-wheeler. The trucker just managed to stop without flattening me. He left his truck and carried me home.

Now it was my turn to visit Dr. Krainin. His office was

a dark suite of rooms above the movie theater in the next town. This time his hypodermic stung my scalp with anesthetic. Then came the buzz of the shaver, the smell of iodine, the tug of sutures. In time the curls returned. As I aged, though, balding emerged not just at the crown, but also on one side. A recent magnetic resonance image of my brain revealed an old hemorrhage on that side as well.

Some lessons here:

1. Not everything you see together is connected.
2. If you want to challenge authority, even of the departed, make sure the facts you wrap your hands around are solid.
3. Do not expect to go through life maintaining whatever symmetry you started with.
4. Memories are not just in the mind. The body bears them, too.

Death and medicine. Round three.

When I was about ten and my brother thirteen and my sister seven, my parents decided we were ready to take care of ourselves while they went to a dinner party. As dusk deepened, we heard a crash. A while later we saw red and blue lights oscillating on the belly of low-hanging clouds toward the west in the direction of Route 104. We walked up the road together to look. At a sharp curve near the crest of the hill we found police cars, an ambulance, a smashed car against a stone wall, slick dark liquid on the road, and near it a body under a blanket whose shape outlined another object near the torso. That, we were told, was the head.

When we got home, I went to the cellar for my Army surplus machete in its olive canvas scabbard. From then on, I kept it under my bed. Good thing I was on the way to graduating from Cub Scouts: "Be prepared."

I was old enough to know that a machete could not protect me from a ghost that had already lost its head, but I was young enough to expect that death in some form would make its way into the bedroom I shared with my brother. I seem to have conveyed that expectation to one of my cats. We had two cats, Mammy, who was innominate for her first year and only earned a name when she gave us kittens, and Nathan, her daughter, named for being born on my father's birthday. Mammy had evidently read Mark Twain's description of a cat in *Puddn'head Wilson* "stretched at full length, asleep and blissful, with her furry belly to the sun and a paw curved over her nose." In contrast, there was no lying-about for Nathan; she was a go-getter. Our yellow-walled bedroom had two adjacent windows with a desk beneath each window, facing each other. We slept with one window open that had no screen. One dawn soon after the car accident, Nathan jumped onto my bed, sat on my chest, and poked my lip with her paw, claws out. I woke to find a gift at her feet—a dead bird. The next day, a mouse. We installed a screen, but it did not keep death from our home.

When I was fourteen I had to replace my brother, who was off to college, in his job helping Mr. Green. Mr. Green had been an advertising executive until amyotrophic lateral sclerosis left him quadriplegic. He lived with his wife in a house up Route 104, beyond the house where the motorist lost his head. I walked past the spot each day. There was no sidewalk. The shoulder was narrow. The roadside foliage was overgrown and laced with poison ivy, to which I was hyper-sensitive. In winter evenings, the trip was dark. Cars climbing the hill behind me unrolled my shadow before me. I hoped the drivers would take the curves more accurately than the man who lost his head. A machete could not protect me. The only thing that could protect me was how other people behaved. These journeys heightened my preference for being in control.

Mr. Green could say little that Mrs. Green or I could make out. That made me Mrs. Green's main option for conversation. How do you get a teen-age boy to listen to you when you have nothing in common to discuss? You feed him. While he chews, your mouth moves, too. Mrs. Green was a proud chef, given to pastas with rich, red sauces.

Once she had fed and regaled me, Mrs. Green would set her husband's tray on a bedside stand. I would move an armchair to abut his bed. Mrs. Green's arms would encircle his legs, mine would reach behind him and under his. On a count of three, we heaved him to the chair. While I read aloud, Dickens mostly, she wielded the spoon; dinner lasted until he rolled his head to avoid it. Then we re-made his bed with a rubber mat, a plastic cover and a sheet, and swung him there. He would call out that he was sliding off; we would reassure him that it wasn't so; he was safe. I'd walk back down the hill as cars' headlights lit up puddles in the road.

Bending over to lift Mr. Green put pressure on my lower back that a full stomach did nothing to relieve. That was likely when the disk between L3 and L4 began to poke out as the interspinal ligament frayed.

Lessons here:

1. There is death around you if you look for it.
2. Machetes and window screens are not the answer. They mean you haven't asked the right question.

3. There is disease around you, too, if you look for it.
4. The sick you help may not get better, but by helping,
   you do, even if it costs you.

What could befall people, it seemed, covered a wide range.
The head might be physically removed from the body, as
demonstrated by the driver on the road past Mr. Green's, or
the body might be functionally disconnected from the head,
as accomplished by Mr. Green's disease. As these reflections
eroded my childhood sense of security, they compounded
the turmoil of trying to fit in with classmates who were
changing as fast as I was.

A stream that fed the marsh behind the back meadow
brought some solace. In tenth grade I wrote,

> I stood on a bridge in frozen weather
> looking to the stream where though
> slowed it still flowed down the center
> of the bed; but more to know
> the edges. There, swirls and eddies,
> all disruptions curled on rocks
> and sticks, all curving crises
> by the banks, were fixed in locks
> of ice, frozen, caught, set,
> transformed from motion into pattern.
> Looking in, I could discern
> my going, coming, being met
> and meeting, the motions I had spent,
> frozen. I went thanking winter.

Years later my intervertebral disk came out further during a squash game at Rockefeller University, and further
still when a frozen pipe burst above my lab. The water iced

a sideways-opening window. I kicked the inward-protruding side of the metal frame to try to swing the window shut. Only after weeks in bed could I walk again. The disk came even further out twenty years after that, when I lifted a kayak from the roof of our sports utility vehicle in Lenox, Massachusetts, where our older son was studying music. My right foot began to flop with every step. I became a noisy walker: slap, pause, slap. I drove home using my left foot.

Back in New York, the orthopedic surgeon I arranged to meet preceded me down a long hallway from a shared waiting room to his office at the end of the corridor. When I caught up with him, before turning around to face me, he said he could make the diagnosis from the sound of my gait—a herniated disk at L3-L4. He promised to show me the offending material in a vial when I awoke from surgery. He did.

The operation was performed on September 3, 2001. I recuperated at home, nineteen miles to the east, up the coast from New York City. I was able to take my first outdoor walk the morning of September 11. From a park on Long Island Sound, my wife Amy and I saw a column of smoke rising on the horizon to the southwest.

Debbie Mardenfeld was the fiancée of my former graduate student, Greg St. John. Debbie and Greg, along with other members of my lab and their partners, had recently been guests at our home. Debbie was on her way to work at American Express just before Amy and I saw the column of smoke. The landing gear of the plane that hit the World Trade Center tower sped down the street at her. It crushed her legs below the knees and sliced her partway up the middle. During Debbie's prolonged hospitalization, her Senator, Hillary Clinton, visited her often. There were no photos or other publicity until Mrs. Clinton attended Debbie and Greg's wedding many months later.

Some healers, like my surgeon and Debbie's doctors, use scalpels, grafts of bone and skin, medications. Some, like Hillary and Greg, use beside visits and honored vows.

Healing takes both.

Death and medicine, round four.

At the end of junior high I began counseling sessions that continued through the first year of high school. I spent the time playing chess with the therapist, Dr. Thurm. He was intent on demonstrating that his patience in waiting for me to speak was greater than my obstinacy in refusing to talk. I was there because obsessive-compulsive disorder had forced me into rituals and restrictions. For example, to protect my family, and in particular to keep my mother alive, I had to say a silent prayer and turn in a circle to the right. I thought I hid these movements or made them look natural, but teachers must have noticed. At the principal's suggestion, I attended a regional counseling center. My parents or older brother would drop me off each Saturday morning and pick me up 45 minutes later.

Two developments finally broke my silence. One was the check I was obliged to hand to Dr. Thurm after each session. I knew my parents had almost no income and I was wasting what little savings were left.

My father had a study where he worked on a big, pale viridian Olympia typewriter that smelled faintly of steel and ribbon ink. When the ribbon wound all the way through, we would economize by flipping the spools and running the ribbon the other way until the type became too faint to read. Near the typewriter sat a huge, single-volume

Merriam-Webster dictionary. I liked to wander through the pages, savoring obscurities and etymologies. One day I came across the pages between "monarch" and "moniker," and there was "money." Also, money. This, it seemed, was the family bank. When no one was around, I kept track of the account. Where there had once been hundreds of dollars there were now rarely more than a couple of tens.

My father had quit his job writing for the hospital fundraising company to make it as a free-lance writer. He placed one piece of fiction, "Manslaughter Eve," in a leading magazine, *The Saturday Evening Post*, but then there was next to nothing.

When I got up at night to go the bathroom, I could hear him typing. He only used two fingers, but he did sixty words a minute and had no time for mistakes. It sounded as if he were at war, defending his family with a machine gun. After his own father died, he became the breadwinner for his mother and two sisters at age 20, supplementing the life insurance money and some stocks. He worked first as a cub reporter for a Berkeley, California, paper, and then as their theater reviewer. Part of those earnings put him through college at Cal. The editor who gave him those chances was named Carl Hoffman. I was named after the man who gave my father the means to support his family, go to college, and meet his future wife.

Acknowledging that help must have meant a great deal to my father, judging from the disapproval with which the choice of my name was met, first by my mother and then by the City of New York. My parents could not agree on a name for me at first, so my birth certificate was incomplete when my mother and I were discharged from Columbia Presbyterian hospital. About a week later a city public health nurse came to the apartment to record the name. She refused to accept "Carl." Germany had surrendered eight months earlier. "Pick an American name!" she said. My father didn't yield, but on her second visit, the nurse did, and I became a legal immigrant.

I was five when I first heard this story. Its significance is that my mother chose to tell it to me when I was of an age to make an inference. She must have meant it as a lesson: Some will see you as an "other." Acceptance, if it comes at all, may be grudging.

Outsiderness intensified toward the end of adolescence. During high school I made four friends. Two were boys from my town; two were from Mt. Kisco, the largest of the four towns that shared the school. Pound Ridge and adjacent Bedford Village had the highest median incomes of the four towns, while Bedford Hills and Mt. Kisco included larger working-class populations. In the spring of junior year, my four friends urged me to run for senior class president. The school required candidates to have grades of 90 or higher in every subject. The eligible pool was small. I agreed. Students from Mt. Kisco rebelled. For too long, they said, class offices went to students from Pound Ridge and Bedford Village. They wanted their own candidate. The only one from Mt. Kisco with the requisite grade point average was one of my four friends. He told me he had no choice. I agreed and encouraged him to enter the race. His campaign caught fire. In fact, his campaigners held night-time rallies at bonfires. They came up with an unbeatable name: Boss Action. As Boss Action's popularity soared, all my friends but one joined the movement. Boss Action won 96% of the votes.

My sympathies lay with Boss Action as well. My town was wealthy, but my family struggled to pay bills. Academic tracking assigned me to classes with students who came mostly from the wealthier towns, but those students excluded me from their social circles. They made me miserable with questions like, "What do you eat for brainfood?" I made them uncomfortable with report cards that branded me an oddball and a threat. Along with pride, top grades brought me anguish—"acid and sawdust," I wrote in my journal.

That spring, I thought the ostracism had ended when a blonde, blue-eyed classmate from Bedford Village who had long ignored me abruptly changed course. We spoke often on the phone, even after my electoral humiliation. I have a vivid memory of one such conversation while I stood under a gloriously flowering tree at the side of the house. Mobile phones did not exist, so what I remember must have been a rehearsal for a phone call or a mental replay of one. I developed a crush; so did she, it seemed. The next fall, we went to the football games together. We hiked the trail in the Mianus River Gorge and sat in its cathedral of 350-year-old hemlocks. We listened to a double concerto, as one bird's trills and another's whoops competed over the aleatory play of rushing water in the river below us. Anticipation rose like the scent from the tawny needle carpet beneath us. When I got home, I wrote:

> Strange dichotomy,
> that we two sitting here splitting sticks
> should converse across a gap two ferns wide;
> I dry-snap twig bits to toss with brown words;
> you sprig-twist green sap-smell

and lean to show me.
Stranger yet,
that an up-tree spiraling wood-bird's
being mate-joined appears to pairs of eyes unpaired;
our mock-scoffs tossed to them go unnoted;
their song sung to the other only
is heard by us.

Back at the school, the magazine *Seventeen* sent two staffers, a man and a woman, to ask for help in preparing a story. The assistant principal called me into his office, along with my three high-grade-average friends. "How many hours a day do you spend thinking about sex?" the woman asked us, a steno pad open on her knee. I don't remember what I said, but it worked for her. She came back a few days later with a photographer to take pictures of me, the girl from the Mianus hike, and some others. The woman pulled the girl's sweater together between her shoulder blades and fastened the fold with a pin, highlighting her breasts. She beamed. We waited eagerly to see the story. A few months later I found the issue at a newsstand. The feature was entitled something like "Average Teens Today—What Do They Look Like and What Are They Thinking?" There were lots of photos of ordinary kids besides us, many homely. None of us spoke of it.

Nonetheless, the following spring, the hemlocks' hint seemed realized; the girl agreed to be my date for the senior prom. The party was planned to last through breakfast. But I had misread the pines; they just told of pining. She left me early in the evening. I didn't know where she was. It turned out she spent the night with the one friend who had stood by me during the election. He woke me at dawn, in tears, to confess. He explained what she had told him. A group of the popular girls had been making collective decisions throughout high school as to which of them would date which boy. After a while, they would decide on a switch. Having run out of other options, they had eventually told the girl that I was her assignment.

From crush to crushed. The ensuing emotional disentanglement took the form of many letters, thankfully unsent. In one I told her,

> Living means growth. Growth means change. Change means risk and losing. June Callwood writes: "The heart of the matter is the development of self-acceptance ... [which] derives ... from the worthiness of an individual's existence: his honesty with himself, his integrity about his responsibilities, his decency toward all forms of life."

Lessons:

1. If you feel the need to give advice, it is likely advice you need.
2. People routinely include you in their experiments without informed consent.

On a recent trip to the Mianus River Gorge, I was struck with the message of any healthy forest: life and death in balance.

My father was 80 years old before he told me about naming me after Carl Hoffman. Growing up, I thought I had been named after Carl Malmberg. Malmberg was a Danish immigrant who shared the hospital fundraising work with my father. When he was working in the New York City office, he would drive each weekend to his farm in New Hampshire to join his wife, Tommy, who tended the goats, the garden, and the orchard that yielded barrels of fermented cider. The summer I was ten, we spent a few vacation days with the Malmbergs. Tommy's vinegary, frugal personality was reflected in her salads and her belief that they constituted lunch and dinner. Carl's jovial independence was reflected in his enjoyment of the cider and his ability to avoid paying town tax on it. His property straddled a town line. He would roll the barrels from one side of his cellar to the other, depending on which town was sending their inspector. Many years later, I attended a Gordon Research Conference in New Hampshire about forty minutes' drive from where the Malmbergs had lived. Carl had long since died. Someone at the town hall knew where Tommy now lived—in a local nursing home. I visited. She did not remember me, or her Carl.

We kids spent the time on the Malmbergs' farm imitating my father by "writing" a play to present. Our stage was a knoll we called Pine Hill. Despite the spicy aroma under the pines and the admiring audience on the lawn below, for me, at least, there was no escape from dread. This was the summer of 1956. That May, the Soviet Union had announced formation of the Warsaw Pact to justify increasing its military presence in countries on its western border; that November, the Soviets would invade Hungary. I must have heard my parents discussing the escalation of the Cold War. I would have understood only that Americans were expecting to exchange nuclear bombs with Russia. In school we practiced responding to a clanging bell by kneeling under our desks and clasping our hands behind our heads. At the

Malmbergs', I woke in the unfamiliar bed to the sight of a brilliant light in the window. I cried out, "The Russians bombed New York!" Thus did a child greet the sun who thought Russians were out to get him and his family.

Early in their marriage, my parents fled the embrace of their families for the excitement of Paris, which they saw as a haven for writers. They planned to pause in New York to accumulate savings for the next phase of the journey. Obstacles arose that put Paris on permanent hold. One was World War II. Another was the birth of their first child, my brother. My father began working as a scout and then assistant play editor for Paramount Pictures, seeking plays that might be turned into movies. Between 1937 and 1948 he filed over 1300 production reports.

New York was not Paris, but there were compensations. My father loved to relate how he and my mother found Gregory Peck one morning sleeping off his drink in their bathtub.

My father also wrote plays of his own. The fall of my second year in Pound Ridge, his *Double in Hearts* took the stage at the John Golden Theater on Broadway. On opening night, he phoned us from the lobby during the first act. He held the phone up and aimed it toward the audience so we could hear the roars of laughter. Walter Kerr, an influential critic for the *Herald Tribune*, was not one of those laughing. As a result, the play closed two weeks later. My father never stopped writing plays. A double-doored cabinet in the basement filled up with drafts.

Lesson for my father: You wanted to write plays, not scout them. Now you've been told that you are an outsider from the world you'd hoped to join.

As I made the weekly trips to counseling, there were new expenses. My brother had been accepted at Harvard. My father wrote to the Harvard scholarship office explaining that his annual income that year was $4,000. I learned the number when I found a copy of the letter in his files after he died. Back then, I was monitoring the worsening situation from the M page in the dictionary, from strained conversations at the dinner table, and finally from the disappearance of conversation.

There was a second reason I finally began to talk to Dr. Thurm. One morning as I waited in the lobby, in walked a classmate, the most popular boy in the school, blond, blue-eyed, handsome, a natural athlete, but a serious cutup. "Brain" and "jock" were stunned to see each other. After that we violated the school's caste system by exchanging barely perceptible nods or narrowing the muscles around the eyes when we passed in the hallways. Seeing him erased my shame at seeing the counselor. I hope seeing me did the same for him.

That day, I told Dr. Thurm that I heard my parents arguing about my father sharing money with his sister in Oakland while my mother struggled to feed us. How she was ashamed to beg Jerry, who had been our barber, to teach her how to give us our haircuts herself. How I was ashamed by the results.

Then I told Dr. Thurm about my English teacher—his faith in me and how I rewarded it. He had encouraged me to submit an essay to a contest organized by the Attorney General of New York State, Louis Lefkowitz. I won. I took my first trip alone on a train. I rode up the majestic Hudson, whose flanking palisades and hills were lined by blazing trees. I reached Albany as the autumn afternoon gave way to early evening. I spent my first-ever night in a hotel, failed to recognize what the red-veloured bellhop was waiting for after he showed me to my room, was given leave by an amused aide the next morning to order both pancakes and strawberries for breakfast, was driven to the capital, and was dubbed "Attorney General for a Day." This meant sitting around until lunchtime, when I got to watch Mr. Lefkowitz gently feed soup to an elderly Assemblyman whose smile was permanent enough to relieve me of any sense of being its object while creating a multi-napkin challenge for the Attorney General. All danger of a career in law or politics was averted.

Other dangers were not averted, as I explained to Dr. Thurm. My English teacher knew that I had spent a summer in a laboratory at NYU School of Medicine. He confided to me that while he himself was not worried, his new wife, a teacher of home economics whom all the students adored, was frightened by his fainting spells. She thought the fainting might be related to his heart murmur. Would I ask the doctor for whom I had worked what he should do?

I made the connection. The teacher saw a cardiologist, then a cardiac surgeon. The next day the teacher pulled me aside and said he had aortic stenosis and was scheduled for valve replacement surgery in two weeks. He was profoundly grateful.

A week later he died. Round five.

I don't know why he treated a young student like a physician who could make a referral. But he did, and I felt it was on me to have done a better job. I knew he downplayed his fainting spells. If I had explained that to the doctor I had worked with, and he explained it to the cardiologist, and the cardiologist told the surgeon, and the surgeon operated immediately, my teacher would have lived.

I told all this to Dr. Thurm, but I was still holding out. There were two things I didn't tell him.

My parents thought a dog would provide companionship for my brother, sister, and me. Zeke, the dog we brought home from a pound, was a mutt with the build of an Airedale, but bigger, about the size of my 11-year-old sister. His idea of the high life was to roam the woods until mealtime, take the entire contents of a jumbo can of dogfood into his mouth with one lunge, and bolt back to the woods. My mother said his manners offended her. More likely, she saw him as adding expense without filling a need. My parents found him a home with a farmer.

We stopped looking for a dog, but a dog did not stop looking for us. Our family sometimes took walks together up the country road after supper. There was neither sidewalk nor shoulder, but automobile traffic was rare. One day, at least a half mile up the road, we passed the house of a woman whose husband had recently died and whose daughters were in college. She had bought a beagle puppy for company. The puppy darted out of her house and tried to follow us. After a few yards of this, we scooped her up and delivered her to the woman's door. A few days later the beagle appeared at our door, no doubt expecting praise for tracking our scent. We returned her again. After a few more cycles, the woman told us she had no intention of chaining the dog and no chance of competing for it, so we might as well keep it. We named the dog Frauncie. Frauncie ate as fast as Zeke but far less, and she said "Please" before and "Thank you" after. Even my mother adored her.

Now I had a friend. We roamed the woods together. I carried a BB gun and followed my imagination; Frauncie carried her ID tags and followed her nose, but always arrived home the same time as I. She also went where I did not. One day she was hit by a car. The vet said her spleen was ruptured, her back was broken, and he had to "put her down." As with the death of my teacher, grief was tinged with guilt. Walked on a leash or chained in the yard, she would be alive.

I could not bring myself to tell Dr. Thurm what it felt like to learn this lesson: Freedom is as risky as loving a being who is free.

Another thing I did not tell Dr. Thurm was that my mother was making visits to Columbia Presbyterian for radiation therapy. I didn't tell him how she and I talked about this: *we didn't.*

Instead, I wrote poems. One I kept to myself:

> From the fireplace
> the quick, soft "wah's"
> of vapor in release
> startle me with memory
> of cat's pads pacing.
> That cat died: tumor.
> Now the fire dies.
> In the farther room
> my father cries.

The other, I left where she could see it. It went like this:

> The world did not call you.
> You came and you shall go.
> It is no mystery, but a simple story

of trees and sky.
You've seen death all your life:
A day is born, and lives, and dies;
And you are born, and live, and you shall die.

I wrote this on the thin, canary-yellow, second-sheet paper my mother and I would later use for letters to each other when I went to college, because it cost less than white paper. She came to my room looking as if she were wrestling with her feelings. She stood in the doorway, tall, beautiful, statuesque, leaning with one shoulder against the frame, as I lay on my bed. After a while, she spoke. "Where did you learn wisdom?"

I shrugged. I couldn't answer, because I hadn't.

But she had, and she did her best to impart it. When I got to college, we could not afford long distance telephone calls, so I typed letters home on the thin yellow paper. Harvard impressed me. I mistook that for my being impressive. Off went my letter. Back came hers. The yellow paper, blank, enclosed a pin. The sight of it popped my swollen ego. She was an even better writer than I had thought. She needed no words at all.

Giving two boys and a girl haircuts on top of running a household was not my mother's idea of taking care of her family; she should be bringing in money by contributing to society. Nor was it enough that she practice puncturing an orange with a pencil to learn how to give me allergy shots. That is what Dr. Boker told her she had to master as we sat in the doctor's office at Columbia Presbyterian, where she had planted multiple skin tests on my forearms and noted which sites rose up in a hive. I was allergic to house dust and

several other antigens (foreign substances). It was assumed
that these caused my asthma, and they often did. It was not
until 1977 that medicine recognized that exercising in cold
air can also trigger asthma in some people. Dr. Boker had
coffee-brown hair and wore wire-rim glasses. Every week
for the next year the mail brought little coffee-brown card-
board boxes whose lids were secured by wire tabs at the
sides. To me they looked like little Dr. Bokers making house
calls. Inside each box was a vial with a rubber septum. My
mother boiled a glass syringe and a stainless-steel needle in
a saucepan, dried them on a dishtowel, assembled the hypodermic, loaded it from the vial and stuck my shoulder.

I know now what the vials contained, and why. Injecting
my shoulder with tiny doses of substances to which I was
allergic was safer than my inhaling them in uncontrolled
amounts. The injections were meant to induce antibodies
against the allergens, antibodies of classes called immunoglobulin G (IgG) and immunoglobulin A (IgA). Antigens
are foreign substances that induce an immune response
against them, such as antibodies. Allergens are antigens
against which the immune response provokes certain reactions that are troublesome to the host, such as wheezing,
hives, rashes, and falling blood pressure. When I inhaled
the offending allergens, these protective IgG and IgA antibodies might find these antigens, bind them, and keep them
from the grasp of antibodies I had already formed that
belonged to a class called immunoglobulin E (IgE). At the
time, IgE antibodies were unknown; Kimishige and Ter-
uko Ishizaka only discovered them in 1966. IgEs are pre-
positioned on immune-defense cells called eosinophils and
mast cells. When my IgEs bound allergens, they would trigger eosinophils and mast cells in my lungs to release mol-

ecules that made my airways constrict and fill with sticky mucus. With extra effort from muscles in my chest wall and diaphragm, I could force air through the narrowed passages, vibrating the stringy secretions—the untuned violins of asthma's hallmark wheeze.

Eosinophils are white blood cells loaded with granules that take up ("like," or *phil*, from the Greek) a dye called eosin. Mast cells are filled with granules with different contents than those in eosinophils. Instead of circulating in the blood, mast cells lie along the tissue side of airways and small blood vessels. When they were discovered by a German scientist, Paul Ehrlich, in 1878, he erroneously thought their function was to feed ("mast") the tissues. There must have been a time in human history or there must be a place where people live where a quick-strike reaction by IgE, eosinophils, and mast cells saves lives. But in my time and place, that squadron of the immune system threatened my life far more than the dusts and danders it tried to keep me from inhaling.

Desensitization immunotherapy was only partly successful. After all, it was not just allergens that triggered my asthma, but also cold, and the immune system cannot make antibodies against the cold. How does cold trigger asthma? In 2021, Ardem Patapounian and David Julius won a Nobel Prize for discovering receptors for temperature and touch. The receptors are proteins that span cell membranes, sensing changes on the outside and propagating signals within.

While I was in college, I described in my journal what these signals did to me: "Walking home, the sky black, the air chill, the street bare except for snow and ice, the trees leafless, the houses with one light behind a drawn shade in the upstairs room, the cars parked end to end without a gap. My boots crunch, ears burn, face stings. To breathe gets hard. First a tiny wheeze, a plaintive woodwind; then bubbling in my lungs, abruptly inelastic; the ribs must force themselves out before air comes in. More wheezes now, a mourning sound; then whining insects, chords, fifths, sevenths. Getting weak. One more step, breathe in, out; step, in, out; step. Home. Settle in a chair. As a ragged breath shakes me, rattle the inhaler like a rag in a terrier's mouth, suspending the drug [isoproterenol, which acts like epinephrine]. Squeeze the air from my chest, hunching, to make room for the medicine; place the tube in my mouth, close my lips around it; press the gas-powered canister down on the pin that opens it; inhale the measured jet of drug. Hold my breath as long as I possibly can—the directions are explicit about that. My heart accelerates; my breastbone shakes. When I think I'm near to blacking out, I exhale slowly through pursed lips. Then comes the metallic taste, unnatural but familiar, the light-headedness, the even more vigorous pounding of my heart, and—like a miracle— sudden unencumbrance of breath. Serenity. I used to think that needing a medihaler was humiliating. I assumed that wheezing was psychosomatic. I wheezed, I thought, when I was weak."

Being her son's immunotherapist was no more the job my mother wanted than being her children's barber. Before she was a mother and a housewife, she had been a social worker. She wanted a job that brought her out of the home while bringing money in.

We needed income. My father produced a long list of ideas for books and applied to a publisher who might front

him an advance for writing them. The publisher said no to
my father but kept his list and got other people to write the
books. That ended my father's dream of self-employment.
He began looking for work in a going business. For a short
while he was a story editor for Disney and then for Dell, but
he quit over what he considered disreputable practices.

Then my father returned to a lesson he'd already learned—
the scientific and health care industries can offer job security. He visited Rockefeller University to interview for a
staff position at the *Journal of Experimental Medicine*. When
that did not pan out, he considered that instead of writing
fund-raising brochures for hospital expansions, he could
write fundraising material for the disease-oriented foundations that were emerging, such as the March of Dimes. It
was the Cystic Fibrosis Research Foundation that best liked
his resume and writing, but they expressed concern with
his lack of scientific background. He came home from that
interview with science review books for seventh, eighth,
ninth, tenth, and eleventh grades. He read them. He got
the job.

Cystic fibrosis results from mutations in a gene that
encodes a protein called an ion channel that spans the
membrane of cells that line the lungs. Normally, this channel transports chloride out of the cells. There, chloride,
matched with a sodium ion, forming what we know as table
salt, attracts water, thinning the mucus that lines the airways to trap the tiny particles we inhale. When airway
mucus has the normal consistency, we bring the mucus up
on an escalator of cilia, little hairs on the mucus-producing
cells lining the airways that move together like synchro-
nized swimmers. When the mucus reaches our mouth, we
can spit it out if we think about it. Mostly, though, we swal-

low it unconsciously. Swallowed mucus dissolves in gastric acid. The acid kills the bacteria in concert with molecules called reactive nitrogen species, about which more later. Without the chloride channel, mucus in the lungs thickens, much as in asthma, but permanently, rather than episodically. Children and young adults with cystic fibrosis struggle to move air in and out of their lungs. Their immune systems struggle to kill bacteria embedded in the mucus. The immune system's ineffectual efforts inflict increasing amounts of collateral damage. Until recently, few cystic fibrosis patients reached middle age.

Dr. Harry Shwachman, chief of the clinical laboratories at Boston's Children's Hospital, was the pre-eminent authority on cystic fibrosis and an important figure in the Foundation. On a drive to New York, he stopped in Pound Ridge and visited our home to welcome my father. Some years later, the Foundation moved to Atlanta. We did not. Our family again needed an income.

While there was money, my mother took classes at the University of Connecticut in Danbury and earned accreditation as a teacher. But what she still dreamed of was what she and my father both dreamed of when they married and headed, they hoped, to Paris—to write. My father's efforts were blocked by the unscrupulous and the indifferent. My mother's were blocked by her womanhood.

My parents concocted a scheme. As an entrée, my father agreed with a publisher that he would write the text for various issues of Classics Illustrated Comics. My mother was the secret author. She did the research, decided what to feature in each panel and wrote the captions and speech balloons. This is how she got to Paris. The study in our house filled up with books on the French Revolution. The chilling cover of the French Revolution comic featured a tumbril carrying a man and woman to the guillotine. It sold.

She was a secret success. It gave my parents what they needed to out themselves to a literary agent, Ms. Jean Ennis, herself a pioneer in the male-dominated world of publishing. Ms. Ennis took up the cause and secured a contract for my mother to write children's books for Random House's Landmark series. By the time my mother was publishing under her own name, she had achieved remission of breast cancer from a treatment so new there were no statistics to suggest how long remission might last. She began with a book of six short biographies, *Women of Courage*, featuring Mary McCloud Bethune, Dorothea Dix, Susan B. Anthony, Jane Addams, Amelia Earhart, and Margaret Mead. That the author was another example was only for her family and friends to know.

The second book she wrote, *The Shy One*, told of her uncle's arrival from Russia and his struggle as an outsider who was older than the classmates he was placed with—the reverse of my experience.

Decades after her death, dozens of fan letters about her books, mostly from eight- or nine-year-olds, continued to find their way to my father. My father replied to all of them. In 1979, a girl named Barbara wrote him back, referring to *The Shy One*: "Dear Mr. Nathan, I've got such good news to tell you! I did a little detective work, and I found the house that your late wife lived in when she was a young girl. . . . As soon as summer begins, and I am out of school, I am going to begin the building of my miniature house." In 1981, Tara wrote, "Maybe you and your family together can write a book about yourselves. It would be interesting to read about a family of writers."

As a writing, fighting woman, my mother attracted dedicated women friends. One was Judith Sulzberger, a physician who later became a philanthropist for medical research. Dr. Sulzberger was the daughter of the publisher of the *New York Times* and later one of the paper's directors. She arranged for my mother's care at Columbia Presbyterian, where she herself had trained. She organized a carpool of women who drove my mother to the treatments when my mother did not feel well enough to drive herself. The experimental treatment offered by the doctor was radiotherapy alone, a radical departure from radical mastectomy, the dominant practice since its introduction in 1894.

My mother wrote a short story, never published, about her trips to the hospital, which was just a few blocks from where we used to live. Here is an excerpt:

> ... Nothing else was as I had known it until, at the far end of the block, I drew abreast of Katz's fish store. There behind his counter, arguing always with a customer, stood my old opponent, Katz ...
>
> ... "An automobile from fifteen years ago don't run like new, either," he was saying, wagging his knife as though it were an extended forefinger. "So why should you expect different?"
>
> The customer shook her neat white head. "There ought to be a pill, a mercy killing. Like they do it for animals ... Each day I eat a little, I live. But what for? So tomorrow maybe I can eat again?" She shrugged her shoulders, infinitely sad. "What's to enjoy?" ...
>
> "Why not start by enjoying today?" I heard myself say. "Look at the marvelous June morning. . . ." I made a

sweeping gesture that took in all the lights and shadows of upper Broadway.

"You mustn't toss life away so easily," I scolded. . . . "I'll tell you why I'm in this neighborhood today, back again in a neighborhood I've hardly seen in twenty years . . . Because I have cancer, that's why."

I could see them recoil from the ugly word.

"Yes, cancer. So I drive myself to the hospital for treatment, every single day. Why? Because I'm fighting for the privilege of staying alive."

My tiny antagonist . . . picked up her parcel and prepared to leave the shop. But as she passed me she stopped to renew the argument . . .

"You don't understand." She sighed. "You talk that way because you are young, young. But I am already seventy-eight. What have I got to look forward to?" . . .

"All right," I said, tacking into the wind. "Supposing I did have a pill, right here in my handbag. Supposing I gave it to you this minute, a pill that would kill you instantly. Would you really, truly, want to put that pill into your mouth?"

She looked at me with those steady, milk-chocolate eyes. "Yesterday my doctor, he's a good doctor, he asked me that selfsame question," she said. "So you know what I answered him? 'Doctor, if I could die here in your chair, right this minute, I would only be glad. I would go saying Thanks, God.'"

We stood there, silent. After a moment the old woman shifted her bundle so she could pat my arm. "Bless you," she said softly. "May you live as long as you want."

"And may you die soon if you wish it," I replied.

Five years later, in April 1966, in my junior year at Harvard, my mother wrote me,

> I am poised to enter the ring for round two in my bout with the enemy: Friday I noticed a spot on my breast. . . . I'll be starting treatment . . . I'd like to do it quietly, without having a community stir about it, for the selfish reason that a business-as-usual basis is my best defense against fear. And that is why I hope you won't telephone home when you get this. I don't want to talk about it, there is nothing more to say, and when people are too nice to me I can't stand it."

I didn't call.

In September, she wrote me that she

> came upon a poem you'd written in April 1961 . . . which started up my current all-too-available waterworks again.
>
> Do you remember it: It begins
>
> The world did not call you;
> You came, and you shall go.
>
> I'm impressed that someone as young as you were (are) could express such a simple, sophisticated philosophy of life and death. It's a view I hold and try to accept, but somehow find hard to do. I can view the death of a day or a leaf with gentle equanimity but for some reason the concept of one's personal dissolution is unacceptable except in the broadest, most general terms.

I did not recognize that this letter revoked her ban on calling. I still did not call.

When I came home for Thanksgiving, I was stunned
to find my mother in bed, taking Dilaudid for broken ribs.
Fifty-three, she looked decades older. Her eyes were wild,
her face gaunt and as gray as her once-chestnut hair. Five-
fluorouracil, she complained, was giving her diarrhea. To
get from bed to the bathroom was excruciating because of
the pain in her ribs and back. "This is no way to live," she
said. She stayed in her room and did not say anything else.

Ignorance and denial can dull one's heartache and wits,
like Dilaudid for emotion and thought. I returned to Harvard numb and dumb.

So it was I could be shocked when my father called me
home about three weeks later, a few days before my planned
return for the Christmas break. By the time I reached the
hospital my mother was unconscious, breathing slowly,
then faster, then stopping for a very long time, then cycling
again. Soon I would learn to call this "Cheyne-Stokes respirations." She woke once, stared in my direction, and said, "I
know what's going on." A short time later she was gone.

Fifty-six years later, I finally opened a box of my mother's
papers that my father had saved after her death and I had
saved after his. Inside was a notebook. After a few ideas
that she mused might make good stories and excerpts from
articles on how to write good fiction, there came a multi-
year gap. When her cancer returned, the notes resumed,
longer, searching. She devoted pages to Montaigne's six-
teenth-century reflections on the naturalness of death.
She pondered the message in lectures she attended at the
American Museum of Natural History, where the biochemist George Wald, one of my Harvard professors, expounded

on the molecules of life and the nature of the universe (he would win a Nobel Prize the following year). Paraphrasing from a *New York Times* interview with an astronomer, she wrote, "We leave out so many real questions. Why is there any matter? Why is there as much as there is & not more or less? How did matter come to be?"

Only from a note written two months before her death did I learn that she had been a patient at Memorial Hospital, across the street from where I have worked for forty-six years: "October 11—1st appearance at Memorial Hospital—I lie on the sofa and sob. Why was I born? On the sunny side of the window a sparrow answers: 'Chirp.'"

Next, just days before she died: "Everything has been said. I am content, all's well, last entry."

Yet there was one entry more.

My mother's last written words were what she remembered of a poem my father wrote before they were married, when her surname was Goldeen:

> High up in a cherry tree
> Who should be but Dorothy G
> Looking for her valentine.
> Come down, Stupid, I'll be thine.
> Hope when you go up again
> It will be as Mrs. N.

The afternoon my mother died, the hospital directed my father, my brother, and me to a local funeral home. When we questioned the exorbitant cost of a casket and internment, the owner's hostility and condescension infuriated us. We opted for cremation.

We went home. I went to bed. The telephone rang. It was for me. Western Union read me a telegram. Dean of Admissions Perry Culver, MD, offered acceptance to Harvard Medical School.

The next morning, I rose early and walked up the road away from the house. The cold felt heavy, a weight pressing the past days' snow against the landscape. As its lid of ice shifted, the lake beyond the meadow groaned with a thunderous crack. I sensed my life split in two. There was a half to leave behind, and a half to choose.

Two motives took shape and began to struggle with each other. I must do something about cancer and other causes of death. Yet I must also understand why death is indispensable to life.

The immune system evolved to prevent DNA that is not ours from replicating within us at our expense. The immune system can tell that DNA differs from ours when it codes for production of a substance that our lymphocytes recognize as foreign—an antigen. Cancer arises because of changes in the DNA of one of our cells. That cell gives rise to many copies of itself, each of which may mutate further, generating potential antigens. Shouldn't the immune system see cancer cells as infection and reject them? Scientists now think that's what the immune system usually does, without our notice. What we recognize clinically as cancer represents a *failure* of immunity—as does any infection serious enough to put us into bed.

Asthma on my back in the snow.

Bacteria in my lungs in a hospital.

A needle-full of allergens in my shoulder.

A walk from my mother's deathbed to a funeral home.

These began as memories to be silenced. With time, they clamored their connection, demanding understanding. Why are we sometimes secure in immunity's protective embrace, sometimes its target, sometimes victim of its limitations?

War Stories

WHEN I WAS about four and out shopping with my mother, we passed a newsstand and saw photographs of piles of bodies at the concentration camps. My mother would not explain.

A boy my age lived in the house behind ours. Most days he crawled through a hole in the fence to play. One day he warned me about sidewalks. "Step on a crack, break your mother's back," he said. I needed to find out what it was about the cracks in sidewalks that threatened my mother so I could protect her from becoming a body in a pile.

When my friend left, I sat on the sidewalk in front of the house with a stick and dug up the ribbon of dirt separating the concrete squares. On the first try, up popped a bright penny, the color of my hair. An old man walking by stopped to watch. "Hi, Red!" he said. "My name's not Red!" I retorted. "Are you looking for treasure?" he laughed. I was furious. I was looking for control. Discarding the penny and ignoring the man, I moved on and dug up all the ribbons between all the squares along the frontage of our property.

The lesson would be reinforced many times: One of the most difficult challenges of inquiry is to judge how often to repeat an experiment that doesn't work.

By junior high I had been relieved of my ignorance about the piles of bodies in the photograph but had not learned how to protect my mother from the threat they conveyed, even as I got the sense that protecting her was my responsibility. Why mine? Was it because, as she later told me, when I was two and a half and she sat on the front porch and opened a telegram and began to weep, I abandoned my toys and climbed to her lap? That's when I learned what a grandfather was, that I had once had two of them, and now there were none. Was it because my father spent years in therapy and struggled with practical matters and physical objects? Because my brother was unburdened by foreboding, and my sister was little?

At five, I gathered in the shrubbery for an anatomy lesson with the boy from the house behind ours and a blonde, gray-eyed girl our age from two doors down. We learned that our bodies were somewhat different, but that had no bearing on the roles we took as we played, running around the yard. To each other we seemed interchangeable, if not one.

Then China invaded South Korea. The girl's father was a pilot. A new war called him. He went. He crashed. He died. The girl and her mother moved away.

I began to play games with toy soldiers. The good guys were called "good guys." The bad guys were called "bad consciences." That's what I thought the word "communists" meant. The Korean War merged into the Cold War. Neither ended. The warring parties continued an experiment that didn't work.

War and its ghosts never stopped invading the peace. In November 1956, Khrushchev said "we will bury you." The newspapers talked of "mutual assured destruction." For a week in October 1962, we were glued to the television each evening, sure that Khrushchev's missiles were about to fly at us from Cuba while President Kennedy threatened to launch missiles against Moscow from Turkey. Cuba was too close to leave time to find a desk for cover. And by then I was old enough to compute the outcome of an encounter between a desk and the incinerating shock wave of a hydrogen bomb.

My concept of what it means to be an "outsider" expanded dramatically in 1963, my senior year in high school. I learned that the discrimination my classmates faced according to their families' means, and that my mother and Jean Ennis faced as women, was just the tip of society's iceberg of cruelty. As I retroactively recognized the real outsider with whom I had shared two earlier grades, guilt grew like a debt bearing compound interest long gone unpaid. Robert was one of the very few Black students in our school. He lived in an outbuilding of a big house in Bedford Village. It was rumored that his uncle was a servant there. He was the best pitcher to try out for the baseball team (I knew, because I was the school paper's sports reporter), but that's as far as he got. He walked the halls head down. He gave a slight smile when I greeted him. But greeting is all I did to include him, and that was more than anyone else. Then he was gone.

Boycotts and marches in Birmingham in the spring of 1963 led to the arrest of Rev. Dr. Martin Luther King, Jr., on Good Friday, April 12. During that incarceration, he wrote his epochal "Letter from Birmingham City Jail." I probably read it in August, when it appeared in *The Atlantic Monthly*. Bull Connor's attacks with fire hoses and dogs on unresisting children and adults peaked on May 3–7. The police backed off on May 10, but on May 11 a bomb went off at the hotel King had just left. On June 11, President Kennedy delivered an address from the Oval Office calling for civil rights legislation. The next day, Medgar Evers was murdered in the driveway at his home. Decades later, my wife would pick up the mantle from my mother, writing books for young readers about the events of that summer and the power of ordinary people to bring change.

In the summer, three of my former high school classmates and I went door to door to collect money for voter registration in the South. I wrote the text for flyers that we passed out and posted. Some homeowners threatened through locked doors to call the police; others opened their doors and wallets. In July, I walked into a factory in lower Manhattan and handed the manager a check for $3000 for a mimeograph press to be shipped to a voter mobilization group in Alabama.

On August 28, 1963, the March on Washington for Jobs and Freedom and Rev. King's "I Have a Dream" speech riveted the country. Eighteen days later, Klansmen Blanton, Cash, Chambliss, and Cherry bombed Birmingham's 16th Street Baptist Church, killing young Addie Mae Collins, Cynthia Wesley, Carole Robertson, and Carole Denise MacNair. The same day, whites murdered two more Black children in Birmingham. A policeman shot 16-year-old Johnny Robinson as the child was waiting for dinner, and a teenager gunned down 13-year-old Virgil Ware as he rode a bike. It was my second week at Harvard.

One afternoon two months later, I looked out of the window of my dorm room in Harvard Yard. The Yard bustled, as usual. Some minutes later, I glanced again. The people were gone, except for a knot around a campus police car, heads bowed toward its open window, presumably listening to its radio. I went out into Harvard Square and joined a crowd reading the ticker over the newsstand kiosk. I learned what I would later see in black and white and then in color: Oswald's rifle had distributed President Kennedy's brain over Jacqueline Bouvier Kennedy's pink Chanel suit.

Returning to the Yard, I saw workmen in the bell tower of Memorial Church. A classmate and I joined people filing into the pews. Distraught, we thought we must get the workmen to ring the bells. We pushed up the aisle, parted the drapes behind the pulpit and passed through the chapel. A side door led to a stairway. As we climbed, we tried each door we reached. One opened into a closet. From there, a vertical ladder rose with iron rungs. This led to a maze of catwalks that crossed what looked like scars where sections of the walls had been stitched together. A steel door opened to another ladder that led to a trapdoor in the belfry floor. We pushed through. There, the great gourd bellowed and boomed as the workmen rang. They had gotten the word. They motioned us back.

We retraced our path. I went out into the Yard. People, silent, stood in groups, facing the steeple.

The workmen tolled the bell. The bell told all. I still hear it. We must all—all toll, all hear.

From these events, a thought took shape. Perhaps much of society's suffering stems from past eons' evolutionary selection for family survival. Perhaps people in recent eras have conflated that drive with struggles for dominance by groups defining themselves or others by religious heritage, political preference, or "race"—a false concept based on surrogates for ancestral geography.

This gave rise to a further thought when I entered the

field of medicine: If competition for resources stamped the biology of human behavior, did competition among species build death into the biology of life itself?

I had a lot to learn before an answer came into focus.

Throughout my childhood, we expected war any minute. We finally found it, but not from Russia. Domestic terrorism by white people against Black people, and by the far right against the rest of us, steeped the country in hate and death, while politicians embraced foreign wars as distractions from domestic failures. The 1963 bombing of the Birmingham Church was the fortieth bombing in Birmingham directed at African Americans—their homes, businesses, and churches. Nine months after Martin Luther King, Jr., stirred our hearts from the Lincoln Memorial, President Johnson fabricated the Gulf of Tonkin incident and ratcheted up a war that ripped open the guts of our stumbling country. One of my Harvard chemistry professors invented napalm. Two days after the Tonkin incident that wasn't, three bodies were unearthed from Mississippi mud—Schwerner, Chaney, Goodwin. On April 4, 1968, a terrorist gunned down King, and two months later, another killed Robert Kennedy. Two months after that, rioters surrounded the Democratic National Convention. When the Chicago Seven went on trial, among them was the father of the resident with whom I was then studying surgery.

Eight months after Chicago, Nixon and Kissinger had an answer for the protestors: they carpet-bombed Cambodia. Sick with grief, I stopped reading newspapers, but the news found me. On the 27th of May, 1970, I got out of bed, ready to report to my surgery rotation with the resident whose

father was on trial, looked out the window, and saw post-
ers on a fence across the way—a girl keening, her mouth an
O, arms outstretched, palms up, a cosmic "Why?", kneeling
by her classmate, prone, gone. Four Kent State students had
died when 29 National Guardsmen let off 67 shots to persuade students to stop protesting the napalming of the vil-
lagers of Vietnam, Cambodia, and Laos.

By 1985, domestic terrorists were no longer confined
to the Klan and other private groups; they operated from
within the military, the elected government, and the tele-
vised press. Lt. Col. Oliver North ran a government within
the government to support Iranian terrorists. Members
of the ruling party protected him from punishment. They
rewarded his treason with fame and lucrative employment
as a political commentator on Fox News. Angry men took
note: terrorism is a sure, cheap route to impact and goes
unpunished.

On April 19, 1995, I was giving a lecture to the Pulmonary Division at Bellevue Hospital. News that made the
audience restless started to filter in. Confusion was followed by gasps of disbelief. Nineteen toddlers and 149 others above the age of six had just perished in the Federal
Building in Oklahoma City at the hands of Army veterans
Timothy McVeigh and Terry Nichols.

On February 6, 1993, Khalid Sheikh Muhammed's basement bomb in the World Trade Center killed six and
injured scores but left the building standing. He took eight
years to take another tack. On September 11, 2001, TV ran
a video loop of people leaping to death before each tower of
the World Trade Center telescoped from edifice to ash. The
CNN commentator, Aaron Brown, was audibly wheezing.
Perhaps stress triggered his asthma. His wheezing wors-

ened in the weeks to come as he tested a new phrase, "the new normal"; soon he was gone from the screen. Having recuperated from my surgery, I resumed commuting to New York on Monday, September 17. My First Avenue bus carried weary World Trade Center volunteers, night-shift guys, on their uptown ride to rest. Their clothes and faces were powdered gray. Their eyes were blank with exhaustion and dismay. The risk of lung disease did not stop them from going back the following day and the next. Some died later from what they breathed. Aaron Brown was not just reporting; his wheeze was forecasting.

Lesson from foreign wars: There is no such thing as a "foreign" war. *War comes home.*

Lesson from our Civil War: *It's not over.* A white flag is often not surrender, but a call to pause.

Lesson for campaigns to make things better: *Most efforts for change fail; they fail and fail, until suddenly, they don't—* or not completely. State-sanctioned slavery ended—but not Jim Crow and economic subjugation. Women vote—yet full parity awaits. Apartheid collapsed—though it can be hard to tell.

Heed this history to scale your expectations to your goals—the worthier your campaign, the likelier it will outlast you. That's no reason not to try.

The same lessons pertain to science as the collective pursuit of understanding. The hurdles are even higher for medicine, when medicine is seen as the collective and equitable application of biological understanding to human well-being.

In the midst of all that, what is the significance of one more personal round of death-meets-medicine? Only that it became my call to war of another sort, a campaign to revive the discovery of antibiotics and preserve the ones we have.

Almost every winter, my asthma worsened, bronchitis set in, and antibiotics became essential. My immune system was failing me in two ways at once—over-reacting to allergens and under-performing against invading bacteria. Thankfully, the antibiotics were still effective. Often, I also needed the anti-inflammatory action of high-dose corticosteroids, though they suppress the body's ability to fight infection. During one such course in the winter of 1995, I rose in the night with fever and nausea, shaking and sweating. Amy had to stay with our two small sons, so she made two calls, one to a car service and the other to a friend who is a doctor at New York Hospital. I brought along a plastic bag and caught my vomit during the ride to the hospital. I made it to a seat in the Emergency Room and waited. When the triage nurse called me over, I said I couldn't get up. She just kept waving for me. I rose and fell. The next thing I knew, I lay on a bed while a young physician stood over me saying "systolic pressure 40" and "come back, stay with us now!" I tried to answer her questions, but my lips, tongue, and brain were each following conductors of different tunes, all of them slow. Then the friend Amy had called arrived. He ordered an intravenous push of vancomycin, a last-resort antibiotic. I spent New Year's Eve in the ICU. Great doctors and nurses used an antibiotic that still worked and pulled me back from septic shock, just as antibiotics rescued me from pneumonia when I was eight months old.

Of those who sink into septic shock, only about half climb back out. Sepsis arises when the immune system, having failed to contain an infection, senses the invader everywhere in the blood and attacks the whole vascular tree. Fluid leaks from the blood into the tissues. In my case, fluid had filled and swelled the sac around my heart. Blood pressure falls; vital organs starve.

Before World War II, doctors and nurses were just as devoted as they are today, but they had no antibiotics. As a consequence, they lost a far higher proportion of their patients. One of them was my father's father, who died in his middle years from something many of us breeze past today: an infected tooth. Right after World War II, penicillin rescued me, but penicillin is rarely used today because bacterial resistance to it is widespread, as it is to most of the antibiotics developed in the post-war boom of the pharmaceutical industry. In January 2022, a study funded by the Bill & Melinda Gates Foundation, the Wellcome Trust, and the government of the United Kingdom estimated that nearly 5 million people died in 2019 with infections caused by bacteria resistant to antibiotics that used to work, and the deaths of 1.27 million could be attributed specifically to the antimicrobial resistance.

In the span of my own lifetime, antibiotics, history's most impactful class of medicines, arrived to rescue us and are on the way to failing us.

Why? We squandered them.

By the time I left the hospital and went back to work, I had learned two things.

1. No need to go on numbering the "rounds." My bouts make a trivial addition to the history of medicine.

2. My own immune system is not the only one that needs help. Most of us have immune systems that fail at times to fend off infectious disease.

That thought became action. What made action possible was my not getting the summer job I sought at age fifteen and getting another instead.

Peace Stories

IN THE SUMMER after ninth grade, to fill the week between gardening for a neighbor on Saturdays, I arranged by mail for a job as a carpenter's assistant building houses. When I showed up on the first day, the foreman, a Ukrainian immigrant, paused his hammering and looked down at me from an unfinished roof. He stared for a moment, shook his head, said, "No," and went back to work.

My parents came up with a backup plan that laid the foundation for my professional life. Their college friend, Lester Grant, had recently opened a lab at New York University Medical School. "I am trying to arrange things," he wrote us, "so that everyone feels he is a part of a project aimed at defining the factors that enter into tissue injury, a vast and important problem in biology of which our work is only a part. This makes doing experiments exciting for everyone and predicting results, often incorrectly, a great deal of fun."

Lester had been orphaned young. His parents left him little but his father's tuberculosis. TB destroyed his knee but steeled his ambition. After years as a newspaperman writing about medicine—he was the medical writer for the New York *Herald Tribune*—he decided to do what he wrote about. He used a prestigious Nieman Fellowship to wangle his way past Harvard Medical School's prohibition on admitting married matriculants with dependents and became one of their oldest graduates. Then, salt-and-pepper-haired, square-jawed, tweed-coated, white-shirted, and bow-tied, he went to Oxford to earn a D. Phil. with Sir Howard Florey. The 1945 Nobel Prize in Physiology or Medicine recognized Florey's work with Chain and Heatley to purify penicillin and demonstrate its medical power. However, Florey's postwar work involved pioneering studies on the role of leukocytes—white blood cells—in inflammation. That became Lester's passion.

That summer—and four more—I commuted to New York City to work as his assistant. The first summer, I used the daily train ride into the city to read Claude Bernard's *An Introduction to the Study of Experimental Medicine*, whose foundational role in medical science I would recognize years later. In the basement where the NYU School of Medicine housed its library, I cracked open the *Journal of Experimental Medicine* to read about discoveries Dr. Grant had got wind of, such as small plastic chambers with two compartments separated by a porous membrane that Stephen Boyden devised to demonstrate leukocyte chemotaxis (directed migration) in vitro.[2] The *Journal of Experimental Medicine* was the first scientific journal I opened for research. Today, I co-chair its editorial board.

The summer before I entered Lester's lab, a friend had given me John Canaday's *Metropolitan Seminars in Art: Great Periods in Painting*. I decided to become an artist. Then my parents showed me a column in the *New York Times* by Canaday, who was the *Times'* art critic. Some of his friends had asked him to advise their own son about his ambition to become an artist. "Do it," Canaday wrote (I'm paraphrasing from memory), "but only if you can't possibly imagine doing anything else." Within a month of working in Lester Grant's lab, I couldn't imagine doing anything else. I was welcomed into a world I hadn't imagined, where doers were thinkers, thinkers were doers, and membership was based on merit. Our team was diverse in ages, colors, and countries of origin. We shared science: a powerful fellowship.

Dr. Grant installed plastic chambers in rabbits' floppy ears. Perhaps he got the idea from Boyden's chambers. The chambers devised by Dr. Grant had a transparent central portion in which an upper plate was slightly elevated above the lower plate. After tissue grew between the two plates, the rabbit was allowed to take its ease on a raised platform near a microscope with its ear draped across the microscope stage. The new tissue was so thin that we could look through the eyepiece and high-powered objective and watch blood cells hurtle through the venules (tiny veins).

Dr. Grant's goal was to understand what causes white blood cells to convert from spheres racing by to amoeboid detectives searching slowly for the source of an injury. He created a tiny injury in the tissue between one venule and another by delivering a small pulse of laser light through the microscope. We would turn away as the laser popped. By the time we swung back and looked through the microscope, white blood cells were crawling on the vessel wall nearest the injury, like bloodhounds tracking a scent. Minutes later, the white cells penetrated the wall of the venule and crawled to the injured site. Evolution has selected for white blood cells to interpret tissue damage as risk of infection and has equipped them with an arsenal of antibacterial weapons, some of which my own lab would later discover.

As described in a seminal book that Dr. Grant and his colleagues Benjamin Zweifach and Robert McCluskey pub-

lished in 1965, *The Inflammatory Process*, what we were wit-
nessing in Dr. Grant's lab is one of the most fundamental
phenomena in medical biology.[3-5] Moreover, inflammation
is the first step in the immune response. To my knowledge,
this was the first study of inflammation using a through-
the-microscope laser and the first to capture images at the
tissue level in a living animal. It opened the way to the
far more sophisticated, computer-assisted approaches used
today by Ronald Germain and others. In 1999, with Lester Grant in mind, I joined John Gallin, Ralph Snyderman,
Douglas Fearon, and Barton Haynes as an editor of a new
book, *Inflammation: Basic Principles and Clinical Correlates*.

In my first summer in Dr. Grant's lab, he said it was
"good to learn science from the bottom up." This was my
introduction to double entendre. Dr. Grant assigned me to
clean the feces-laden trays from the rabbits' cages, wash the
trays and cages, and refill the food baskets.

On my first day, a woman at a desk in a windowless room
gave me a social security card (it was only in the late 1980s
that social security numbers began to be assigned at birth).
A man behind a half-door in the locker room in the basement of the Medical Sciences Building handed me a green
uniform. I changed at my locker, surrounded by Black men
with expressions of effortful indifference or outright surprise. In the animal room, Felix, a gentle Dominican, used
gestures and inflections to train me, as I had no Spanish. He
showed me how to gather supplies at the loading dock and
deliver waste to the incinerator.

One day, as I slung a fifty-pound sack of rabbit chow,
a nub of intestine popped out through a tear in a muscle low in my abdominal wall. In the hospital a few days
later, a male nurse apologetically shaved away my recently

acquired pubic hair to prepare me for surgery. A few hours after the operation, the surgeon came to my room to see me how I was doing.

"It hurts," I said.

"I know, he said. "I got my hernia fixed right after I did yours."

Lesson: man up, nude pubis or no.

The following summer I took notes on index cards in the library and reported to Dr. Grant while he operated, installing the transparent plastic chambers in the rabbits' ears. The lab and its operating room were on the second floor. There, almost everyone I passed was white. Their indifference to my presence was effortless. So simply can a young person be informed where he belongs. The third summer, gowned and gloved, I assisted at surgery.

Dr. Grant's team consisted of one or two medical students, a college student, two high school students, and a technician from Puerto Rico who had been a sergeant in the Army. Dr. Grant treated all the members of his team the same, to the consternation of the medical students. He introduced us to any luminary colleague he could inveigle to give a chalk talk. This is how we met an extraordinary roster of pioneers in immunology, infectious disease, and experimental pathology—William Tillet, H. Sherwood Lawrence, Chandler Stetson, Jonathan Uhr, Robert McCluskey, Baruj Benacerraf, and Lewis Thomas.

H. Sherwood "Jerry" Lawrence, the chief of infectious diseases and immunology at NYU Medical Center, believed that immune responses, including "delayed type hypersensitivity," could be transferred to a new host by injecting a small protein released by lymphocytes (cells found in lymph, lymph nodes, and the blood) from an immunized host (a person or animal that has been injected with or otherwise encountered a foreign substance that induces an immune response). The "transfer factors" he described in 1954 were never conclusively identified. Nonetheless, his work bolstered the idea that lymphocytes are the class of cells in the body responsible for recognizing antigens (foreign substances) and controlling antigen-specific responses. That idea was so controversial that when I studied pathology in medical school in 1969, my textbook stated that "Lymphocytes are small, round cells of unknown function."

In fact, the function of lymphocytes was first demonstrated in 1942 by Merrill Chase, a foundational figure in immunology who worked at Rockefeller University, about thirty blocks north of NYU School of Medicine. Six years earlier, Prof. Chase's wife had developed bacterial pneumonia in her eighth month of pregnancy. Antibiotics were not yet available. She was treated with serum from an animal, most likely a horse, that contained antibodies against the type of bacteria growing in her lungs. She had a hypersensitivity reaction called anaphylaxis and delivered twins prematurely. Both babies died. Chase devoted himself to trying to understand hypersensitivity reactions. Influenced by his colleague René Dubos, Chase turned to the study of tuberculosis. He managed to transfer a delayed-type hypersensitivity immune reaction against tuberculosis from one set of guinea pigs to others. He took lymphocytes from animals that had been immunized with the bacteria that cause tuberculosis, injected the lymphocytes into naïve recipients, challenged the recipients with tuberculosis antigens, and found lymphocytes and other white blood cells accumulating at the injection site. If the donor guinea pigs had not been immunized, no cells accumulated at the injection site in the recipients. He concluded that lymphocytes are the cells responsible for recognizing foreign antigens.

In 1977, when I joined the faculty of Rockefeller, Merrill Chase had just retired. I hired the technician who was the last member of his staff and went to check on Prof. Chase to see if he needed a hand with cleaning out his lab. Eighty years old, he was tottering on a lab bench, trying to reach a box atop a wall-mounted cabinet. I helped him down. He rewarded me with the box, which he had planned to discard. It contained the dissecting glasses, forceps, and metal sieves he had used to make the suspensions of lymphocytes for the historic experiments that launched the field of cellular immunology.

As a Jewish immigrant, Baruj Benacerraf, another colleague of Dr. Grant's who briefed us, had been denied admission to every medical school but one, the Medical College of Virginia, where a personal connection to the head of the college prevailed. Through brother-sister matings, Merrill Chase had developed inbred strains of guinea pigs that did or did not have hypersensitivity reactions to certain antigens. Benacerraf discovered that some strains of inbred guinea pigs could mount an immune response to a given antigen while other strains could not, and this was determined by what he called "immune response genes." His further studies of what came to be called the major histocompatibility complex led to his sharing the Nobel Prize in 1980. A few years after his award, at a symposium at the Institut Pasteur in Paris, Benacerraf was the speaker who immediately preceded me. While there was no one taller mentally, physically he stood only a little higher than the podium. He had bent the microphone down flat before he began to speak. As he left the podium and I approached,

I considered that pulling the microphone back up might seem insensitive, so I left it where it was. Unfortunately, the result was that my voice didn't carry well. I had to bend down to be heard, calling even more attention to the contrast in our heights. One makes many bad decisions. It's striking how the small ones outcompete the big ones for space in one's memory. My embarrassment survives the decades.

Another of our guest speakers in Lester's lab, Lewis Thomas, had been chair of pathology and had pioneered the field that came to be called "experimental pathology." He spoke of his work on inflammation and immune response to infections. He went on to become dean of NYU School of Medicine, dean of Yale Medical School, and president of Memorial Sloan Kettering Cancer Center. He won two National Book Awards, including for *The Lives of a Cell: Notes of a Biology Watcher.* Years later, when I got a letter of acceptance to NYU Medical School signed by the dean, the signature was his. He gave me something else as well— the notion that a physician-scientist could write a book that people from other walks of life might read.

Lesson: Lester Grant taught us that science is solving puzzles through teamwork.

Dr. Grant shared that message in several ways. The workday morning began with an effort to solve the daily *New York Times* crossword puzzle by committee. Drinking coffee from a beaker heated over a Bunsen burner, Dr. Grant sat in an old armchair chair covered in cracked cordovan next to a deep steel sink alternately filled with trays from the rabbit cages or laboratory glassware. The rest of us crowded around on wheeled lab chairs and struggled with the "Downs" and "Acrosses." Another puzzle-solving exercise was to bring his team to Shakespeare in the Park as often as possible. The following day, the research could only begin after we had dissected the plots and characters to his temporary satisfaction, only to re-dissect them at our communal lunch.

We dissected rabbits, too. It was my job to clasp the struggling creatures against my chest while Dr. Grant placed a needle in a vein at the margin of an ear to inject an overdose of Nembutal, a barbiturate. When the necessary tissues had been collected, Dr. Grant would puddle the carcass into a U and drop it into a wax-coated paper bag. It was my job to take the bag to the eighth floor, accessible by a service elevator. White-coated in more ways than one, I rode with men in uniforms of green or gray who carried mops or tools or pushed garbage cans on wheels. They held the door for me to enter, pressed the button for my floor, and, without speaking, asked what brought me there. I said, "dead rabbits." This brought some smiles and jokes, except from one man, who said, unsmiling, "Bring 'em back to life," and said it again, louder. I got out on eight, slid aside a concrete disk on the floor, and dropped the bag into the flames.

The second summer, I was nearly fired. In the cafeteria, Dr. Grant spotted a distinguished colleague, Severo Ochoa. The Spanish Civil War had driven Prof. Ochoa from his lab in Madrid. After his wanderings brought him to NYU, he made fundamental discoveries regarding the synthesis of nucleic acids, for which he had just shared a Nobel Prize. Dr. Grant sat our team down at Prof. Ochoa's table and introduced us. I sat next to Dr. Grant, toying nervously with a mustard packet. Suddenly it broke and sprayed Dr. Grant's face and seersucker suit, narrowly missing his red bow tie. I grabbed napkins from a dispenser and rubbed his face, but the napkins were poorly absorbent and only distributed the vile yellow more widely. Dr. Grant was furious. Dr. Ochoa was not amused. Back in the lab Dr. Grant changed out of his suit into operating room scrubs and told me I had to return the suit, cleaned, by commute-home time the next day or I should not come back. I ran from one cleaner to another before finding one that thought he could save the suit. In my first forays into science, I barely cut the mustard. Today, I chair the board of trustees of the Open Lab Foundation, which supports academic-industrial collaboration for the treatment of tuberculosis, malaria, leishmaniasis, and other infectious diseases at a campus of a major pharmaceutical company, GSK (GlaxoSmithKline), outside Madrid. Their buildings are located on Calle de Severo Ochoa.

In the June of my sophomore year in college I went to a party at the apartment of my brother, who was in graduate school. A slender, ash-blonde Radcliffe student with brown eyes arrived. I offered her the last chair, which was next to mine. My roommate was at the party, too, along with his new girlfriend, whom I hadn't met before. She came up to the two of us seated side by side and pointed to me. "You're going to be a doctor," she said. Then, pointing to the girl seated at my right, she said, "You're going to marry him." I didn't even know the name of the girl in the chair, and I had no idea what I was going to do after graduating with a degree in history. Moreover, the prophetess seemed to think that medical knowledge was pre-installed in anyone destined to practice medicine. She pulled her skirt up to ask me what caused the red spot on her upper thigh. A year later she was hospitalized—not for red spots, but for mental illness.

But she was right. The young woman who took the chair married me. She taught me most of what I know about the world beyond science and medicine. None of that sociological knowledge was pre-installed. My ignorance included a superficial understanding of America's racism, so much more virulent than my brushes with anti-Semitism. My wife was able to teach me about racism because she was already launched on a life-long course of teaching herself, after growing up in segregated Baltimore. Amy began her remedial self-education decades before the murder of George Floyd led much of the country to open its eyes to America's four-hundred-year tradition of domestic terrorism and its hundred-and-fifty-year obliviousness about the post-slavery continuation of domestic terrorism. Amy investigates that history, meets and works with principals, writes books, and teaches teachers, school kids, and me. She did not restrict her search for understanding to discrimination by race but included discrimination by gender as well. She found "women of courage" in the civil rights movement, in the military, and in the arts. She met those women, helped tell their stories, and tells them still.

When my mother died and I accepted the offer from Harvard Medical School, Judy Sulzberger, my mother's friend and a doctor, decided to honor my mother by lending me money for tuition. When I invited Judy to my wedding, which was to take place the month before the start of medical school, she called to tell me that she had made a similar mistake in her own life. Marriage and a medical school education don't mix, she said. One, the other, or both will fail. I should choose medical school, she advised. Marriage could wait. If I insisted on the early wedding, I should not expect the loan.

I chose the wedding.

Amy and I got married in Baltimore in the Presbyterian Church where her father was an Elder. He was an office-based doctor with admitting privileges at Johns Hopkins who still made house calls. When he first heard my name, he raised no objection. When he laid eyes on me, he still raised no objection. On the contrary, he welcomed me in the most meaningful way he knew how: by giving me a copy of Osler's 1892 textbook, *The Principles and Practice of Medicine*. Osler was a saint to the doctors of Johns Hopkins. His book was considered a major milestone in the incorporation of science into medicine, though on reading it, I found it was more a matter of intent raised to the level of commitment: a fitting pre-wedding gift.

My father-in-law was wise and kind. Many of his patients were physicians from whom he would accept no payment. At Christmas they gave him artwork, liquor, and wine. He accepted the bottles graciously and emptied them privately—in the toilet. Others of his patients were poor and paid him not at all. The descendant of mid-1800s German immigrants, Amy's father would not have had any-thing to do with the piles of bodies in the photographs.

Graciously, Judy Sulzberger did extend her loan after all. From Amy's and my shabby walk-up on Worthington Street in Boston, furnished with bricks, boards, and fruit crates from Quincy Market at Faneuil Hall, on the shaky table where we rushed through dinner (often beans and franks) so I could study, I wrote $100 checks every few months to pay Judy back. The money came from Amy's father. At that rate, I figured, repaying the loan would only take eight or nine years. Finally, Judy sent back a check torn in half and asked me to stop embarrassing her. The loan became a gift.

There have been so many gifts, among them a seat in Lester Grant's salon, Judy's financial support, and the failure of Judy's prediction: I emerged with both a medical school education and a marriage of fifty-five years and counting.

There was one girl I felt close to throughout junior high and high school. She was one of the few Jews in my class. In seventh grade we sat side by side in geometry, she to my right. One day, she slipped her left hand into my right front pocket and left it there all the way through rhomboids, a discussion that kept the teacher's face to the blackboard for miraculous minutes. It was a surprisingly warm and powerful declaration of comradeship.

Four years later, in the fall of junior year of high school, when I could drive, the gentle, white-haired geometry teacher invited me to attend a meeting of the Society of Friends. The Quaker meeting house was a small stone building dating to colonial times, now nearly secluded among the orange and yellow leaves of the surrounding maples, hickory, and ash. As we entered, the teacher explained that anyone who wished could speak or respond. Otherwise, we would meditate. The Friends, few and elderly, sat in contemplation on wooden benches in the cool, dim interior. After about half an hour, the teacher stood. He put up his hand and turned it this way and that. He spoke in praise of the miracle of the human hand and the meanings it can convey. Then he sat. After another half hour, the congregation dispersed. I wondered if he had noticed my experience in his classroom four years before and had waited all this time to tell me that he understood.

In August, at the start of my junior year of college, my former geometry classmate—the girl with her hand in my pocket—joined me and two other former high school classmates for an overnight escape to Cape Cod. What is "young"? Young is when you're on the road and you think that finding a place to sleep is of no concern until the night is young no more. Hotels and campsites were full. Only the Cape Cod National Seashore at Provincetown was empty, but for a reason. Each in our own sleeping bag, we were awakened by sharp kicks from heavy boots and bright lights blinding us to our assailants. Park rangers chewed us out and chased us off. As the east began to light the dunes, we saw we had camped in a field of poison ivy.

By the next day, Lester Grant had arranged for my admission to NYU Medical Center in the care of Dr. Rudolf Baer, chairman of the department of dermatology. I have delayed-type hypersensitivity to oils, called urushiol, that come from *Rhus radicans*. Covered with massive, weeping blisters, I received my first course of high-dose, immuno-suppressive corticosteroids. Asthma would bring many more such courses in the years to come.

All my life, my body has been inviting me to understand immunology. Why does my immune system over-react to urushiol and to the allergens that Dr. Boker taught my mother to inject me with? Immunity routinely cures many of my infections. Why does it fail to protect me from others?

When I got home, I found a blue aerogram from Europe. The traveler was the young woman I had met at my brother's party in June. I looked her up when I got back to Cambridge. We married just under two years later.

One bitter winter evening of my first year in medical school, the high school friend I had last seen two years before when we were expelled from the Eden of Provincetown came to Boston to see me and meet Amy at our apartment, as we had arranged. The landlord, who lived below us, let her in. I was studying intensely in the school library. Amy was there too, because the library was heated and our apartment was not. I forgot the time. The library closed at 11 pm. By then, after a long wait, our guest had left. Later she sent a gracious note. She had become a labor organizer for migrant farm workers in California. Her parents had died, the house in Pound Ridge was sold, and she was not likely to come back east again for some time.

A few years later, in her early thirties, she died of breast cancer.

She was another good person with breast cancer I not only failed to help, I failed to support and even failed to say goodbye to, at what proved to be the last opportunity. I had been studying medicine so hard I missed the point.

Choices One

IN THE SPRING of my junior year of high school, the administration invited me to undertake an enrichment project. I could stay home for two months and do whatever I wanted, as long as a teacher would give credit for it and I completed the requirements for the courses I would miss.

At that point I still thought I might become an artist. I had not taken into account the advantage of talent. I was operating under the presumption that one models oneself on one's parents, yet somehow strikes out on one's own. My parents created communicative materials out of their imaginations. I would create something communicative, but it would involve work of the hands.

This idea that visual art involves building something as well as representing something was reinforced by a friend of my parents. Josephine "Lizzi" von Miklos was a Hapsburg baroness with a PhD in fine arts from the University of Vienna who escaped Austro-Hungary between the World Wars. She arrived in the US in 1930 and worked as a designer and photographer, with a stint in a munitions factory during World War II. There had been a husband. She lived with another woman in a house she built herself while living in her car. The house was hidden among trees alongside a brook. Her home was equipped with a bandsaw, a drill press, and other tools she used to make models for her

industrial designs, like the iconic box for Kleenex. When
my sibs and I were toddlers and my father returned from
his work in other cities, as soon as he walked through the
door we would tackle him to the floor and tumble all over
him, relenting only when he opened his suitcase and pulled
out his gift box of Fanny Farmer candy. Lizzi had designed
that box, too. Her swirls of white hair framed flaming red
cheeks and ice-blue eyes. She wore lumberjack shirts and
baggy pants. "Vat are you going to do for money?" she would
press me. "You think your father always can pay for you?"
Her bedroom was set off from the living room by a wall of
shelves in whose hundreds of closely spaced holes stood
glass bottle stoppers, some fashioned into hands, swan's
heads, suns or stars, purple, crimson, clear, pebbled, no two
alike. The corresponding bottles ranged around the living
room on shelves beneath the eaves—spheres, prisms, figu-
rines, canisters, vials, crocks. Below the bottles, the walls
were lined with books, on art—the Cretans, Carolingians,
Aztecs, Merovingians; or religion—the Book of the Dead,
the Vedas, Latin and Germanic writings of the Christian
mystics, Hebraic texts. One wall was devoted to migrations
and mythologies, another to typography and examples of
the craft. One summer, Lizzi took me with her on a tour
of New England towns while she photographed fences; this
turned into her book, *Good Fences Make Good Neighbors*.

In my sophomore year of college, I was browsing a used
book sale in Harvard Yard. There, for ten cents, was a manual of courage—*Training Manual, Royal Flying Corps, Part I*
(May 1914). For example, on page 76, it spelled out what you
can do when you find "All cylinders firing irregularly ..."
Short answer: Not much, but you will climb into the cock-

pit anyway. Another steal, at ten cents, gave advice on how
to cope in the rough. It was the US Army's Philippine-
American War instruction manual for baking bread in a
field kitchen. It advised, "Remove nails and weevils from
the flour while the stones are heating in the pit." Out of that
tome fell a slim book of Lizzi's poetry in German, published
in Vienna when she was twenty-five, with an inscription
on the flyleaf in a small, cramped hand, dated 1942. This
volume gave me a lesson as well—not in courage or how to
cope, but in how the past sends us messages by circuitous
routes. Not seeking those messages is no protection from
receiving them. When I visited Lizzi on Christmas Eve and
she unwrapped my gift, her eyes glistened. She quickly re-
inscribed the book to me in large, looping letters, thrust it
brusquely back and turned away.

When I was in high school, Lizzi inspired me to build
things. I began with a shed to shield the garbage cans from
raccoons. Then I took it up a level for my father's birthday. I
roped my brother and sister into helping me clean the basement and rebuild its workbench. I screwed the lids of jam
jars to the underside of the wooden shelf above the bench.
We sorted the heaps of screws, nails, nuts, and bolts into
separate jars by type and size and hung each jar by twisting
it into its lid. I organized the scraps of lumber and hung wall
racks for the tools. Our efforts gradually revealed the surface of the bench, from which we scoured the grime. When
we led my father downstairs, took off his blindfold and sang
"Happy Birthday," he burst into tears. This was the only
time I saw him cry. (There would come a time when I would
hear his tears in another room.)

The other influence on my choice of project was my art

teacher, Herold Witherspoon, who would later be a guest at my wedding. Witherspoon, as we called him, used a blowtorch to sculpt graceful, soulful animals from blocks of wood: he used heat to find cool. Witherspoon also took devoted care of his wife, who had inflammatory bowel disease.

When I was an intern at Massachusetts General Hospital, I lost two patients with inflammatory bowel disease—a young man during his fifty-sixth admission who had not responded to one drug, and a young woman who had a lethal reaction to another. In inflammatory bowel disease, the immune system treats the bacteria residing in the gut not as house guests but as home invaders. The immune reaction damages the intestinal tract. In another autoimmune disease, rheumatoid arthritis, the immune system acts as if certain joints are infected and nearly destroys them. Scientists have yet to find a living infectious agent in those joints. How can we gain control of such misdirected power?

Witherspoon's artistic influence found fertile ground. Color fascinates me. As a child, I added and subtracted mentally, according to a scale that assigned a different hue to each decade from 0 to 100. I experimented with polarized filters to cadge rainbows from wine glasses and windowpanes. I dreamed of translating choir singing into a moving map of shifting colors. I sought to learn why flames from burning wood flicker red, orange, yellow, green, and blue. An aspiration to make art took root when my father brought home long-playing record albums—Ornette Coleman, John Coltrane, the Modern Jazz Quartet. The harmony between an album's cover and the sounds coming from the disks mesmerized me. I raided my savings to buy oil paints, linseed oil, brushes fine and fat, canvas boards, an easel.

I tried to capture the silhouettes of maples in snow and the viridian of cedars in the meadow beyond the marsh in summer sun. Trees are like music—they yearn, reach, and teach. I also tried to paint them with words.

> Tree's branches bared,
> aspirants to the sky,
> ask me why each limb
> and twig grows only
> to its place in the shape
> of the dome that signifies
> identity.
> When to branch, at what angle,
> how far to grow—
> how does each know?
> If I can't answer this
> (much less touch the crown)
> what makes me the higher species?
> So deftly does a tree cut me down.

Most recently, on turning seventy-five,

> Snow limned
> limbs of beech
> maple ash oak,
> tracery of cedar
> hemlock pine—
> miracle.
> I've seen this
> twenty forty sixty
> nearly eighty times—
> miracle.

My terminal journey down the road of art began when Lizzi von Miklos gave my parents a full set of John Canaday's illustrated series on art history, published by the Metropolitan Museum of Art. I read them all and chose my junior year project: *fresco a secco*.

For the practical side of the project, I built a large wooden frame in our now tidy basement and hung chicken wire in it. I went to the New York Public Library's reading room and took notes from an English translation of an Italian recipe for fresco plaster. It called for a certain grain-size of washed sand, a certain kind of lime, and a certain proportion of goat hair.

I built a sand sieve and a sand box. I bought sand from a local quarry, washed it and sieved it. Lime arrived by truck. As former captain of the local Yankees fan club, I had a connection with a fan whose family kept a goat. I have no idea what they thought of my request, but who can turn down a free haircut for their goat? I held the goat's collar with one hand and tried to use kitchen scissors with the other, but the goat jerked about and I was afraid the scissors might hurt it, so I got astride and trimmed. I got off and scooped the stinky, sticky hair into a paper bag.

I mixed the plaster and applied it. I neglected to consider its weight. The chicken wire bulged out at the bottom. In profile, my wall had the belly of the Guinness-loving overseer on the estate whose grounds I would later mow. No matter. I turned the radio to opera and painted a landscape: the hill behind the house.

At last, Witherspoon made his inspection. "What is it?" he said.

"It's the hill," I said.

"It looks like a large turd," he said.

When my mother died in my senior year of college and my father sold the house, my brother, who had to empty the place, saw that I had constructed the fresco frame bigger than the basement door. He took a sledgehammer from the well-organized rack on the wall.

Lessons:

1. I would have to find a way other than visual art to express what that hill meant to me, or what anything meant.

2. Whatever I would build in the future, I would have to take into account that the world does not stay any one way for long, and neither will what you build.

3. Nothing exists only in itself. Everything is a part of something else, including its surroundings.

4. Written instructions are no match for apprenticeship. Consider the practice of medicine.

5. Look at what the immune system inflicted on the Witherspoons by savaging the wife's gastrointestinal tract. Can we train its power on cancer?

My art career came to its close in college. In my role as managing editor of the *Advocate*, the literary magazine, I was responsible for choosing other people's art for each issue. I picked some from what students submitted and others from Harvard's collections. Albrecht Dürer's Rhinoceros (1515) made my favorite cover, perhaps because it best expressed what I lacked (armor) and what I felt ("back off!").

Failures One

IN JULY, AS a newly minted college graduate in possession of the family's car, I drove from Boston to Baltimore to help plan our wedding. I stopped to visit Ola in Pound Ridge.

Ola, who hailed from Sweden, lived directly across the street from the tiny cemetery that housed Captain Miller's monument.

My first summer in Pound Ridge, when I had just turned nine, I knocked on the door of Ola's trim red house looking for work so I could save money for college. What got me the job was the name that drove away the public health nurse nine years before. Ola had married a man named Carl the day before he shipped out to World War II. Carl died in battle. Ola gave birth. She named her daughter Carla.

My first job was to weed a rectangular plot of land between a hedge and the street, directly across from Captain Miller. I sought to impress. Soon there was nothing living above ground in that space. Ola was shocked. I hadn't known that "weeding" meant making a cultural distinction as to which plants sharing a given space are considered fit to live and which are designated undesirables, even though all had mastered the synthesis of chlorophyll and could capture the light of the sun.

Ola did not give up on me. I graduated to sweeping, then to mowing, and eventually to jack-of-all-trading. In time I met Ola's new husband, who spent most of his time in his city apartment. His cheerful goofiness and New York accent were odd matches for Ola's Swedish reserve and lilt; his age, paunch, and gray-fringed pate a contrast to her youth, trim figure, and golden coils. He worked hard to wash away her sadness with his doting. He used a pin to slice her breakfast banana before she peeled it. He left notes around the house with doggerel rhymes in a childish hand. He slept in one bedroom, she in another, where carved, painted wooden horses and brightly colored crocheted pillows recalled her homeland.

As the years went on, my savings grew. One of Ola's husband's friends, a cruise ship tour leader who gleaned investment tips from travelers, recommended ComSat. Communications satellites were the wave of the future, he told the crowd of gin-and-tonic fired house guests as I trimmed a hedge nearby. He took pity on me and offered to swell my college fund. He helped my parents put my savings into an account at a firm called A. G. Becker with a young broker named Richard Gilder. The stock price fell, my savings disappeared, and we closed the account. Then ComSat rebounded. So did Mr. Gilder, who founded his own firm and became a major philanthropist. For better or worse, this helped shape my attitude toward money. I needed to earn it and spend it but did not understand it well enough to make it reproduce.

There were compensations. Ola became one of my mother's best friends. She took turns in the radiation therapy carpool. They shared books and iced tea on summer afternoons. Ola bought a new car and gave me her old one. I learned to drive. The gift was not for me; it was for me to relieve my mother. No longer did she have to chauffeur me to or from after-school events or friends' homes. I could drive the three miles for the newspapers, the ten miles to the supermarket.

My mother had died in December. I graduated from college the following June. I would begin medical school in September. My fiancée and I were to marry in August. That July, I was driving from Boston to Baltimore to meet my fiancée at her parents' house. I got off the highway at Stamford, Connecticut, and drove to Ola's house for lunch. I was concerned that she had not answered the wedding invitation.

Ola put out a sandwich for me, nothing for herself, and hardly spoke. After the first bite I sensed her stress and left the sandwich on the plate. Ola rose and went to another room. She came back with a package wrapped in brown paper and handed it to me. It was heavy. Inside was an urn. In the urn were my mother's ashes.

His wife gone, his kids in college and graduate school, the silent rooms in his house resounding with memories, my father had fled for a hotel room in the city, where he began looking for an apartment. Knowing he was leaving but not knowing where he was going, he had given the funeral home Ola's address. In his grief, he neglected to tell her. Or me. Or my brother or sister. We each assumed he had a plan. My mother's death highlighted what she was in life: without her, our family fell apart. Without her to plan a commemoration, there was none.

The urn was about the size and shape of the capstone on Captain Miller's tomb across the road. It was not as heavy, but it knocked me just as dumb. This time there was no one to carry me home to my mother. It was my turn to carry my mother home. But now my family did not have rights to any of this earth.

Ola turned her face from me. I took the urn outside. I got a shovel from the tool shed. I walked to the farthest field on Ola's property, the edge of the area I used to mow. I buried the ashes. Then I buried the secret for twenty years. But not the shame.

Soon Ola's husband died. Ola gave me and Amy some of her furniture, sold her house, and moved to Portugal. I saw her once more before she died, at a meeting her daughter arranged in New York. Ola honored our bond by not hiding that she was unforgiving.

One day, long after Ola's death, I returned to the red house and knocked on the door. I said I used to live nearby and keep the grounds. I asked if I could walk around the property for memory's sake. The woman at the door looked concerned but gave her consent. I walked out back and sought the grave. The property had been parceled. The gravesite lay beyond a fence. A house stood there now.

As much of this was written, COVID-19 slowed the rush of my professional life, though I continued to work hard, often to the point of exhaustion. Three hours per day were no longer devoted to commuting, two to three days a month no longer spent on travel. SARS-CoV-2 magnified and vivified the possibilities of imminent illness, prolonged incapacity, or death in isolation. Reflection became possible and advisable in equal measure.

Turning over a heavy stone, I see how my fear of a circular firing squad was unnecessary, for my family was too loving to pull triggers.

My mother had had Cheyne-Stokes respirations in the

hospital because she was being injected with large doses of morphine. My father revealed this as we walked from the hospital to the funeral home. My mother had persuaded a doctor to end her suffering at a time of her choosing. Assisted suicide was illegal. Amy has suggested that fear of repercussions for the doctor may be what deterred my father from holding a ceremony where people would gather and talk. For the date of her death, my mother chose the holiday break of her children's college and graduate school terms so as not to interrupt their studies or their mid-term exams. This was in character—loving, thoughtful, protective of our prospects.

I should have been grateful. Instead, I was angry that she denied us the chance to say goodbye. More fundamentally and irrationally, I was angry at my mother for abandoning her family. Perhaps I was angry that she abandoned me before I had the chance to abandon her, in the small but meaningful ways that children do as they establish independence. I was angry at my father's complicity. Now I was furious with him for ignoring her remains, though also concerned about whether he could survive the collapse of his world.

There was another person I was even angrier at: me. I could have phoned, or come, when my mother revealed her cancer had recurred.

When Ola handed me the urn, I could have kept it. I could have contacted my father, brother, and sister, and we could have decided together what to do.

Why did I respond to the urn as I did? I felt horror at handling my mother's remains. I grew dizzy. My mouth went dry. I heard and felt my heartbeat in my ears. If I revealed the urn to my family, it would indict my father at his lowest, most vulnerable moment, just seven months after her death, turning my brother, my sister, and my parents' friends against him, as it had turned Ola against all of us. If I put the urn in the trunk of the car, it would follow me to my future wife's parents' house where we planned our wedding—a wedding that some said was indecently soon after my mother's death, a wedding to a woman my mother had met only twice and of whom she said she was not yet ready to approve.

Twenty years after my mother's death, my father, brother, sister, and our families gathered to commemorate her. They learned how I buried her urn, heard my burden and dispelled it. The time had come for the living to forgive the dead, the dead the living, the living each other and themselves.

If faith is believing what cannot be proved, I have faith that had my mother and wife had the chance to know each other, they each would have seen in other a "woman of courage" and heartily approved.

More years later, when my father died, the ceremony my brother, sister, wife, sons, and I organized was well attended. The photographs, music, and loving talks by friends, family, and caregivers commemorated my mother as well. A few months after my father's death, the family gathered again to set his ashes free in the Hudson River. They coursed by the island he loved, then headed toward Paris at last.

Choices Two

WHEN I WAS growing up, my father told me why our family moved from Teaneck to Pound Ridge: he and my mother felt oppressed by the insistence of the Jewish community of Teaneck that they join it. While we were in Teaneck, even unrelated members of the Russian émigré Jewish community of Brooklyn expected our attendance at Passover Seders. One of my earliest memories is of a heavyset man with a thick accent growing increasingly angry at me as I stood baffled by his order, "Go! Go find the afikomen!" My parents had fled California for a similar reason—to escape pressure to stay within their families' immigrant groups.

My parents did not talk about their parents. They shielded me from mention of pogroms and the holocaust. Their protectiveness may have encouraged my tendency to suppress whatever might set me apart.

In junior high, one classmate liked to say, "Hey, lend me lunch money." The first time, I did, but the mistake was asking him for it back a few days later. "What a Jew!" he said, laughing and shoving. "Hey, lend me money!" was his standard greeting long after there were no replies.

My mother invited the new Latin teacher, a recent immigrant, to dinner. Someone asked about her family. "They are all dead," she said. Someone asked her to pass a dish. Her gaunt arm poked out from the sleeve of her blouse, revealing a tattooed number. There were dark half-moons beneath her eyes. An upside-down half-moon formed the curve of her mouth. In the classroom she jumped instead of laughing at students' pranks. When a student asked her, "Who cares about Latin, since it's dead?" she answered only with tears. Soon she was gone.

Recently, when my haircutter, trying to cope with my mop's unruliness, asked, "Are you Jewish?" I said, "No." I meant it; I did not answer that way because she was Polish and holding scissors. Much earlier, around 1980, while I was working at Rockefeller University, I collaborated with an elderly scientist in Switzerland. This was long before email or Facetime; we communicated by letter. He decided to visit. He arrived in my lab late in the afternoon, excited to meet. He handed me a wrapped gift. It was a long-playing record of Klezmer music. My face fell. "You have no idea how hard this is to find in Switzerland," he pleaded, searching for gratitude. And yet, one day years later when I walked past the Kabbalah Centre on East 48th Street and a man dashed out in front of me saying, "Are you Jewish?" I said, "Yes." He took me by the arm and pulled me inside. A few men were praying. I was on the way to work and he no longer had anything to say to me, so I turned to leave. "You can't go! We need a minyan!" the man shouted. "You can't tell me what to do," I said, walking out. He shouted after me, "Go to hell! You're no Jew!"

I bridle if I'm told what to think or how to pray, but I embrace a heritage—humility before the immensity of creation, love of learning, an aspiration to live ethically and help others. My parents did not forsake their heritage when they fled the constraints of an immigrant community and censored mention of what sent their forebears to sea. Amy, our sons, and I joined Seders arranged by my father's second wife. Amy held Seders and Hanukkahs at home to further our sons' education. As Jennifer Weiner wrote: "... a Jewish identity has little to do with whether you ... attend services every Friday ... and everything to do with ... the way you see the world and the way the world sees you. It is an identity we can't slip, even if we want to" (*New York Times*, September 30, 2020).

As hard as this is to believe, as I was growing up, the twin information blackouts—externally imposed by my parents, internally imposed by myself—were so effective that when I entered college, I thought I had been named for a Scandinavian (Carl Malmberg) and descended from English grandparents on one side and Russian grandparents on the other. I began studying Russian and chose Russian history as my major.

By sophomore year, the picture came into focus: People speaking Russian (or Ukrainian) drove away those of my maternal ancestors they failed to kill. Moreover, because the US was preoccupied with the Cold War with Russia, the field of Russian studies was well-developed. It was time to choose a major with less emotional baggage and more intellectual space.

At about that time my father was finding meaning in a book of philosophy, *Zen in the Art of Archery*. The book fascinated me, too. My mother, in a bid to move beyond Landmark books, was writing a biography of Fukuzawa Yukichi. Fukuzawa was a nineteenth-century Japanese samurai who taught himself Dutch, thinking it was the universal language of the West, taught himself English when he learned

otherwise, and joined Japan's first diplomatic mission to the
United States. He embarked on that journey in 1859, just six
years after Admiral Perry forced his way into Japan, violat-
ing the Tokugawa shogunate's prohibition on foreign contact. When Fukuzawa returned to Japan in 1860, he began
full-scale importation of knowledge of the Western world.

Over 100 years after the exploits of Fukuzawa, I wondered if any comparably adventurous Americans were
bringing knowledge of China to the United States. After
Mao took control in 1949, China closed itself off to the West
much as the Tokugawa shoguns had closed off Japan. To
most Americans, China remained a cypher. A few Americans had taken up the challenge. Leaders among them
were Harvard professors John King Fairbank, Benjamin
Schwartz, and Ezra Vogel, while Edwin O. Reischauer
became an expert on the history of Japan. In time my
brother would join their ranks.

It dawned on me that my high school history text, Palm-
er's *The History of the Modern World*, confined itself to
Europe. Was Europe the extent of the "modern world"? My
embarrassment over my willful ignorance of my ethnic origins fueled my outrage over this hypocrisy in my education.

I took a course in East Asian history taught by Fairbank,
Schwartz, and Reischauer. Then I took a course in Indian
cultural history taught by the brilliant anthropologist Cora
Du Bois, only the second woman to be awarded tenure in
the Faculty of Arts and Sciences at Harvard. I was awed by
the ancient and advanced cultures of China, Japan, Korea,
and India. I found my new major: East Asian history.

By my sophomore year, I realized that the escape into a
new intellectual world did not bring with it an escape from
needing money for tuition, room, board, haircuts, clothes,

and for gas and tolls so I could get a ride with anyone who might be passing a highway exit near my home at holiday times and semester breaks. My father paid his taxes with bad checks, hoping the IRS would not cash them until he had filled the account. When I needed a winter coat, he sent me his. Since age eight I'd been listing earnings and expenses. Now my parents and I told each other our respective sums. It was worth a five-cent postage stamp to tell me they had deposited $35 in my account, while my fifteen-minute phone call earned a scolding, delivered with another five-cent stamp. I was not willing to make do like the student who owned two pairs of pants, each with large holes in different places. He wore both at once, never washing either. His ability to recall the score of any major league baseball game ever played did not compensate for his odor. It was time to find a term-time job.

The job I would soon land was a key part of my Harvard education. So was the weekend before I found it. Despite being literally in the same boat, I was not figuratively in the same boat as a friend who invited me to spend that weekend with him, not "on" Cape Cod but "off" Cape Cod. We met at the Cambridge garage near campus where he rented a parking space for his sports car. We drove to Woods Hole, where his family kept a motorboat. Four miles across the water lay the island of Naushon. We got there at dusk, found another family car at the dock, and soon reached his family's many-roomed home on the far side of the island, by the water's edge. The routine for breakfast, he explained the next morning, was to tell the maid what you would like. She relayed the information to the cook. Like the bedsheets, the tablecloth and napkins were starched linen. The coffee service was sterling.

The morning's sport began. We piled into a sailboat with his father at the helm and headed out among the Elizabeth Islands. Total freedom included his father stripping naked, peeing from the railing and then jumping into the ocean to swim—his way of boasting how many knots we were making and how strong a swimmer he was that he could catch up with the boat.

Then the wind failed. Part of utter freedom was having no engine. The hours drifted as slowly as the boat. By two o'clock the most conspicuous freedom was the freedom from food. The father managed to dock us at a flat little island that held nothing but a large field of corn, a tiny house and a dock to which was tied a one-person fishing boat. A white-haired couple came out of the house and greeted the father in Portuguese. He answered in kind. Clearly, this had happened before. The woman boiled corn and fed us the cobs at their table. When we were done, my friend's father offered money. Our hosts refused. It was late afternoon. The wind was up. We returned to the world from which we had come.

By that Monday I was back in Cambridge, resuming my job search. The one I found was life-shaping. For ten to forty hours a week for eleven months, beginning at $1.55 an hour and ending at $2.50 an hour, I assisted Roger Revelle, director of Harvard's recently opened Center for Population Studies.

I worked in the basement of an old, converted wooden house on Bow Street. Prof. Revelle occupied an office on the top floor that was expansive enough to accommodate his six-foot, four-inch frame, vast intellectual interests, and wide government connections. He had headed the Oceanographic Section of the Navy Bureau of Ships during World

War II and helped found the Office of Naval Research. He had come to Harvard after directing the Scripps Institute of Oceanography, where he had discovered that carbon dioxide is accumulating in the atmosphere. He impressed that on a Harvard student two years behind me, Albert Gore, who recounts the experience in his film, *An Inconvenient Truth*. Watching that movie when it came out in 2006 was the only time I wondered if I had chosen the wrong career. Why fight human disease when it's more important to keep humans from being a lethal disease for Earth?

The Center's inaugural concerns were with population growth and water resources. The scholars Revelle gathered in a family-like team ranged from Arthur Dyck, a pioneer in the field of bioethics, to Rose Frisch, a fruit-fly geneticist and Manhattan Project alumna who was discovering a correlation between girls' body weight and age at menarche and the impact of malnutrition on fertility.

Lessons: Big problems call for creative solutions. Creativity thrives in interdisciplinary groups with an interdisciplinary leader.

President Johnson's Science Advisory Committee commissioned Prof. Revelle to prepare a *Report on the World Food Supply*. My job was to calculate the available land area in Central Asia, Pakistan, and India suitable for agriculture but not yet farmed, based on annual precipitation, water table levels, soil type, and mean temperature. This would allow a prediction as to whether potential regional food supply could meet the needs of the growing population. The approach required producing a contour map based on data collected from locations spaced at close intervals across those regions. I was astounded that such information existed and that it resided at MIT. I spent hours at MIT collecting the figures. Personal computers did not yet exist; I used a hand calculator to process the numbers.

I was working on this one Sunday in the Bow Street office, when Dr. Revelle and his administrative assistant came in and saw me. "Do you want to have lunch?" he asked.

"Sure," I said, "I can go get something. What would you two like?"

"Oh, no," he said. "We have food."

On the way to his office, we passed a well-stocked kitchen, and more; Dr. Revelle asked me to choose the wine. Over the next ninety minutes he regaled us with stories of John von Neumann and JFK. Wrapping up, he told the administrator to go ahead and let me recruit another student to help with my work, and by the way, I might deserve a raise.

The White House published the report in 1967. I also drafted a monograph on multilateral aid that contributed to another of the Center's publications, "International Cooperation in Food and Population" by Roger Revelle. Published in 1968, the paper began with a generous acknowledgment to "the extensive help given by Carl Nathan in many aspects of the preparation of this essay."

For a student to be entrusted with such responsibility and to be treated with such collegiality made an enduring impression and served as model to aspire to when working with students of my own. And I was drawn to learning about people in other countries and what they need for healthy lives.

In my junior year, after one of Professor Fairbank's lectures in the East Asian Center at 2 Divinity Avenue, I was using the men's room. Prof. Fairbank came in and chose an adjacent urinal. As we moved to the sinks to wash our hands, he asked me my name. He nodded at my answer, which he seemed already to know, then invited me to attend one of the weekly teas he held at his home for graduate students, faculty, visiting scholars, and government officials. This was a rare honor for an undergraduate, said my brother, who had studied with Fairbank. I went to one of the teas. I met Westerners fresh back from China and Mongolia. How had they evaded the ban on travel by Americans? The mystery was intoxicating, as was the prospect of glimpsing the unknown.

As senior year began, Professor Fairbank agreed to be my advisor. He would help me choose a topic for a thesis. His secretary gave me a piece of paper with a phone number on it and a time I could call him—7:30 am. I was impressed that he would be in his office that early. My brother explained that the number was reserved for undergraduates. It rang a phone in the professor's home on the wall next to his toilet. After calling that phone, I was granted a thirty-minute, in-person appointment in the professor's campus office. He waved me to a chair, dialed a phone call and spoke softly for about twenty minutes. I heard my name but could make out nothing else. He hung up, handed me another piece of paper with another phone number on it and waved me out. That was the extent of his advice about my senior thesis.

It was great advice. It validated my thrill in conducting challenging investigations, demanded independence, took me out of Cambridge and myself, set me down at an important but almost unknown intersection of Western medicine with East Asian history, and helped shape my life.

The area code of the phone number provided by Professor Fairbank was for New York City. The elderly woman who answered the phone was expecting my call. She identified herself as the widow of the American consul to Harbin in Manchuria. When I visited her in her apartment in Peter Cooper Village on the lower east side of Manhattan, she told me over tea that I might be interested in her husband's reports to the State Department. They could be found in the National Archives in Washington, D.C.

So it happened that my first trip to Washington was to a reading room in the National Archives. The next three trips were during medical school: to testify in the Senate about a perverse practice of drug companies; to petition Speaker of the House Tip O'Neill to end the war in Vietnam; and to march on the Mall in protest. The first visit was more productive than the second, third, and fourth.

An attendant at the National Archives brought out shoebox-like files stuffed with cables and newspaper clippings. These were full of intelligence-based insights into the clash of imperialist powers, the impact of pneumonic plague on their designs, and the surprising rise of a first-rate, Western-style, Chinese-run medical system that deprived foreign powers of a pretext for invading Manchuria. (Twenty years later, Japan invaded without bothering with a pretext.) One of the reports of the North Manchurian Plague Prevention Service listed a Westerner as a staff member, Dr. Robert Pollitzer. I recognized his name as the author of a book on plague published by the World Health Organization that I had not been able to find. I called the National Library of Medicine in search of the book. The woman on the phone said, "Why don't you come talk to him? He works here." I went to Bethesda, Maryland, and found Dr. Pollitzer in a basement cubicle. Now in his eighties, he had fled service in the German Army of World War I by crossing Siberia. He eventually found employment in a field hospital of the Plague Prevention Service created by Dr. Wu Lien-teh. After I turned in the thesis, I had another meeting with Professor Fairbank. This time he had words for me, four of them: "We will publish this." The Harvard University Press monograph is titled "Plague Prevention and Politics in Manchuria, 1910–1931."[6]

Published or not, what could an East Asian history major do who did not speak Chinese, Japanese, or Korean, was interested in the intersection of medicine, science, and government, but could not consider medicine as a profession, given that no one in his family had ever done such a thing? Moreover, except for my mother's use of a hypodermic, my parents seemed incapable of using technologies. My mother's borscht-filled pressure cooker exploded, requiring us to repaint the kitchen. My father's frustrations with forward and reverse gears on the five-horsepower Gravely walk-behind tractor had made mowing our lawns my responsibility. Presumably, this problem with objects was hereditary and would preclude my using the tools of medicine.

The answer seemed obvious: work on public health in English-speaking India. I called the Harvard School of Public Health, made an appointment, took the MTA to Boston and met a professor who studied public health in India. The professor looked sad. His cubicle was covered with stacks of papers, not just on his invisible desk and file cabinets but all over the floors. Those I could see were tables filled with numbers. He pointed out that action in public health, as opposed to scholarship about it, usually required an MD before a public health degree. The distinction he drew between scholarship and action was as new to me as the distinction had been between favored plants and weeds when I began my career as a groundskeeper.

A thought grew. Why not medical school? I was in awe of the egalitarian teamwork I witnessed in my summers in Lester Grant's lab at NYU Medical Center. I was dazzled by the subcellular structures revealed by the history-making electron micrographs that Keith Porter displayed in his biology class at Harvard, based on his work at the Rockefeller Institute with George Palade and Christian de Duve, who soon thereafter shared a Nobel Prize. I had no trouble maneuvering the walk-behind Gravely or driving the tractor in Chappaqua. And perhaps there was some way I could help others avoid my mother's experience.

I submitted applications to the medical schools at Harvard, NYU, and Case Western. The first response was a call from the admissions office at Harvard. A young woman gave me a date to come for an interview. Then she tried to set up another kind of date. "I've read your application," she cooed. "You seem like a very nice man. Would you like to go out with me?" I began to sense the privilege of the path I sought to enter, where a presumption of earnings could act like a pheromone.

I got to the admissions office at Harvard Medical School at the same time as an applicant from Dartmouth. The attractive blonde who checked us in turned out to be the one I had turned down on the phone. She said we were both to meet Dr. Funkenstein. "Oh no!" shouted the man from Dartmouth. "I've heard about his stress interviews! I don't want any part of this." He left.

I had not heard of stress interviews. I was told later that Dr. Funkenstein was reputed to nail his office window shut, ask you to open it and berate you because you couldn't, or leave his office and call the phone on his desk, then return and berate you if you had answered it or berate if you had not. I don't know if any of that was true. As I approached his office, I thought the Dartmouth man might have been referring to the need to walk through an open ward full of psychotic people in Massachusetts Mental Health Center, because Dr. Funkenstein conducted his interviews in an office at the far end.

Dr. Funkenstein sat me down in front of his desk and asked me one question: "What football games have you attended at Harvard?" I began what would have been a very short reply, but it became even shorter when he cut me off and told me about the games *he* remembered. He had attended many, and his memory was sharp. I stayed awake and listened politely. After 45 minutes he sent me on my way. It was a stress interview after all, perhaps the most grueling ever devised.

Later I wondered if being propositioned by the woman in the admissions office was another part of the test. It was deflating to think her interest may have been feigned. I allowed myself to think that perhaps it was not.

PART TWO
A Fight

Medical School

THE SCHOOL that admitted us wanted to be sure it had not erred. That first month, each first-year student had to meet with a psychiatrist. The one interviewing me focused on my mother's recent death. Apparently, he wanted to find out how destabilized I had become. "Can you describe your mother in a few words?" he asked. "Democratic," I said. "She believed in fairness. Fairness in the family and in the world." His eyebrows shot up, then down with an air of disappointment. The interview ended shortly after that.

Before the first lecture began, out came Dr. Funkenstein with a stack of papers for the class to fill out: the "Strong Vocational Interest Inventory for Men." I went up to him at the front of the amphitheater and said, "Dr. Funkenstein, there are women here." He said, "If they're here, it's the right test." This may be what set me on an anti-authoritarian path, or, as we say now, this really pissed me off. Later I got back the results of my own test. It said that my interest was highest in being an artist, then a psychologist, only then a physician. My antipathy was greatest for the profession of mortician. Four contrasting ways to engage with life's chances and challenges.

I joined a group of fellow students who did not think drug companies should give medical students expensive gifts any more than the companies should give prescribing physicians costly gifts to promote sales of their drugs. The pharmaceutical company Eli Lilly had presented each incoming student with a leather bag containing a stethoscope, percussion hammer, tuning fork, and tape measure. Today the items would probably cost over $400. Those of us who objected built a pyramid of the gift bags in a conference room for the *Boston Globe* to photograph.

As one of the lead instigators, I was summoned to Washington to testify to Senator Gaylord Nelson's Select Committee on the Present Status of Competition in the Pharmaceutical Industry. My testimony listed additional gifts of educational materials we received in our first two years of medical school, many of them branded and some bearing advertisements for specific drugs. They came from Geigy, Lederle, Abbott, Upjohn, WarnerChilcott, and Merck, Sharpe & Dohme. I described how the medical school sought money from drug companies to support students' research projects without the students' knowledge, then at the end of the projects, the school instructed the students to write a letter of thanks to the company that had supported them. "The gifts we received were ultimately paid for out of the pockets of the patient," I testified. "They represent a hidden part of the cost of the drugs. . . . This constitutes a form of income derived from the patient without his knowledge or consent." The senators were skilled anesthetists. Recording our words, they put the issue to sleep.

Back in Boston, I returned my gifts to Lilly and dipped into scholarship money to replace the items. Medical students stopped getting free bags. Nothing else changed, except for a pronounced decrease in my local popularity and the slow germination of a campaign I finally began in 2004 to create "Open Labs," an idea I proposed for academic-industrial collaboration in the development of drugs, based on medical need and without regard for market potential.[7]

First-year classes had nothing to do with cancer, but given what had befallen my mother, I was not going to wait. A few evenings a week I took the MTA to Massachusetts General Hospital for Paul Black's course on cancer virology. The idea that viruses might cause cancer was radical. Convincing evidence for the idea only came much later, and with it the 2008 Nobel Prize for Harald zur Hausen's discovery that papilloma viruses lead to cervical cancer, the second most common cancer in women.

Even more radical was the view of my assigned advisor, the pathologist Hermann Lisco. His studies of chromosomes from cancer cells convinced him that cancer arises from genetic changes. We know now that there is no cancer without mutation. Dr. Lisco's insight was decades ahead of its time.

Thirty-three years later I learned from Dr. Lisco's obituary how he came to that view. After he fled Germany in 1936, he was recruited to the Manhattan Project, working first in Chicago and then at Los Alamos. He studied the impact of plutonium on chromosomes and conducted the first autopsy on a victim of radiation poisoning. The violence that he fled, the violence that his Manhattan Project colleagues helped to inflict, and the violence that he detected in the genomes of cancer cells that go on to inflict their own violence must have been deeply buried beneath his gentle mien. Perhaps those experiences fueled his penetrating prescience and perceptive guidance. He listened to my interest in cancer, told me his theory of its genetic origins, and stunned me by predicting that its control would come from a better understanding of the immune system. He recommended I do research with a rising young immunologist, John David, at the Robert Breck Brigham Hospital.

So it began. Twenty-two years after meeting Hermann Lisco, I became Associate Scientific Director of the Cancer Research Institute, the chief philanthropic driver behind research in cancer immunology. As this is written, the Scientific Director is Jim Allison, who shared a Nobel Prize in 2018 for demonstrating the curative potential of cancer immunotherapy.

Forty-four years after Hermann Lisco sent me to see John David, I joined John and his wife Roberta at John's eightieth birthday party at Gramercy Tavern in New York, a gathering of family and friends organized by his son Joshua, a founder of New York's Highline. Five years after that, I celebrated John's and Roberta's fiftieth wedding anniversary at a symposium where I hailed their "modus operandi": "Choose key questions. Apply scientific imagination, experimental rigor, unbelievably hard work, and an all-embracing humanism, so that a love of people—all kinds of people—forms both the team's scientific vision and its style." Three years later, Joshua invited Amy and me to the restaurant Il Buco to celebrate the life of Roberta, whose ashes would soon go to sea. Two years after that, just before COVID-19 closed down New York, I sat next to John at Gramercy Tavern once more, at another party Joshua put together for John's birthday, this time his ninetieth.

Failures Two

ONCE I COMMITTED to spending a year in John David's lab during medical school, I became eligible to apply for a scholarship from the Life Insurance Medical Research Fund. My application was approved. Founded in 1945, the Fund sought to encourage physicians in training to pursue research. By 1968, when I won one of the scholarships, their intent was more specific: to encourage students pursuing the MD to pursue a PhD as well. That idea was new. The first MD-PhD program in the country was launched in 1956, at Case Western. NIH began funding such programs in 1964. Harvard Medical School would not have a dual-degree program until 1974.

Today, fellowship awards from outside entities are deposited with the institution where the trainee is enrolled. The institution accepts responsibility for seeing that the expenditures conform to the donor's intent. In the pioneering program of the Life Insurance Medical Research Fund, however, these policies had not yet taken shape. The funds came to me in a check. The check was orders of magnitude larger than the monthly support from Amy's father and on a par with Judy Sulzberger's loan-become-gift that allowed me to enroll in medical school.

In celebration, Amy and I spent two weeks in Denmark, Sweden, and Norway. In Stockholm, I visited Peter Perlmann at the Wenner-Gren Institute to discuss his research on malaria. In Bergen, we visited the Leprosy Museum that commemorates Hansen's discovery in 1873 that a bacillus now called *Mycobacterium leprae* causes leprosy, which used to be prevalent in Norway. I had no idea I would later participate in developing new drug candidates for malaria or discover a new treatment for leprosy.

At midnight in the snowbound Myrdal railway junction station on the high Norwegian plateau, we waited for the early morning funicular that would bring us to sea level at Flåm. From there, the ferry to Balestrand glided past towering verticals of rock kissed by silvery freshets plunging into the waters of Sognefjord, reminding us how much greater the world is than what humans create. When we exerted ourselves to our utmost and climbed part way to the summit over Balestrand with legs like jelly, the cows grazing there that must have preceded us up the same vertiginous path gave us an even humbler perspective. In short, to spend a hunk of the Life Insurance Medical Research Fund scholarship on an expedition to Scandinavia was a sound investment in my education as a human being.

On the other hand, to skip the opportunity to earn a PhD was a failure of judgment. Most of the mentors and role models in research I had met up to that point, such as Lester Grant, Lewis Thomas, John David, and K. Frank Austen, were MDs. A few, such as Manfred Karnovksy, had PhDs. Only Heinz Remold held both degrees, and his PhD was in entomology. For many years to come, additional role models in research continued to hold only the MD, such as Ralph Steinman, Lloyd Old, Maclyn McCarty, Sam Silverstein, Zanvil Cohn, and Ralph Nachman. René Dubos and

Tony Cerami had PhDs. Very few, like Seymour Klebanoff, had both.

However, a lack of dual-degree holders as role models did not excuse my failure. On November 23, 1969, the front page of the *New York Times* trumpeted the work of my medical school classmate, Larry Eron, with his mentor, Jonathan Beckwith, in an article entitled "Scientists Isolate a Gene; Step in Heredity Control." As the *Times* put it, "Ultimately it may also be possible to pin down the exact sequence of chemical units that make up individual genes. . . . It is widely thought that diseases like cancer are fundamentally cases of the genetic control mechanisms having broken down." Even with evidence as compelling as this for a seismic shift in science, I did not appreciate the magnitude of the coming impact of molecular biology as a driving force and computers as a tool, jointly giving birth to genomics, followed by computational biology. Foregoing the opportunity for formal training in those emerging concepts and techniques meant I had to play catch-up to take advantage of each specific application as it appeared, such as isolation of monoclonal antibodies, expression of recombinant proteins, and knock-out of genes.

Playing catch-up does not mean catching up. When science moves as fast as it does now, there is no catching up. One leads where one can, and otherwise tries not to fall too far behind.

The challenge, as usual, is to learn from mistakes. I compensated for the missed opportunity in two ways. One was to bridge disciplines—medicine, immunology, microbiology, biochemistry, and chemical biology. This involved learning enough of the premises, terms, opportunities, and constraints of other scientists' disciplines to be able to collaborate discerningly, meaningfully, and appreciatively. This was as stimulating as it was rewarding.

The other compensation was to help others earn both an MD and a PhD. By 1991, I had spent nearly ten years at Rockefeller University and five at Cornell University Medical College (CUMC). CUMC anchored three different NIH-funded MD-PhD programs: Cornell-Cornell, Cornell-Rockefeller, and Cornell-Sloan Kettering Institute. NIH sent site visitors to review the programs. The resulting critique ended with an instruction to merge the programs or lose them, followed by an expression of doubt that the institutions would manage to do so. The reviewers were likely aware that at the time, many of the faculty at each institution referred to the other two institutions vaguely, dismissively, and collectively by the term "across the street." Remarkably, moreover, the leaders of the three institutions had apparently never met.

Ralph Nachman, chairman of the Department of Medicine at CUMC, asked me to lead the effort to combine the programs. Working with Ralph Steinman at Rockefeller, I wrote a constitution for trilateral collaboration. I became the founding director of the Tri-Institutional MD-PhD Program, which offers full financial support for its students and research mentorship at any of the three institutions. I sat in the office of David Baltimore, the Nobelist who was president of Rockefeller, as he signed the document along with Richard Rifkin, the director of Sloan-Kettering, and Robert Michels, dean of CUMC. With that in hand, I launched a program called Gateways to the Laboratory to bring under-represented minority students to campus each summer to gain the research experience needed for successful applications to programs offering the dual degree. This was the first such pipeline program in the country. By the thirtieth year of the program, 84% of 296 Gateways alumni had completed or were still pursuing an advanced degree in medicine or science, including 66 earning combined MD-PhD degrees.

Launching the Tri-Institutional MD-PhD program and its Gateways to the Laboratory program was such a heavy lift that I stepped down from the directorship in 1993 to concentrate on research. Nonetheless, members of CUMC's Board of Overseers (now called Board of Fellows) must have noticed the effort. In 1995, the dean of CUMC invited me to become the medical college's first senior associate dean for research. I accepted. I launched CUMC's first core facilities for shared technologies and bridge funds for researchers whose grant applications just missed the cut-off for funding and were being resubmitted. I reassigned tens of thousands of square feet of lab space from one department to another for more productive use.

One day the following spring, I was working in my laboratory. As usual, I came in early, treasuring the serenity. I set out an absorbent, plastic-backed paper sheet on the lab bench and laid out what I would need: an alcohol-soaked pad, a venepuncture kit, several rubber-stoppered glass tubes containing small amounts of an anticoagulant substance in a vacuum, a sterile gauze pad, a Band-Aid, and a rubber tourniquet. I rolled up one sleeve. I wrapped the tourniquet around my biceps and knotted it, borrowing from surgical training in medical school, where we learned how to tie sutures with one hand. I used the alcohol pad to clean the crook of the elbow, inserted the needle at one end of the venepuncture kit into a bulging vein and the needle at the other end of the tubing through the rubber stoppers of the glass tubes, whose vacuum drew in the blood. I released the tourniquet, pulled the last tube away, withdrew the needle from my arm, pressed the gauze to the wound for a few moments, placed a Band-Aid to protect my shirt sleeve from a stain, and inverted the tubes to mix the blood with the anticoagulant. I used an electrically powered pipet to draw up the blood and transferred measured amounts to plastic centrifuge tubes containing a cushion of clear cell-separation fluid of a specific density. I put the tubes in holders designed to fit in a centrifuge and used a pan balance to make sure that the holders that would reside opposite each other on the rotor each had the same weight. Otherwise, at high speeds, the rotor could break, destroy the machine, injure people nearby, and spray the lab with blood.

Centrifugation forced the blood into different bands according to the density of plasma (the fluid portion of blood) and the density of the cells of different types. Red blood cells, the densest, collected at the bottom. White blood cells called neutrophils rested in the colorless fluid just above the red cells. Above the colorless fluid itself, a cloudy layer contained lymphocytes, monocytes, and plate-lets. Above that floated straw-colored plasma. I collected the neutrophils, diluted them in a chilled buffer solution, cen-trifuged them again, resuspended them in the buffer, and plunged the tubes in a bucket of ice to keep the cells from metabolizing until the experiment began. I took a small sample of the suspension and counted the cells under a microscope, made a calculation, and diluted the rest of the suspension to a chosen concentration. Then I dispensed measured numbers of cells to a plastic tray with 96 identical wells to begin a carefully timed experiment to test the cells' ability to release bacteria-killing molecules called reactive oxygen species, closely related groups ("species") of chemically modified forms of oxygen that can change the structure ("react with") other molecules and change their functions.

I was discovering that human neutrophils can release over 100 times higher quantities of reactive oxygen species than they had been known to be able to do.[8] The secret was that neutrophils needed not one but two signals to do so. The first signal was to convince them that they had left the bloodstream and were in the process of crawling out of blood vessels into the tissues, or had already arrived there. I could persuade neutrophils of such whereabouts by letting them adhere to a plastic surface coated with proteins found in the extracellular matrix, the collection of substances that occupy the spaces between cells in our tissues. Neutrophils sensed these proteins through transmembrane proteins called integrins.

The second signal was a protein recently discovered by Lloyd Old and his colleagues at Memorial Sloan-Kettering Cancer Center across the street, called tumor necrosis factor, or one of several other proteins that promote inflammation. On receipt of both signals, it took ten to thirty minutes for neutrophils to disassemble the cable-like filaments of a protein called actin below their outer membrane. Those filaments kept the cells spherical when they hurtled through the bloodstream. Now, these filaments reassembled at the bottom of the cells, where the cells' integrins contacted the matrix proteins. This ten-to-thirty-minute lag period ended when the cells began crawling on the surface. Then, for over an hour, they poured out reactive oxygen species. In earlier studies with neutrophils studied in suspension rather than adherent and with stimuli other than the inflammatory proteins I was using, this so-called "respiratory burst" (sudden consumption of oxygen) was tiny, lasted about five minutes, and was not seen at all without addition of a substance called cytochalasin. The cytochalasin was an actin-disassembling poison from a fungus. Its use in such experiments was an artifice rationalized by the presumption that the cytochalasin took the place of something physiological that remained to be identified.

My findings were drastically altering the understanding of what neutrophils can do—release vast amounts of reactive oxygen intermediates when they leave the blood, enter the tissues, and encounter both the extracellular matrix and signals of inflammation. There was an intense sense of fulfillment in discovering something new, reproducible, and susceptible to ever-deeper mechanistic analysis.

Just as I was about to launch that day's experiment, in walked the dean, along with two other men in suits. "What are you doing?" he said.

"An experiment," I answered.

"Can you talk now?" he asked.

"No," I said. Astonishment and anger fought for space on his face. "We have dedicated scientists," he told his companions. They all turned and left.

A few days later, the dean called me into his office. "A Board member asked me about you," he said. "He wanted to know if you are as naïve as you seem, or if it's just an act." I didn't have to answer, because it wasn't a question. It was a warning. As I learned later, the deanship was about to become unexpectedly vacant.

Shortly after that, Hunter Rawlings, the new president of Cornell University, urged me to step in as acting dean. By the third time Hunter called—early on a Sunday morning—I realized that, as a seasoned leader, he had learned to remove "No" from his incoming vocabulary, while retaining it for outgoing messages. I spent the second half of 1996 as CUMC's acting dean.

July 1, my first day in the dean's office, began with disaster. I had been given a key. I let myself in around 7:30 am to find a note from one of the secretaries informing me that the executive administrator had resigned a few weeks before. The note-writer expressed her regret that no one had been allowed to warn me, no effort had been made to find and orient a replacement, and consequently there was no one to introduce me to the job's routines, responsibilities, and remedies.

Within two weeks, I recruited an excellent head of the CUMC dean's office staff. Twenty-one years later, when I was dean of the Weill Cornell Graduate School of Medical Sciences, a long-time member of that staff who was Black pulled me aside. "Do you know what an impact you had when you were acting dean of the medical school?" she asked. It ran through my mind that I helped launch the college's first set of strategic plans, set a dollar value for the donation that led to re-naming the medical college, and so on. But she meant something different. "Your executive administrator was the first Black person ever to work in the dean's corridor. During the day, that is, before the night cleaners," she explained. "We all noticed."

At about 8 a.m. that first day, the phone rang. I was still the only one in the office, so I picked up. It was Paul Marks, President and CEO of Memorial Sloan Kettering Can-

cer Center (MSKCC). He told me in exceptionally color-
ful language that the outgoing administration had allowed
the affiliation agreement between CUMC and MSKCC to
lapse, effective that day. Our medical students and residents could no longer rotate at MSKCC, nor could MSKCC
residents rotate at CUMC. I laughed. He asked why. I told
him I admired expertise, including his mastery of cursing.
That did it—we were friends. Putting down the phone and
resuming my inspection of files stacked high on the desk,
I pulled out the thickest one. It described a long-standing
decision to terminate a tenured faculty member for cause
and the expectation of an ensuing lawsuit. The termination
had been postponed so that it would fall to me.

With those first steps, I boarded a hurtling train. In
the next few months, CUMC approved the merger of
New York Hospital and Columbia's Presbyterian Hospital,
escaped takeover by Columbia's medical school, launched
a physician's organization, wrote its first strategic plan for
research, and recruited a new dean. I persuaded my colleague Olaf Andersen to take over leadership of the Tri-I
MD PhD program, and he guided it to national eminence.

In retrospect, my insistence that my deanship last no
more than six months helped make these successes possible. To the University President and the medical college
Board of Overseers, my disinterest in continuous attention
and chauffeured rides made it clear that the self-imposed
six-month term-limit would be real. They saw that it was
urgent for them to get deeply involved. They did, and they
were magnificent. For my part, I could make or endorse
decisions without regard to their popularity. On January
1, 1997, I returned full time to my lab, enriched by inter-

actions with the extraordinary men and women who had steadied the medical college and readied it for growth.

Before that interlude, I had felt that CUMC was sliding backwards. Edward Scolnick, head of research and development at Merck, had invited me to become Merck's executive director of immunology and inflammation. I went to see the dean whose later exit would lead to my interim service in that role. I expressed my concerns, hoping to hear that he had a plan to turn CUMC around. All he said was, "Come see me before you go." I accepted Merck's offer. In the end, I withdrew my acceptance at Merck when it became clear that I might not be able to address family concerns that the move would entail. Serving as acting dean gave me a chance to help make CUMC a place where I was glad to remain.

When the next dean stepped down after fifteen years of service, he published a history of the medical college in which the period of July through December 1996 went unmentioned. Good decision: what happened in that time could fill a book of its own. But not this one.

At a dinner celebrating the selection of the next dean, a member of the Board of Overseers asked me why I had not stayed on in that role. "If you'd asked, it could have been yours," he said.

"I like what I'm doing," I said. I had long since committed to a different path, based on patients I saw and professors I met in medical school. Their stories follow.

Choices Three

THREE YEARS after my medical school admissions interview held at Mass Mental, I was back in its own admissions office as a medical student sharing a night shift with a psychiatry resident. While the resident ate his dinner in a back room, I held down the fort out front. A young man walked in, sat down in the chair facing my desk and said, "I cut off my penis." I asked, "Why did you do that?" He said, "The voice told me to." He pulled down his pants. The voice was imaginary; the amputation was not, though the bleeding had stopped. "You were right to come here," I said, and led him to the resident.

About an hour later, a barefoot girl of about seventeen walked in wearing only a nightgown. "They're chasing me," she said. "Who is?" I asked. "Here they come!" she screamed. She jumped up and ran from the office. I ran after her. She was already out the door and far down the street, her white gown flailing faintly in the dark. I caught up and took her hand. "Let me help you," I said. "Thank you," she said. We walked quietly back to Mass Mental, hand in hand.

At best, I may have kept her from being hit by a car, or mugged, as I had once been in the wooded area she was approaching. How could I have been of more help than that, with what little we knew about the workings of the brain?

Two of my neuroscience teachers, Edward Kravitz and David Potter, had just discovered the major chemical compound, gamma-aminobutyric acid, that one neuron in the brain uses to suppress the electrical response of another neuron. Two other teachers, David Hubel and Torsten Wiesel, had just discovered that sensory experience can affect the formation of neural circuits, for which they won a Nobel Prize. Many years later, after Torsten Wiesel retired from the presidency of Rockefeller University, we served together on the Board of Trustees of the nearby Hospital for Special Surgery. Back then, the message I took was to study cells rather than people, look for chemicals as specific as neurotransmitters, and conduct experiments I could control.

The difference between neuroscience (trying to understand how the nervous system works at a molecular and cellular level) and neurology (diagnosing dysfunctions of the nervous system and recommending preventions and treatments) was reinforced when I began my neurology rotation with the eminent Prof. Norman Geschwind at Boston City Hospital. He specialized in deducing the location of brain lesions that affected people's ability to speak or read. On the first day of the rotation, as we students in our short white jackets joined the professor in his long white coat, we crowded around the bedside of a patient who struggled to reply to the professor's questions. After a few moments, Prof. Geschwind announced that the patient had a brain tumor, predicted what part of his brain it had destroyed and stated that there was no effective treatment. He congratulated himself with a smile. The patient burst into tears. I quit the rotation and went back to John David's lab, where I had already spent a year. Fortunately, I had enough credits to graduate despite bailing from neurology.

Surgery was far more attractive. Definitive interventions helped people and often cured them. Dr. Donald Glotzer at the Beth Israel Hospital was the personification of humanism and dedication. Making rounds with him, I thought I had found my calling. However, it seemed that the demand for perfection before, during, and after surgery could crowd out the search for underlying causes. Moreover, some of the research in which I was asked to assist reminded me of social science classes in college, in which I saw the social but not the science. For example, I was asked to interview patients on the evening before the ulcer-bearing parts of their stomach or duodenum would be removed. The goal was to test the hypothesis that ulcer disease was caused by a "Type A" personality. Surprise! Patients facing surgery were anxious. Anxiety is a hallmark of Type A. In short, the patients' ulcers were their fault and they should take tranquilizers in addition to antacids. About thirteen years later, Barry Marshall and Robin Warren discovered that the cause of most gastric and duodenal ulcers is infection by a bacterium, *Helicobacter pylori*. They won a Nobel Prize. Much of ulcer surgery gave way to antibiotic treatment.

After my time with Dr. Glotzer, I rotated with a towering figure in surgery, William Silen. He was intent on reducing "EBL" (estimated blood loss) to less than 5 milliliters (one teaspoonful) per case, whether he was meticulously identifying each over-active parathyroid gland in his patient's neck or removing a mass from her abdomen. The operating room was his classroom. His favorite lesson was the need for fortitude under stress. The fortitude training through which he put chief resident Dr. Kravitz took the form of testing his tolerance for escalating verbal abuse. "See Kravitz' hands starting to shake," Dr. Silen said to me.

"He's no better than a frog." Frog was a surgeons' term for internists, whose inability to remove disease with a scalpel or Bovie cautery tool was taken as a lack of manliness. "How can he be a surgeon if his hands shake? What if he's nervous and he sweats and his sweat falls into the operative field?"

Then Dr. Silen turned to me and said, "I think I remember an article about this operative approach. It was by (so and so) in the journal of (such-and-such) in 1966. Why don't you go to Countway and check it? Come right back and tell us about it." This meant doffing the gown, mask, cap, shoe covers, and gloves, which had only been donned after a twenty-minute scrubbing of hands and fingernails. In fact, Dr. Silen required students to prepare for the operating room by immersing our hands in lampblack and scrubbing until no trace of it remained. On this errand, I had to run half a mile to the medical center library, find the journal, read the article, run back, and scrub in again. "Well?" asked Dr. Silen, when I returned. I rattled off the information he was looking for. "Oh, that's not the one I meant. Go back and check this other one."

When one of Dr. Silen's patients bled into his abdominal wound around 4 a.m. the morning after surgery, Dr. Silen was furious not just that it had happened but that the resident had not phoned him the moment he detected the swelling. As punishment, the resident had to call Dr. Silen every hour for the next 48 hours with the patient's vital statistics. As the resident's student and co-malfeasant by default, it was my job to collect the numbers: blood pressure, heart rate, and respiratory rate. The nurses were not allowed to use my measurements for their records, so they collected them again after I did. Clearly, Dr. Silen did not need sleep, nor, apparently, did his wife, his resident, or his student, but I pitied his patient.

I found that I could sometimes make a difference *without* cutting people open. A resident led a group of students to the bedside of a patient in the intensive care unit and began her lecture. The cardiac monitor on the overhead shelf suddenly showed ventricular tachycardia, a lethal rhythm. I slammed the patient's chest with my fist. I had read that this can produce an electrical current that is sometimes enough to revert the heart to its normal beating. It worked. The resident stopped mid-sentence and stared at me. The nurses stared. Everyone stared. I was as surprised as they were.

The next day the resident called me over to a patient on a respirator. It was necessary to draw arterial blood to measure his oxygenation, but after many needle "sticks" over the past few days, the artery was scarred and the resident was having trouble locating its pulse where the thumb meets the wrist. My fingertip faintly sensed the beats. I thought of my mother popping a pencil into an orange and then popping a hypodermic into my upper arm. I popped the needle and watched the patient's pulse push the plunger up in the syringe with bright red blood. I gave the resident the now warm syringe. She plunged it into the waiting bag of ice and left for the lab. I sat on the bed for the requisite five minutes' compression of the puncture site. Once again, I was holding a patient's hand. Soon I was good at placing intravenous lines in people's necks, finding the internal jugular vein while sparing the carotid artery.

I remember everything about these experiences except the people. I had spoken few words to any of them and none to some. I only remember their parts—chests, wrists, necks, arteries, veins.

I did not choose surgery.

The late 1960s and early 1970s were within the "golden age" of antibiotic development. We did not know that very few novel antibiotics would be discovered in the decades to follow. Antibiotics were the first small chemical compounds found to act in biological systems by binding to specific, identified molecular targets, and, by inhibiting them, create a change that reveals their function. Scientifically, antibiotics launched what came to be called chemical biology. Medically, they became the most impactful drugs in human history. For a long time, antibiotics were the only drugs that routinely cured disease in the strict sense: returning a person to his or her previous state of well-being without the need for continued use of the drug. In that regard they struck me as the internist's equivalent of surgery.

My medicine rotation at Massachusetts General Hospital introduced me to Dr. Morton Swartz, chief of the Division of Infectious Diseases and master user of antibiotics. Besides the curative power of antibiotics, what dazzled me about Mort Swartz's approach to medicine was that he did not use the subspecialty as a way to limit the scope of his responsibility for diagnostic acumen or therapeutic judgment. He used it as an entry point to all of medicine, because infection can take hold in any organ, alter the function of any other, and reveal itself by changes in many.

I realized that cancer has the same three attributes and is also an entry point to all of medicine. In a fundamental sense, cancer is an internally arising infection: cells whose

genome differs from the one we were born with proliferate in our tissues and damage them. At last, my intellectual preferences and emotional imperatives in medicine
came together in one place: oncology. But where surgeons
and infectious disease physicians could cure people, cure
was almost always out of reach for medical oncologists at
the time. The magnitude of the challenge beckoned, much
as the vastness of Western ignorance of East Asia had
attracted me in college.

Oncologist Dr. Robert Carey sensed the gradual coales-
cence of my decision as I followed him on his rounds, made
rounds myself on his patients, and reported to him before
we visited them together. He invited Amy and me to spend
a November Sunday afternoon at a small home he and his
wife kept near Crane Beach, about an hour up the coast
from the hospital. Given how many hours he spent at the
hospital, it was a special gift from both him and his wife to
share some of their rare time together with us. Shoes in our
hands, socks in our shoes, he and I walked on the cold sand
of the empty beach as surging gray waves reflected hus-
tling clouds.

As Robert Carey described it, *medicine* was what psychologist Erik Erikson called it the following year when he
spoke at my class's medical school commencement—*mediation* between the patient and her or his illness. Doing what
you could, and being there when that was all you could do.

The shoreline added its own message to our conversation. A few weeks before, Amy and I had visited a colleague
of hers from work. A widow, she lived alone in a small, historic house in Salem, on the coast some miles south of Crane
Beach. Despite the season and the weather, she excused herself for a while to go swim in the ocean a few blocks from

her door. She said she swam every day throughout the year. She began doing so the day her son, an only child, went swimming and did not come back. She had gone out looking for him. She looked for him still.

Medicine

INTERNSHIP AT Massachusetts General Hospital was to begin July 1, 1972. Except that it wasn't. A letter arrived courteously asking if I wouldn't mind coming on June 23 to prepare for total immersion. I still have a handout from that week's bootcamp. It lists major medical emergencies and is covered with my handwritten notes of what to do in each. The hospital gave us our on-call schedules—two days on, one night off, alternating with three days on, one night off. A "day on" meant twenty-four hours. They gave us short white coats with wide side pockets. On the left would be my ophthalmoscope, tuning fork, and knee hammer; on the right a small, thick, three-ring binder where I kept lists of differential diagnoses and drug choices, doses, and side effects. Around my neck, the stethoscope. They gave us white pants that closed with buttons and white, short-sleeved shirts that closed with snaps. Presumably the logic was that we could take off the shirt even if we were too tired for buttons, but we should keep our pants on at all times.

Most important, they gave us pagers. On July 1, mine began its adrenalin-evoking beep-beep-beep. I would rush to find a telephone and dial the page operator's number. A honeyed voice with a mix of urgency and concern would say, "Dr. Nathan, you have a patient for admission in the ER," or even the dreaded "You have three patients for admission in the ER."

Dr. Silen was right to train me to rebuild my neural circuits in sleep periods lasting under an hour. The problem was not so much the duration of those rest periods but that there were so few of them. It was particularly challenging to carry the code-call beeper: its claxon call meant rushing to resuscitate someone in cardiopulmonary arrest. Sometimes that meant setting off at a run before waking up, a circumstance that proved the wisdom of leaving one's pants on when in bed. Running while asleep sometimes meant running in the wrong direction, colliding with another person, and losing the contents of both pockets in my white coat.

On one evening off, I took the MTA as usual back to Cambridge, where Amy and I now lived. I suddenly noticed that my hand was on my forehead. My forehead felt damp. The dampness was blood. The blood came from a cut. The cut must have come from my glasses, because they lay broken on the street. Even without glasses I was close enough to the cause of their breakage to identify it: a telephone pole. I had fallen asleep walking home.

On another of those few evenings off, Amy and I invited one of my fellow interns to come to our apartment for dinner. It was his night off as well. Amy served a stew. Our guest fell asleep at the table so abruptly that his face hit the stew. More surprising, he continued to snore. We cleaned him up and sent him home, never mind about supper.

The only other time I saw comparable disregard for a stew was thirty-two years later at a meeting in 2004 that the Scripps Research Institute and the Karolinska Institute co-hosted in Palm Springs. I was invited, I learned later, as an audition for recruitment by Scripps. I gave a talk entitled "Host Pathogen Relations as Competitive Genomics: Lessons from *Mycobacterium tuberculosis*." After my talk, a tall man wearing sunglasses came up and asked if I would join him for dinner. I had no idea who he was but did not want to reveal my ignorance and was glad for company. We met that evening in the hotel restaurant and ordered from the menu. Then the man declared, "God gave us all these beautiful chemical compounds and it's our responsibility to use them. Let me get my laptop, I have to show you!" He hurried back to his room. Meanwhile, our entrees arrived. His was a stew. He returned, pushed aside the stew, set the laptop in its place and gave an exhilarating talk about chemistry. When I returned to New York I learned that my dinner companion, whose name, Barry Sharpless, I saw on the title slide of his presentation, had won a Nobel Prize three years before. The prize was awarded for his discovery of ways for oxidation reactions to produce a given chemical compound rather than the compound's mirror image. As our friendship developed, he helped me learn more about chemical biology. He shared his collection of compounds for a technique he made famous, click chemistry, that I would use in my work.

In 2019, Dr. Sharpless was quoted in the *Dartmouth News* while visiting his alma mater. The interviewer asked him, "What would be the highest, best function that might come from the click chemistry that you've been pioneering?" He replied: "Right now we're working on resistance to tuberculosis. . . . Tuberculosis is a horrible disease. . . . So we found an inhibitor . . ." On October 5, 2022, K. Barry Sharpless was awarded a second Nobel Prize—this time for click chemistry. He shared the prize with two other scientists who pioneered click chemistry, Morten Mendel and Carolyn Bertozzi. Dr. Bertozzi was also applying click chemistry to the management of tuberculosis.

In the hospital, my sense of responsibility increased my workload and nearly got me fired.

One evening, our ten o'clock dinner of free access to that day's cafeteria leftovers was interrupted by a code call. My fellow first-year resident and I arrived at the bedside to find that the patient in cardiac arrest was his. "I'm still hungry," he said. Confident in what would follow, he went back to the cafeteria and nourished himself for the successful career in research that he later pursued. I stayed behind, compressing his patient's chest until the defibrillator got there and I could switch to that.

A recent technological advance in the Emergency Room was the provision of typewriters for preparation of the write-ups. Broken keys accumulated along with ink-depleted ribbons. One night a woman arrived by ambulance from a local restaurant. She wasn't breathing. I tried to intubate her but could not. I called the anesthesiology resident. When he could not intubate her either, he looked into her airway with a flashlight. He ran out of the room and came back with long forceps, reached down her trachea and pulled out a hunk of chicken. She was dead. Later that year, thoracic surgeon Henry Heimlich introduced the now famous maneuver of chest compression that can rescue people who choke on food.

Also dead was the typewriter I tried to use to prepare the report. I picked it up and stuffed it partway into a wastebasket. It was quite a bit bigger than the wastebasket, so most of it projected out conspicuously and the basket threatened to tip. That suited my purpose. The next typewriter was dead, too. I junked that one as well. And the next. A few days later there were new typewriters throughout the Emergency Room.

I had hated how we made rounds when I was a student. Doctors and doctors-to-be filled the patient's room, which was rarely a private one. The resident who had been on duty the night before rattled off the signs, symptoms, differential diagnosis, and test results, using as many abbreviations as possible in the interests of speed. This ensured incomprehensibility for the patient, a sure way to promote anxiety. Then the attending physician or others in the team would turn to the patient, sometimes raising their voice as if to overcome the lack of comprehension they had just engendered, and fire off questions for the patient to answer. Then orders would be issued for tests and treatments, again in the form of abbreviations or jargon, and the team would leave. As a resident, I organized my own team so that doctors, nurses, students, and others, such as a nutritionist, made rounds together. We would meet in advance in a conference room to discuss the patient; enter the room to talk only to the patient and only in lay terms and at normal decibel levels; then meet again in the conference room to update our understanding and our plans.

The nurses welcomed being included. They began to call on me for special matters. For example, they called me when a patient's mattress caught fire, though the patient was not mine. The goose-necked, wall-mounted lamp over the bed was limp. It drooped toward the mattress next to the patient's head as he sat up in a bed that had been motored into chair form. The lamp's bulb protruded beyond the metal shade and touched the sheets. The heat was enough to

ignite the mattress. The white smoke gave the man a halo—
premature, and perhaps undeserved. I lifted him to a chair,
dragged the mattress into the shower and soaked it. After
the second time that I extinguished a mattress, I wrote to
the head of the hospital. Lamps began to change.

My next campaign had to do with cardiac monitors.
Sometimes there were not enough of them to hook up to
everyone who needed one. One of my patients was going
repeatedly into a dangerous cardiac rhythm and there was
no monitor available that could alert me or the nurses at
a distance. Instead, we hooked up a portable EKG machine
and kept it running while we took turns sitting next to it
and reading the rhythm strip. It was late at night, but I got
the telephone operator to give me the home number of the
man who ran the cardiac monitor service. I woke him and
told him if he didn't get me a monitor in the next thirty
minutes, I would put the patient in an ambulance and take
him to our cross-town rival, the Peter Bent Brigham Hospital. Thirty minutes later, a monitor appeared.

Then it was brain scan reports. I ordered a brain scan on
a patient whose care I had just assumed. When the report
came back a few hours later, it was dated five days earlier.
The previous intern had ordered the scan, but there was no
record of it in the chart, and that's how long it took to get
the result back. The scan I had just ordered was unnecessary. That set me up for the next patient who needed a scan.
The scan was done in mid-afternoon. When the report had
not arrived by five p.m., I called the chief resident in radiology. He said the office was closed and locked and there was
no way for him to get in and find the result until the next
morning. I asked him who had done the procedure and he
gave me the name. I paged that doctor but got no response. I

called the operator and demanded the doctor's home number. I reached his wife, who said he was playing tennis at a court in a nearby town and had left his pager at home. I called the police in that town and asked them if they would mind going to the tennis court, finding the doctor and asking him to call me. They were delighted to oblige. Call he did.

"Hello, this is Dr. (X). What is the emergency?" he said.

"I'm sorry to interrupt your game," I said, "but the brain scan you did was urgent and I need to know the result."

"I can't help you," he said. "I'm an orthopedic surgeon."

It turns out there were two Drs. X on staff. I next phoned the chairman of the department of radiology at his home. He came into the hospital, unlocked the department office, found the scan and read me the result. There was no lesion—not in the patient, anyway.

Sometimes I found ways to solve problems without phoning anyone in the middle of the night. One afternoon I was called to the ER to admit a young college student. I found her in a remote overflow corridor on a stretcher. She had a high fever. She was breathing fast and hard and her lips were blue. She needed close observation. Her disease might be contagious. She needed a single room. I called the floor but the room was not ready: Housekeeping had not yet cleaned it after the previous patient's discharge. I called Housekeeping but they said they were busy and it might be a few hours before they could get there. I hurried up to the floor, raided the utility closet for a broom, disinfectant, bucket, mop, and rags, and cleaned the room myself. I rushed back to the ER, did not even consider calling Dispatch, and wheeled the patient up. The patient made a recovery. A physician cleaning a room made history.

Medical residency taught me how variably people react to death: to the sight of it, the fear of it, their sense of responsibility for it, knowledge of its imminence. Here are examples of each.

At Massachusetts General Hospital at the time, the wealthy, the middling, and the poor bedded in different buildings. The wealthy enjoyed the amenities of Phillips House—private rooms, fine meals, silver service, and linen to cover the wheeled bedside tables. Amenities were not for the help. One evening when I was on call in Phillips and reached for something to eat, the head nurse scolded, "You can't take supper until the last patient has been served."

Disease, being indifferent to privilege, stalked the halls of Phillips House. A woman in her late twenties moaned and tossed in her room near the end of one corridor. A drug she had taken for inflammatory bowel disease led to Stevens-Johnson syndrome, a sloughing of much of the skin. There was a risk that bacteria would breach the breaks to bloom in her blood. Of all the patients on my watch, she was my main concern. Late one night I went to the nursing station to check that her private doctor's orders had been followed, then to her darkened room. In the glare of my penlight, the clipboard hanging at the foot of her bed told me that her vital signs held steady. She answered my question with "I feel the same." I tried to offer words of comfort.

I went to the on-call room two doors down, flopped atop the cot, and dove steeply to sleep. I woke sometime later to find myself opening the door. Perhaps there had been a knock, perhaps not. A young nurse stood there, sobbing. "I've never—seen—a dead person," she gasped, working to keep her cries in the corridor to a whisper. "I—just started. This is my first week. I don't—I don't know what to do."

"Who?" I said, over and over.

In time her heaving chest kept breath enough to say, "The woman with the missing skin." Most likely, sepsis had swung its scythe.

Giving comfort is one of the most important skills a doctor needs. No one trains us. Now I tried for the second time that night. I failed both times.

Another woman in a private room on a higher floor in Phillips House had a different kind of pain and a reaction opposite to moaning and tossing. Middle-aged but petrified of dying, she had lain silent and immobile in bed for weeks. Her physician had no remedy for her mental state. She had no other illness and received no medication. The pages in her chart where doctors wrote orders recorded each day's date, followed by nothing but the next date stamp. Dismayed, a group of us residents finally wrote: "D/C [discontinue] dates."

She remained in her room at least as long I remained in Phillips House. The distorted economics of healthcare lasted even longer.

I was escorting a man in his thirties with heart disease from the Bulfinch Building, where we cared for the poor, to the cardiac care unit, because he had begun to have irregular beats. Near his left hip on the wheeled stretcher sat a portable cardiac monitor, by his right a portable defibrillator. As we rode up in an elevator, the monitor sounded the alarm. His heart had stopped. I activated the defibrillator, but it was dead. Its battery had lost its charge. I began manual CPR. When the elevator opened, others helped me rush the stretcher to the cardiac care unit, where defibrillation was applied, to no avail. I did not telephone anyone.

I marched to the office of the chairman of the department of medicine, Prof. Alexander Leaf. "He's busy, you can't go in," said the young lady at the desk. I moved past her, flung open his door, walked in, and laid out my complaints about monitors and defibrillators. "Go home," he said, glowering. "You are too upset. Go home now if you want to keep working here."

Nonetheless, near the end of my second year as a house officer, one of the chief residents told me I was invited to stay. I thought about the clinicians there I admired, like the cardiologist Roman DeSanctis. It was rumored that his wife would know if he had been home on any given night if she found the toilet seat up in the morning. I thought about patients I admired, like a forty-year-old man from Haiti with metastatic prostate cancer, no visitors, and no stateside kin.

Charles Huggins and Clarence Hodges at the University of Chicago had won a Nobel Prize eight years before for discovering the temporary benefit of castration or estrogen treatment for prostate cancer. This man was past that. He was suffering from disseminated intravascular coagulation, a paradoxical combination of clotting and bleeding. His body was using up its clotting factors so fast that he was bleeding into his muscles. In the economically segregated manner of the time, he shared a large open ward in the historic Bulfinch building with about twenty other men of limited means; another open ward served economically disadvantaged women. Every few hours I drew blood from a vein in his arm and measured his red blood cell count and his clotting time in a small laboratory between the men's and women's wards. I had advance notice about his clotting time because the venipuncture sites oozed much longer than normal. Next to the laboratory was the communal men's bathroom, which had no door. As I made my measurements, an elderly man with an enlarged prostate of his own stood in agony at a urinal. A young nurse stood at his side, rubbing his shoulder and urging him on, "Pee, Mr. Haggarty, pee! You can do it! Listen to the water." She had opened a faucet at one of the sinks.

Gushing water, seeping blood. As my patient's blood leaked into his tissues, the resulting anemia cut the delivery of oxygen to his brain and heart. As his clotting factors fell, he couldn't stop the leaking. I had been giving him transfusions, but their only effect was to increase the swelling and rigidity of his musculature. The paradox in his blood created a paradox in his appearance, as the more his body came unbuilt, the more he looked like a body builder.

Finally, I sat on the edge of his bed and told him I had nothing left to offer; today or tomorrow would likely be his last today. He pulled himself up from his bed, tied the straps of his white "johnny" behind his back, and began to parade slowly and stiffly around the ward. Men in the neighboring beds who knew him best began to cheer and clap. Then all the men did. He raised his arms over his head, began to smile and picked up speed. The nurses joined the clapping and cheering. I joined. Arms high, triumphant, he circled the ward twice before allowing me to help him back to bed. "I know you tried," he said.

The movie *Rocky* appeared two years later. I had already seen it.

In the Bulfinch's open ward, when doctors examined a patient, the nurses closed the curtains surrounding that patient's bed. When it was time to remove someone's body, the nurses closed the curtains surrounding all the other patients' beds. Each was left to examine himself.

I took stock of my two years at Massachusetts General Hospital: amazing doctors, nurses, and patients, all of whom needed more tools, including better medicines. Nowhere was the lack of fundamental understanding more glaring than in how to treat cancer. I decided to join a lab at the National Cancer Institute. I wanted to learn how the immune system can kill cancer, as Hermann Lisco prophesied.

First, there was the receiving and giving of thanks. One of the patients I saw most frequently in my weekly clinic— he had congestive heart failure, chronic obstructive pulmonary disease, cirrhosis, and diabetes—managed to keep working part-time in a fish market in Little Italy in the North End. He paged me to say how sorry he was that I was leaving and that he had left me a gift at the reception desk in the lobby. Two days later, my shift ended. I picked up his gift on the way out. Wrapped in layers of brown paper around layers of waxed white paper were perhaps five pounds of fresh fish. At least it had been fresh two days before. I had to go some distance from the hospital before choosing a trash can so as not to drive new patients away.

The last step in my departure from medical residency at MGH was to meet the page operator whose sultry voice had so often disturbed my sleep. She must have used that seductive tone to minimize the fear of failure that she knew every page call aroused for a physician in training. Her voice reminded me of the young woman in the medical school admissions office who had asked me for a date. I bought a bouquet of flowers and imagined her receiving it—she would be in her twenties, svelte, a trifle bored by yet another young doctor bearing a gift. I found her in an attic-like room in near darkness, her smiling face lit by a glow from her switchboard. She was white-haired, likely past seventy, well past plump, and flabbergasted. All the better.

Between Medicine
and Science

MY TWO YEARS at the National Cancer Institute (NCI), one
of the National Institutes of Health (NIH), at the NIH campus in Bethesda, Maryland, were a mixed experience that
left me undecided as to how to allocate my time between
research and patient care.

On the plus side, these years were a crash course in
immunology. I met extraordinary scientists at a time when
the field was growing so rapidly that new questions took
shape faster than old ones could be answered. The yeasty
confusion that resulted was as promising as the scent
of rising dough. At the Immunology Branch of the NCI,
Thomas Waldman was discovering the basis of immunodeficiency diseases and learning from them the fundamen-
tals of immune system physiology. Dorothy Windhorst
was characterizing chronic granulomatous disease (CGD),
an immune deficiency that predisposes one to life-threatening infections. Years later, I would help introduce interferon-gamma as the first medication to prevent infections
in CGD. David Sachs and others were trying to understand the function of the major histocompatibility complex
(MHC) molecules so as to improve transplantation medicine. Sachs had just discovered what we now call MHC class
II molecules, but no one knew their function. His future

work would lay the foundation for today's implantation of kidneys and hearts from genetically modified pigs. Gene Shearer was mapping immune response genes and wrestling with the concept of T cell suppression. Pierre Henkart was identifying cytotoxic enzymes in killer T cells. Michael Potter and collaborators were discovering that the antigen-binding portion of antibody molecules is itself an antigen that can be recognized by other antibodies. I shared a lab with Richard Hodes, who had been a year ahead of me as a resident at Massachusetts General Hospital and who went on to become director of the National Institute on Aging.

I learned a great deal from Tom Waldman, Dorothy Windhorst, David Sachs, Gene Shearer, Pierre Henkart, Richard Hodes, and others, and from the manner of their brainstorming. The intellectual interactions mirrored the volleys David Sachs and I exchanged as we played squash on weekends. As Public Health Service officers, we had the use of courts at the Pentagon. We did not feel out of place there. Our mission, like the armed forces', was defense; in our case, learning how to help the immune system better defend people's health.

My branch chief, William Terry, was leading the effort to bring the People's Republic of China (PRC) into cooperative programs for the study of tumor immunology. At his home in an upscale suburb, he hosted what I believe were the first scientists from PRC to visit the United States. Wearing blue-gray Mao suits, they and their identically tunicked handlers sat stiffly in Bill's living room for slow, guarded, historic discussions. Bill was similarly active in trying to free an imprisoned immunologist in the Soviet Union whose criminal offense was that he was both internationally famous and Jewish.

But while Bill was focusing on trying to bring more freedom of movement to China and the Soviet Union, we were all ignoring restrictions on freedom of movement at home. The invitation to meet the visiting Chinese officials at Bill's home extended to everyone in the branch, including the lone Black person, who worked as a supply clerk. He asked me if I could give him a ride to Bill's house. I knew he drove to work, so I said I'd be happy to, but it would be a longer trip for him than if he went directly. He said it would not be safe for him to drive alone through Bill's neighborhood. He would fear for his life.

Additional issues on the negative side at NIH ranged from bureaucracy to sabotage. Personal computers were still in the future. I needed a typewriter. I was directed to a cavernous room on campus that housed hundreds of manual typewriters that had been discarded in favor of electrics. I could pick any one I wanted as long as I filled out a requisition in thirteen copies. When I brought the copies to the clerk, she photocopied them.

One day, a fire broke out in one of the many machines lining the corridor outside my lab, a scintillation counter that was used to quantify the amount of radioactive isotopes that immune cells had incorporated or retained. I pulled the fire alarm. Firemen came and put out the fire. A senior administrator called me into his office. "Are you an idiot?" he said. "Why did you pull the alarm instead of just putting out the fire yourself? Don't you realize it's illegal to have all these machines in the corridor—the counters, the freezers, the ultracentrifuges, the refrigerators? What if we have to move them now—where are we going to put them?" The order to clear the corridors never came.

After the firemen, we had two other kinds of visitors—a

scientist and the police. The visiting scientist was dating a recent Miss New Zealand. One day she came to my lab in a white lab coat. "I have a cough," she smiled. "Diagnose me!" She threw open the coat, revealing that it was all she wore. Richard Hodes continued pipetting, and I continued to read optical densities. She scowled, wrapped up again, and went down the hall to join the audience for a seminar that began shortly thereafter. Word of the event followed her to the conference room, which proved to be a substantial disadvantage to the speaker. The police arrived shortly after that. It was not indecent exposure that concerned them. They came to arrest the visiting scientist for unpaid parking tickets. There was a lively chase. The scofflaw escaped, but not permanently. He went on to become a pharmaceutical company executive and was convicted of insider trading.

My studies of tumor immunity were based on cells from mice. The scientist in charge of granting space in the animal facility was pursuing similar inquiries in his own work. He denied my request, saying he needed all the mouse space for himself. He advised me to take advantage of the National Cancer Institute's auxiliary Fort Detrick facility in Frederick, Maryland, about an hour's drive away. Fort Detrick was also used for anti-biowarfare research. It became famous in 2001 when a worker there mailed anthrax spores to people in the news media. For each trip to Frederick, I had to requisition a government car, a process similar to acquiring the typewriter. After a few trips I mastered the maze of unmarked access roads and interior corridors at Fort Detrick, which were designed to thwart spies. At the same time, I realized that my assignment to Fort Detrick was meant to thwart my work. Not only would it impose needless travel time, it would deny me the help that animal room staff routinely provided at the Bethesda campus. The lab I shared with Richard Hodes included a large walk-in closet behind a folding glass door. I used it to set up my own animal room. Adding up the weekly hours, I spent an estimated three of my 24 months at NIH changing water bottles, filling food holders, changing bedding, and cleaning cages for my mice, an echo of cleaning rabbit cages at NYU and cleaning the hospital room at Mass General.

I wrote a paper and offered courtesy co-authorship to a scientist in another branch who had made a minor contribution. I gave him the manuscript to review for corrections and for permission to include his name. He took months to give it back. During that interval he published his own paper on a topic so similar that there was no longer any point in submitting mine.

Lessons:

1. Scientists' personalities span the range of human personalities.
2. An institution large enough to ensure internal competition was not the environment for me, despite how much I learned.

I decided to pursue clinical medicine. I applied for oncology fellowships. At Memorial Sloan Kettering Cancer Center, the fellows rotated from one organ of the body to the next, handing off their patients as they went. At Yale, each fellow followed his or her own patients for the duration of the fellowship, or the duration of their patients' lives, whichever ended first. I chose Yale.

My experience at Yale was mixed, though in different ways from my time at NIH. The division chief, the eminent

Dr. Joseph Bertino, was on sabbatical at Stanford. While he was there, he put his home on the real estate market. We found out because he chose the wife of one of the oncology attendings as his agent. This was misinterpreted as a sign that he would not return. Most of the faculty began to look for jobs elsewhere and stopped making rounds with the fellows. To learn the nuts and bolts of oncology, I relied on a skilled physician's assistant, Burdeen Camp, who was assigned to Hunter 5, the cancer ward. The one faculty member in the Division of Hematology and Oncology who continued to teach won a large cash prize from the Department of Medicine in honor of his teaching skill. The other faculty in the division held a meeting at a time when they knew he could not attend. They voted that the prize honored the whole division, so the money should be shared.

I prepared a manuscript on a clinical problem that included a case report, a review of the literature, and an analysis of potential mechanisms. I asked the acting division chief for comments. He said it was good, but as a trainee, I lacked standing to publish it, so I should list him as the senior author. I threw the paper out. I chose a trash can distant from his office, drawing on my experience at Mass General with spoiled fish.

Patients taught me what I most needed to know. A high school student who left the hospital to die at home shared his bitterness at our failure to cure him. The tobacconist whose lung cancer I could not restrain thanked me for my efforts with a pipe and pouch from his shop. His wife's eyes beseeched me to thank him kindly. The bartender who told me that her breasts brought her the tips that helped pay her rent begged me to tell her that her surgery had preserved her symmetry. More than just livelihood, symmetry was dignity. The professor who came down with the same type of leukemia she cultured in dishes in her laboratory chose to die in the company of no one but Mozart. From a portable record player at the head of her bed, Mozart told of immortality, his hymn low, the door closed, the conversation private.

One day a seventeen-year-old high school student returned to the emergency room with a fever. Her acute myelocytic leukemia was rapidly advancing. Hunter 5 had no open beds. I told the admitting office she would have to go to one of the general medical floors.

The house staff marched up to protest having her on their service. They said her care would be too demanding. I had no sympathy for such a complaint. My sympathy was with the girl, whose leukemia was incurable. Still, she had a goal: to walk across the stage at her high school graduation.

Two days later, a bed opened on Hunter 5 and the patient was transferred. Her lungs were infected by Aspergillus. Aspergillus is a fungus whose spores we all inhale daily and dispose of readily. White blood cells called neutrophils and macrophages engulf the spores and kill them with the help of molecules called reactive oxygen species. The girl's leukemic cells were immature neutrophils that lacked that ability. The leukemic cells filled her bone marrow, crowding out the cells that would have become functional neutrophils and macrophages.

Neither the leukemia nor the infection was responding to treatment, the best that medicine then offered. The girl began to cough up blood. This meant the fungus was invading blood vessels in her lungs.

The next evening, the amounts of blood increased considerably. I tried to reach her mother, who worked at night. The chart listed only the home number and did not name the mother's workplace. No one answered.

Around midnight, the girl's coughs became continuous and the hemorrhaging copious. I called her home repeatedly, but there was no answer. Around 4 am, she began screaming in fear and pain. When the bleeding became torrential, she no longer could get enough air to scream. She whipped her head and shoulders from side to side in panic as her cheeks went gray and her mouth bubbled red.

Morphine's mercy had unmoored my mother from her cancer's agony. She slipped from my present into my past, as memories, and into my future, as motives. Those motives brought me to this moment by this patient's bed. Here, medical science had failed. But what about medical responsibility?

A decision was in my power. I would have to make it quickly. No time for consultation.

It would not be in my power to forgive it.

I gave an order. From a cord around her neck, the night nurse, grim-faced, took a key, unlocked a drawer. Eyes moist, staring, she handed me a syringe and a logbook to countersign.

Our patient slowed her thrashing. Still, she choked, wild-eyed, spouting blood.

I signed the log again.

I held her hand as she drowned.

As the black sky grayed, I phoned the girl's home again. Her mother answered. She had just returned from work.

Her daughter was gone. Her howls live on.

Dawn came. The ward was quiet. I finished the paper-
work and went to the staff cafeteria for coffee.

The tables were empty except for one woman my age
with auburn hair, wearing a tweed suit in the same hue. She
sat in slanting sunlight from the eastern window, a plate of
scrambled eggs before her, a book to the side.

"May I join you?" I said.

"OK," she said.

"Are you a physician?" I asked.

"I'm training to be a chaplain," she said. "What kind of
medicine do you do?" she asked.

I said, "I'm an oncology fellow."

"How unpleasant," she said. "Dying, I mean." She put
down her fork, pushed away her eggs and reached for her
book. "Look, I have studying to do. If you don't mind, I don't
want to talk."

I took my coffee to another table. The sun, a bit higher
now, poured in like a searchlight.

PART THREE
A Search

A Path

THE DYING GIRL in the cancer ward drove home how much science lacked. So did Mrs. C, my dying clinic patient, when she shoved me against a wall and told me to go seek better treatments. My hand on the girl's, the woman's hands on me: these encounters set me on a path, but the path was unmarked, and it stayed that way. Years later, I confronted that feeling in a forest where Amy and I were hiking. At a fork in the trail, we found a tree whose trunk bore seven signs. One sign aligned with one trail and one with the other. The other five angled all over the place. On all seven the weathered wood was mum. It's just a presumption something once was written there. *That's me, on the tree*, I thought. I go in tow to my own wandering thoughts and the comings, goings, interests, talents, and limitations of the people I work with.

Only retrospection discerns an arrow's arc between my start—hoping to control cancer—and all that followed, including tackling tuberculosis. Emotion can defy logic but can also evolve it—that is, exert selective pressure on logical choices. What's straight about my path is its emotional logic.

At the start are three hungers: to understand how things in nature work; to share understanding; and to share understanding verifiably. Communication in music, art, lit-

erature, and dance is limitless in intensity and indispensable for my equanimity, but indeterminate in accuracy. The
paintings of Paul Klee move me, but there is no way to be
sure I understand what he felt or meant. In science, we can
repeat an experiment. If others get the same result, they
understand. We can build on that.

Understanding shared with whom? The first test can be
whether a new understanding is shared by those who contribute to its development. Hence the rewards of working
in a team—more is learned and sharing can be sure. Those
rewards scale with the group's diversity in skills, outlooks,
and origins, until growth in numbers hinders.

How to achieve verifiability? It is not enough that observations be quantitative and reproducible; they must be
clearly defined and described. Clarity requires specificity—
the basis for something having the meanings or impacts
that it does and not others. As I continued to work toward
clarity with words, I became fascinated by how nature
achieves specificity—its own clarity.

For people to share understanding requires language—
symbols spoken or sung, written in words or equations,
or generated by musical tools, movements of the body, or
works of art. What languages do cells use to share understanding? We knew about hormones carried by the blood.
We understood that some cells release autacoids, chemicals
that diffuse a short way to the cells around them and change
their behavior. We knew that nerve cells release chemicals
called neurotransmitters, which diffuse no farther than the
sealed-off spaces between one neuron and the next neuron
or between a neuron and a muscle cell to which the neuron
connects. These chemical messages bind receptors on or in

those cells that have an evolved ability to respond to messages that help them execute their functions.

But how does a cell of the immune system tell a cancer cell or a bacterial cell to die—a cell that is not there to cooperate with the organism in which it finds itself, but to do the opposite? After all, cells that kill and cells that die are made of the same stuff: salts, sugars, fats, amino acids, nucleosides, vitamins, certain metals. Some of these components are dissolved in the cell's water. The rest are assembled in its carbohydrates, lipids, proteins, and nucleic acids. How can one ensemble of these substances exert life-or-death control over another ensemble of the same? Multicellular organisms, such as people, kill other multicellular organisms with trauma, poisoning, burning, suffocation, and starving. Which mechanisms are available to cells of the immune system? (All of them, it turns out.)

I needed to understand the biochemical messages that immune cells send that kill other cells. I needed to understand how and when the host avoids self-destruction in the process.

How can we learn the most in what little time we have? Ideally, an inquiry into the biology of one phenomenon teaches us about others. You can go wide in learning by drilling down from organisms to cells to molecules, because the more fundamental a process, the more likely it is to be present in multiple species on different branches of the evolutionary tree.

Recognizing convergence is another powerful way to leverage understanding, such as by recognizing similar properties and functions of products made by independently evolved, structurally unrelated enzymes that act on different molecules as their substrates. For example, it is striking and instructive that evolution has conserved the ability of organisms to use different enzymes and the electron-donating molecule NADPH to produce two different gases with profound and overlapping biological effects. Both of them are radicals—molecules with an unpaired electron. One family of enzymes produces a radical called superoxide from gaseous oxygen. Another family of enzymes produces a radical called nitric oxide from the amino acid arginine.

Cells die in a programmed way during an organism's development. Early cells give way to later ones with more specialized functions. Killing is different. Killing comes from combat—predation and defense, major forces for selection in evolution. Cancers are predators, but the majority of cancers arise after an individual has reached reproductive age, presumably giving cancer relatively little impact on evolution. In contrast, infections start to take a toll from birth, even before. The rules and tools that the immune system uses to kill cancer cells invading from within likely evolved for defense against infectious agents invading from without.

This is how emotion and intellect collaborated to pick a path. Emotion guided me to fight death from cancer by helping the immune system bring death to cancer cells. Intellect advised me to learn how to do this by studying how the immune system kills infectious agents.

A High View

FIVE THEMES from my time in science illustrate how a path that seems directionless can turn out to be as direct as an arrow's flight, because personal history and personality guide and shape what a scientist studies and how. Here is a high view.

Cancer is a great divider. It separates the dying from their loved ones, carving families' lives into before and after, held apart by a lasting scar. Yet cancer can unite. Doctor and patient, each scarcely knowing the other, may share experiences in ways rarely attained outside the companionship of family or the comradeship of combat.

Cancer showed me many deaths. Cancer medicine gave me opportunities to reach across divides that separate people of different backgrounds. And I could apply that idea in research by including scientists of different disciplines.

Macrophages are energetic cells of the immune system with wide-ranging responsibilities. Heart cells stay in the heart, connected to other heart cells; lung cells stay in the lung, connected to other lung cells. Macrophages move. Each goes alone, brooking no limitations on location. Macrophages wander through every organ, nurturing other cells, checking their health, collecting and dismantling those that wear out, all the while on alert for signs of foreign genes and damaged tissue. Sensing invasion, macrophages pick up weapons and fight. Their weapons include chemically reactive, charged-up versions of oxygen and nitrogen. Given the risk of collateral damage, the decision to arm is not left to the macrophage alone. The immune system uses dual-factor authentication. Full battle mode for macrophages requires a second signal from lymphocytes, which are immune cells with independent means of discriminating invader from self. The major signal is a protein that lymphocytes send out, called interferon-gamma. When a battle's won, other signals tell macrophages to put their weapons down and help heal the wound. Although macrophages can see cancer cells as tissue-damaging invaders and kill them, cancers can escape attack by disguising themselves as wounds, inveigling macrophages to help them heal.

Like a macrophage, as a scientist, I take on disparate directions and responsibilities. My lab and I go alone, resisting limits on topics and methods. I am a healer who left medicine for research in the hope of becoming a better healer. I am a worrier, on alert to protect family, and not only my own by birth and marriage. My expectation that everyone will care about fairness, about each other, about Earth, leaves me as naïve as macrophages deceived by cancer's masquerades.

Reactive oxygen species and reactive nitrogen species are closely related groups ("species") of chemically modified oxygen and nitrogen that can change the structure of ("react with") other molecules, changing their functions as well. Their seemingly promiscuous destructiveness defied conventional thinking about the chemistry of life. Even as evidence for their role in biology emerged in the last few decades of the twentieth century, I invited disinterest, dismay, and disbelief by joining those who studied them.

When I shared my thoughts about the biological role of reactive oxygen and reactive nitrogen species with colleagues to invite a dialog and they did not respond, the feeling was familiar to someone who grew up odd-man-out. It was hard for some to contemplate or countenance these often-toxic, sometimes cell-killing molecules, which seemed like intrusive disruptors in the body's order. But that is how death seems, too, and death is natural. I could ignore these disturbing molecules and move on, as one might try to get over a loved one's death, or I could seek to understand them, as part of an effort to understand biology by questioning death's necessity.

Antibiotics are miraculous drugs that have saved more lives than any others. Before we had antibiotics, an infected tooth felled my father's father when my father was the age I was when cancer carried off my mother. Babies with pneumonia died who were born only a year before penicillin arrived and cured my own pneumonia.

At a molecular level, antibiotics attain a goal I share: the ability to deliver a message that is understood as meant. An antibiotic is a chemical compound that binds within a bacterium to a specific molecular target that carries out an essential process, changing the target in such a way that if the dose of antibiotic is high enough, the bacterium dies, or at least stops growing.

Yet it's not so simple. The disorder that an antibiotic creates in a bacterium leads the bacterium to generate metabolites—small, self-produced chemical compounds—that react with other molecules. Chief among these reactive metabolites are the reactive oxygen species discussed above. We are just beginning to understand that these reactive oxygen species interact with additional targets in the bacte-

rium and give rise to other messages. Some of those secondary messages contribute to bacterial death. But sometimes
these secondary messages are not strong enough to cause
death, yet are strong enough to cause mutations or metabolic changes that confer resistance to the antibiotic—they
allow the bacterium to survive, or even grow, in the antibiotic's presence.

Over millions of years, bacteria and fungi invented antibiotics to communicate and compete. Most antibiotics we
use in medicine are man-made versions and variations of
the antibiotics invented by bacteria and fungi. No wonder
bacteria understand the antibiotics we throw at them, and
how to resist them, better than we do.

Yet bacteria have something more profound to teach us.
The ability of bacteria to adapt as individual cells and share
what they learn with other bacteria gives them prodigious
resilience in problem-solving. Collectively, they have intelli-
gence without consciousness or cognition. Their individual
units, capable of metabolic adjustment and tunable levels
of genetic mutation, communicate via secreted molecules,
resembling a nervous system that allows adaptation. Rapid,
multiple, independent opportunities for evolution and selection constitute species-level computation. We think of ourselves as the most intelligent among very few intelligent
species, but, unlike bacteria, we share relatively poorly—we
seem to be unable to solve problems that threaten our existence without creating more of them. Vastly outmatched
by infectious agents in our rate of evolution, we must make
far better use of what distinguishes us from microbes: consciousness and cognition.

For example, we are letting ourselves run out of antibiotics that work, by misusing, overusing, and underusing

(diluting for profit) the ones we have, and not making new ones fast enough. These self-defeating social errors have created a crisis called "AMR" after one of its components, the rising incidence of antimicrobial resistance. The future of antibiotics and of the medical and surgical practices that depend on them are endangered by divides that separate old convictions from new ideas, biologists from drug developers, academics from drug companies, food production from health care, and business models from medical needs. To solve this problem, like so many others, we need to cross divides.

Tuberculosis is one of the life-threatening infections that has been becoming harder to treat as resistance to antibiotics spreads. It is an indictment of science and society that drug-*sensitive* tuberculosis, which is curable, was nonetheless the world's leading cause of death from infection before COVID-19. COVID-19 reminded us yet again that infectious disease has no borders. This is truer than ever, as climates that were once regionally confined now migrate to other swaths of Earth, both driving and pursuing larger and larger numbers of migrating people. If we fail to control tuberculosis and climate change both, imagine the global toll as health systems crumble and migrations mount.

The tuberculosis bacterium spends most of its life in macrophages, constrained, often for years, by macrophages that have geared up in response to the lymphocyte-derived protein interferon-gamma. Yet tuberculosis resists being eliminated by macrophage-made antibiotics like reactive oxygen species and reactive nitrogen species, just as it excels at resisting antibiotics that scientists have struggled to find and drug companies have found scant profit to make.

How tuberculosis diminishes, deflects, and springs back

from macrophages' chemical attacks can help us understand how cancer cells do the same. If we can come together
to discover, develop, and distribute new antibiotics for
tuberculosis, that can show us how to do so for other infections, and perhaps how to work better and faster to improve
the treatment of cancer.

Cancer, macrophages activated by interferon-gamma,
reactive species of oxygen and nitrogen, antibiotics, tuberculosis—all seem so different. Starting my journey from
cancer, I had no idea that these diverse themes of study lay
ahead, nor that each would link to the others.

In 1977, a few days past the loving shove from my dying
patient, Mrs. C., I shelved clinical oncology. Amy and I
rented an electric typewriter, sat at the kitchen table and
took turns transcribing my handwritten and rough-typed
drafts of a paper for submission to the *Journal of Experimental Medicine*, as well as an application for a fellowship from
the Leukemia Society, a grant from NIH, and a request for a
position on the faculty at The Rockefeller University. Four
acceptances later, I joined Zanvil Cohn's interdisciplinary
collection of laboratories at Rockefeller and set up my own
group. About ten years after that, I moved to Cornell University Medical College, renamed Weill Cornell Medical
College in 1998 and Weill Cornell Medicine in 2015.

At the outset, all I knew about my path was that I
wanted to harness the destructive power of white blood
cells against cancer cells. Clinical medicine is replete with
examples of the immune system destroying infected tissue, such as forming an abscess to help contain an infection
from spreading. The immune system can destroy any tissue

that seems to signal infection, even when medical science has yet to find infection, such as in joints of people afflicted with rheumatoid arthritis. What is the chemistry by which some living cells can instruct other living cells to die?

Neutrophils, macrophages, and lymphocytes—white blood cells of the immune system—can destroy any tissue in the body that emits signals of two events—presence of infectious agents and damage of tissue.[3] If we want to focus the destructive power of non-malignant cells on malignant cells, we need to understand what chemistries some cells encode that kill others, and by what mechanisms cells deploy, restrain, or resist these chemistries. To learn these things became my goal.

Viewed from memory's height, it looks like my lab-mates and I traveled a path that we read off a map.

There is no map. The path is what we make as we pass.

The image of the U. S. Army surplus machete I kept under my childhood bed to dissuade a headless ghost stayed with me through the years. I swung the machete metaphorically as my colleagues and I hacked through a jungle of ignorance, confusion, error, and doubt. At times the jungle stalled us with thefts, deceits, or betrayals. These were painful and sometimes scarring, but not influential; they get no notice here. In contrast, the failures are worth discussing; they teach.

I had no map, but I did have an internal compass. Describing its guidance through dialog can give order to the stories. Below, the dates in parentheses refer to initial reports from my work in John David's lab at Harvard, Richard Root's lab at Yale, or from my own lab, first at Rockefeller, then at Cornell. Other groups took different routes to some of the same places and arrived at about the same times. It was good to see them!

By the mid-1960s, when I was in college, scientists had found that macrophages can kill bacteria, parasites, and tumor cells if lymphocytes tell them to gear up for it. No one knew how macrophages killed, and no one knew how lymphocytes told them to. Let's start with the messaging. How do lymphocytes send that instruction?

Surprise: by releasing information in the form of a protein (1971). The protein is different in kind from antibodies (1973), the only sort of protein that lymphocytes had previously been known to release.

What is the protein that delivers the instruction?

Another surprise: interferon-gamma (1983). Its function had been unknown.

After receiving instruction, how do macrophages kill?

Yet another surprise: in part, macrophages kill by producing large amounts of a family of chemicals that are forms of oxygen more reactive with other molecules than is oxygen itself. Their actions resemble those of household bleach. In fact, one of them is the active ingredient of bleach. The modified oxygen molecules are called reactive oxygen species. The first reactive oxygen species that macrophages make is superoxide. Superoxide is classified as a radical because it has a free electron, that is, an electron that's not in a bond with another atom. Radicals are unstable until their lonely electron forms a bond. Superoxide quickly does this by bonding with hydrogen ions (the simplest form of acid) in the surrounding fluid. The product is hydrogen peroxide. Hydrogen peroxide can pour out of macrophages (1977), oxidizing what it meets.

Is that all?

It isn't. A *killer* surprise: Macrophages and other cells can make large amounts of another small, radical chemical compound, nitric oxide, which gives rise to a family of additional reactive nitrogen species (1989). The effects of reactive nitrogen intermediates overlap with those of reactive oxygen species. Moreover, the two families interact to make molecules that are even more reactive.

How can the body afford to generate such noxious chemicals?

There is no end of surprises! It turns out that we depend on small amounts of both sets of these reactive molecules to regulate our cellular circuits and coordinate our normal functions. When our bodies sense danger, we ramp up the amounts. Then these reactive oxygen and nitrogen species can kill nearby cells by blowing their circuits (2003).

Facing all that firepower, why aren't tumor cells and pathogens always killed?

They try to prevent these attacks in the first place. Failing that, they have enzymes that help protect them from lethal injury, acting at every level we can imagine (2000 on).

Can't we make drugs that inhibit those enzymes?

Yes, now that we've identified the key enzymes, many of which were not known to have such a role (2000 on). We began with enzyme inhibitors for tuberculosis (2008), then saw opportunities in malaria (2018). Making drugs to modern standards takes more than a village. Part of the process and much of the effort becomes organizational.

Why not take that approach for cancer?

That was the hope. Thankfully, in a broad sense, that is what many are now doing.

Tuberculosis as Teacher

BOTH CANCER CELLS and infectious agents have genomes that differ from the genome of the host. Both invade and damage tissue. Both metastasize. Contagious infectious diseases metastasize not only within hosts but also between them. To direct immune cells against cancer cells, we would do well to learn how immune cells fight infectious agents—pathogens. "Pathogen," from Greek, means an agent that causes disease, but medical history reserves the term for infectious agents.

Which pathogens can best teach us what we need to know about immunity, the better to understand cancer and control it?

Mycobacterium tuberculosis, the bacterium that causes most cases of tuberculosis (TB), has co-evolved with us over tens of thousands of years. Like cancer, TB usually lingers within us long before it speeds up in some of us and kills. In fact, TB lurks in latent, symptom-free form in about one-fourth of humankind. It comes out of its closet to cause clinically evident disease in about five to ten percent of those with latent (asymptomatic) infection, at which point it will kill about half of those who go untreated. Even with treatment, TB was the world's single leading cause of death from infection in 2019. By 2020, COVID-19 snatched that crown, but will likely give it back when enough people are immunized against SARS-CoV-2 by infection or vaccination. Yet, in contrast to the AIDS virus, which cripples human immunity, the TB bacterium appears to be the strongest stimulus yet discovered of the widest range of responses that the human immune system is known to mount.

How surprising, then, that humans are the only species in which *Mycobacterium tuberculosis* completes its life cycle—multiplies in one host and sends its descendants to do so in others. TB has cast its lot with us. What does it mean that after tens of thousands of years, neither we nor TB has eliminated the other?

TB's long ride with us despite our vigorous immune response to it suggests that TB has learned not just how to withstand human immunity, but how to use it. Indeed, the human immunity that TB incites eventually liquefies lesions in the lung that surround the bacteria until they erode into the larger airways, the bronchi. There, lipids released by TB provoke the coughing that sends infectious aerosols into the air that others breathe. In this way TB takes a ride on an immune response vigorous enough to kill many of the causative bacteria but not all.

It seems that TB can read the textbook of human immunity better than I can. Can I learn more about human immunity by reading the genome of TB? In time, I began to try to think like the bacillus:

How shall I, *Mycobacterium tuberculosis*, resist being eradicated by human immunity? I need that immune response to help me spread, but I can't survive the full brunt of it, so I will weaken parts of it. That still leaves me exposed to too many of its bacteria-killing molecules, so I will break some of them down. I can't manage to destroy all of them, so I will learn to detect those that get by my defenses and adapt my metabolism accordingly, the better to withstand them. Some of my important mycobacterial molecules get badly damaged anyway, so I will repair them. Some are too far gone to repair, and the damaged forms are disruptive to my normal functions, so I will take them apart and use the building blocks to make new copies. Some are so badly distorted that they don't fit into the machinery I use for breaking them down, so I will throw a cloak around them and gather them to one side. When conditions improve enough for me to make new molecules and divide in two, I will ask one of my two bacterial descendants to sacrifice for its sib and hold onto the damaged molecules, while I endow my other offspring with new copies of everything it needs. With the next attack, the burdened cell will likely die, but the chosen one has the best chance to survive that I can provide. It only takes one of them to infect another host and start the disease anew.

My lab has identified enzymes in *M. tuberculosis* that carry out each of the defensive maneuvers I imagined. We have also identified inhibitors of most of those enzymes.[9–16]

Perhaps humans and *M. tuberculosis* have co-existed for so long because for much of our history, there were benefits to human populations from latent (asymptomatic) TB infection, and about 95 percent of TB infections remain latent. For example, given that TB puts our immune system to use, perhaps our immune system puts TB to use as well.

The world's most widely administered vaccine, BCG (bacille Calmette-Guérin), gives us reason to think so. The BCG vaccine was developed when Drs. Albert Calmette and Camille Guérin, working at the Institut Pasteur in France, repeatedly took small samples of a form of tuberculosis-causing mycobacterium from one laboratory culture and used it to start a fresh culture. By the time they had done this 239 times over 13 years, the mycobacterium was attenuated—it had lost its ability to cause disease. Since 1921, caregivers in many parts of the world have been inoculating newborns with BCG. The vaccine not only protects from childhood tuberculosis, as intended, but from a variety of other infections, presumably by boosting immunity in a general way. Also, it seems likely that latent TB infection would boost immunity well enough to protect us from some other infectious killers. Clinically active TB has a fatality rate of about 50%, but if only some 5% of people infected with *M. tuberculosis* face that risk, and the other 95% are protected from diverse infections, perhaps our relationship with TB reflects evolution's hard bargain: the death of some of us is a price our species evolved to pay for guarding a greater number from other ills.

Or perhaps humans did not evolve an immune response strong enough to eliminate TB in a greater proportion of the infected population because an even stronger response against a pathogen lurking in our lungs could have left our ancestors badly out of breath. Then they might have failed to catch the prey they chased or been unable to outrun whatever or whoever chased them.

Cancer may mimic TB in benefiting from an immune response against it that falls short of eradication. An immune attack can affect cancer cells' gene expression in such a way as to speed cancer's evolution, aggression, and evasion. Moreover, as with TB, our immune response against cancer is constrained by the need to protect healthy tissues from destruction. Today, the immunologic treatment of cancer (immuno-oncology) consists largely in relieving those constraints through what is called "checkpoint blockade."

Such was my thinking about TB and my belief that studying TB could reveal principles relevant to an immunologic approach to the control of cancer.

In later years, that line of feeling-guided thinking brought a new conviction: that an understanding about a disease mechanism is not confirmed unless that understanding helps prevent the disease or treat it. Strictly speaking, this is an unreasonable standard. Yet it drove me into a world new to me—drug development.

Although emotion can guide logical thinking, there is a point on my path where logic leads and emotion lags. I was scarcely past childhood when my mother died. As I told the psychiatrist who interviewed me at the start of medical school, my mother prized fairness. She would wish for anyone suffering from any disease, including TB, as much of a chance to watch their children grow as she would wish for herself and hers. Logic tells me that my failure to protect her or others like her from cancer does not mean I failed her. Yet that emotion will not yield to reason. After all, I stood powerless by her bed as she left.

Reactivity and Specificity

FOR MUCH OF my research I explored two biochemical pathways that turned out to be both conserved in biology—shared by widely different species—and convergent in evolution—exerting closely related biologic effects through the action of enzymes so unrelated in structure and mechanism that they must have arisen independently.[17, 18] These conserved and convergent pathways produced two classes of products—reactive oxygen species (ROS) and reactive nitrogen species (RNS). In biology, conservation and convergence invite fundamental insight. ROS and RNS appeared earlier in this book. Here we go deeper into what they are, how they are formed, and what they do.

What are reactive oxygen species? To understand that, let's begin with what we do with what we eat.

Our cells extract energy from food in intracellular organelles called mitochondria. The term "mitochondrion" comes from Greek for "tiny, thread-like granule." An organelle is a membrane-bound structure inside a cell. A cell itself is a lot like an organelle that houses other organelles. The human cell lives in a low-protein, salt-water environment. It carries out biochemistry under the protection of a water-repellent, lipid membrane that separates the high-protein, viscous interior of the cell from the more fluid outside, where the salts are of different concentrations than inside. However, the membranes of cells and the membranes of the organelles within cells are not just fatty, water-repelling wrappings. Different membranes are equipped for special tasks.

Mitochondria have two membranes—inner and outer. The inner membranes are equipped with enzymes that separate protons from electrons during the metabolism of food. Mitochondria pump the freed-up protons across the inner membrane into the inter-membrane space. Because protons have a positive charge, the imbalance in concentration of protons (more outside the inner membrane, fewer inside the inner membrane) sets up an electrochemical gradient. As protons flow back across the inner mitochondrial membrane to correct the charge imbalance, they turn a molecular rotor embedded in that membrane. The rotor's movement is coupled with the formation of specialized chemical bonds, which store the energy of the rotor's motion. These are bonds between an atom of oxygen and an atom of phosphorus in a carrier molecule called ATP (adenosine triphosphate). ATP moves out into the cell and bides its time. When the cell has the need, it breaks ATP's high-energy bonds and uses the energy that is released to power enzymes that make DNA, proteins, and lipids. In short, high-energy bonds are currency with which the cell pays its enzymes to make what the cell needs.

So far, so good, but the process began by stripping electrons off certain food-derived molecules to get ahold of the protons with which the electrons had been paired. What can the mitochondrion do with the leftover electrons? If cells can't stash the electrons somewhere safe, the cells will electrocute themselves. This is not the sort of problem to sweep under a rug. After all, if we can't make energy from food, we die.

Mitochondria solve this problem by giving two electrons at a time to each atom of oxygen in the form we find it (O_2) in the air we breathe. When this goes well, the product is two molecules of water (H_2O), a life-sustaining substance that accounts for about sixty percent of an average person's weight. But the process of handing off electrons is not perfect. Some proportion of the time, O_2 gets only one electron, not two. This turns it into a radical ($O_2^{\cdot-}$)—a molecule with an unpaired electron, symbolized in the chemical formula by a superscript dot. This oxygen radical is called superoxide.

We all make superoxide. Biochemists see its production as an awkward imperfection in the mitochondrial machine. Nature, I would argue, sees it as an essential component of a bigger machine—the cell itself. The production of superoxide is an indicator of how much fuel we are processing, and at what rate, and with what efficiency. The corresponding flow of superoxide serves as a signal to regulate other processes in the cell accordingly.

Lesson: Nature's "mistakes" are rarely that by the time we find them. By then, they've been put to use. What is lacking is our understanding.

Superoxide is the founding member of the family of chemically reactive molecules collectively called "reactive oxygen species" or ROS. Through a series of interactions with other atoms, superoxide can give rise to hydrogen peroxide (H_2O_2), a strong oxidant, and hydroxyl radical ($\cdot OH$), the strongest known oxidant in biology. With the help of an enzyme in white blood cells that has iron in its active site, hydrogen peroxide can react with salts called halides (chloride, iodide, bromide, and fluoride) that circulate in body fluids. One such product is hypochlorite, the active ingredient in household bleach, such as Clorox®. All told, ROS are superoxide, its acid (called hydroperoxyl), hydrogen peroxide, hydroxyl radical, an excited state of oxygen called singlet oxygen ($^1O_2$), and hypochlorite (as in Clorox®), and its relatives.[19] Our bodies make all of these.

It shocked biologists to learn, beginning in 1968, that nature would do something so seemingly self-defeating: make forms of oxygen so reactive that they can damage many of our own molecules. It turns out that's the cost of doing business, because we fuel our cells' power plants with oxygen through a process that's leaky. As noted, this strikes some scientists as imperfect, and for that reason, implausible. In fact, we have come to depend on these reactive oxygen species in more ways than one. It is not just that low amounts of ROS help a cell coordinate its metabolism. Some of our immune cells can make much larger amounts of ROS by a different route and fire-hose them against infectious agents. Then, instead of coordinating a cell's metabolism, ROS scramble it. The cell getting bollixed is one the body means to kill—usually a bacterium, a fungus, a protozoan, a cancer cell, or a host cell that has been taken over by a virus.

Our cells have no glass or plastic bottles in which to store ROS like Clorox® and its relatives. This means our cells can't stockpile ROS in advance of needing large amounts of them. Instead, our most abundant white blood cells, called neutrophils, make bursts of ROS on demand as they eat bacteria and fungi, and use the ROS to kill these pathogens. People born with mutations that disable their neutrophils' ability to make large amounts of ROS suffer a disorder called chronic granulomatous disease that puts them at high risk of life-threatening infections.

I discovered that another host defense cell, macrophages,

can make large amounts of ROS as well. First, though, they have to be instructed to do so by cells that recognize that something foreign has arrived. That recognition is the job of another type of cell in the immune system, lymphocytes.

As will be described below, in 1983, I identified interferon-gamma as a key macrophage-activating signal from lymphocytes.[20] In 1986, I reported in the *New England Journal of Medicine* that interferon-gamma can reduce the number of leprosy bacteria in human subjects suffering from that disease.[21] That finding inspired Alan Ezekowitz, a physician-scientist at Harvard Medical School, to recruit me, John Gallin (Director of the Clinical Center at the National Institutes of Health), and others to test the effect of interferon-gamma in people with chronic granulomatous disease. As reported in the *New England Journal of Medicine* in 1988,[22] the subjects in this study were protected from bacterial and fungal infections. This led the U. S. Food and Drug Administration to approve interferon-gamma for use in that disease. At first, we were stunned to find that while the patients were protected, their neutrophils did not produce more ROS.[23] In retrospect, we should not have been surprised, because it turned out that the subjects in the study had structural mutations in the major enzyme that phagocytes use to produce ROS—defects that interferon-gamma could not fix.

That left a major mystery: what else does interferon-gamma induce that helps the body fight infection? From 1988 through 1997, my colleagues and I reported a series of discoveries that provided an answer. Appropriately instructed ("activated") macrophages can also make another radical, nitric oxide ($\cdot$NO), that can also kill infectious agents. Nitric oxide can turn into other reactive molecules. Nitric oxide and the reactive molecules to which it gives rise are collectively called reactive nitrogen species (RNS), just as superoxide and the reactive molecules arising from it are called reactive oxygen species (ROS). Moreover, additional RNS arise when nitric oxide reacts with oxygen or with superoxide. The reaction of nitric oxide with superoxide makes peroxynitrite ($OONO^-$), which promptly decays into two radicals, nitrogen dioxide ($^•NO_2$) and hydroxyl ($^•OH$). Both are highly reactive, and, as noted, hydroxyl radical (one of the ROS) is considered the strongest oxidant in biology. All told, the RNS are $^•NO$, HNO, $^•NO_2$, N_2O_3, N_2O_5 and NO_2^-. Like ROS, RNS can attack a variety of other molecules. Like ROS, RNS are necessary for the host to survive infections by certain viruses, bacteria, and protozoal parasites.

In sum, nature doesn't make just one family of small chemical compounds that can potentially harm the cell that produces them or its neighbors, but at least two such families. The parent compound in the family of reactive oxygen species (ROS), superoxide radical, is an atom of oxygen that carries an extra electron that seeks to form a chemical bond. The parent compound in the family of reactive nitrogen species (RNS), nitric oxide radical, is an atom of nitrogen joined to an atom of oxygen, where the nitrogen carries an extra electron that likewise seeks to form a chemical bond. Moreover, these two families—the reactive oxygen species (ROS) that include and arise from superoxide, and the reactive nitrogen species (RNS) that include and arise from nitric oxide—can react with each other, producing additional highly reactive products.

Neither superoxide nor nitric oxide contains carbon. Both are volatile (they become a gas) at the temperatures and pressures of life on or near the surface of the earth.

In chemical terms, these features designate them as *inorganic radical gasses*. That label scared off many biologically oriented scientists in a period extending roughly from the late 1960s to early 1990s, convincing them that formation of superoxide and nitric oxide by life forms is out of the question.

After mounting evidence forced the scientific community to concede that ROS and RNS are authentic products not only of atmospheric and industrial chemistry but also of living cells, more layers of resistance remained. It seemed implausible that our own cells can produce dangerously reactive molecules in large quantities, as seen first with neutrophils and later with activated macrophages. Evolution, it was felt, was too good an engineer to bequeath us so much risk of self-destruction. This view ignored what physicians see routinely—the immune system mistakenly destroying joints in rheumatoid arthritis, making abscesses (pus-filled holes) in infected lungs and livers, causing septic shock. Immunity can be messy.

My goal was not to disparage evolution, but to better understand the problems to which evolution's best solutions seem so costly.

Still more baffling at the time, from the 1990s on, others began finding that production of ROS and RNS at levels thousands of times lower than made by activated immune cells plays key roles in everyday biologic processes, ranging from the decision of yeast cells to divide to the decision of tomato plants to flower.

For example, insulin is a hormone released into the blood by the pancreas in response to glucose, a sugar in a meal. When the level of glucose rises in the blood, so does the level of insulin. When insulin reaches various cells in the body, it binds to a protein called the insulin receptor that protrudes across the cells' outer membrane. The binding of insulin to the part of the receptor that lies outside the cell leads to a brief puff of ROS inside the cell. This leads to a chemical modification of the intracellular portion of the insulin receptor. That modification leads in turn to the transmittal of signals that activate certain enzymes in the cell. The active enzymes help the cell adjust its metabolism—for example, to use the circulating glucose for growth if that is needed, or to take up excess glucose and store it as glycogen, which is similar to starch.

Small amounts of RNS briefly produced in "puffs" are also critical for normal bodily function. One example of physiologic signaling by RNS earned a Nobel Prize for Robert Furchgott, Ferid Murad, and Louis Ignarro in 1998. Each time the heart beats, the rise in pressure of the blood pushing against the cells that line the arteries triggers those cells to make nitric oxide for a second or so. The nitric oxide diffuses into the underlying muscle cells in the vascular wall, transiently activating an enzyme that makes muscle cells relax. If the vessels did not relax on cue, the systolic blood pressure—the higher of the two numbers that healthcare workers record—would shoot even higher. Such pressure can blow a hole in the arterial tree, and if it does not, it could soon wear out the heart.

As these examples show, we do not just tolerate ROS and RNS as noxious products of metabolism, and we do not just turn on their production in large amounts to kill infectious agents. We depend on small quantities of them every minute of every day to coordinate bodily functions.

How can the same mechanisms whose killing of infectious agents is necessary for our survival of infection also click on with each sweet meal and each beat of the heart, maintaining what Claude Bernard called the "milieu intérieur"?[17] Today we call this "homeostasis"—preservation of cellular and organismal health through coordination of diverse functions.

Coordination depends on communication—what cell biologists call signaling. In time, I recognized that each of these seemingly opposite activities—emergency killing and homeostatic signaling—is predictable from the other.[24] Organisms did not have to evolve different sets of molecules to kill invaders and to keep order. On the contrary, killing at the cellular level can result from forcing an opponent into maladaptive signaling: signaling that is excessive in amount and duration and wrong for the time and place. That the same chemical compound can contribute to normal cellular function and to cellular death is no stranger an idea than that lymphocytes, macrophages, and eosinophils help tissues develop and function, but also both damage and repair them—a major theme in immunology that took hold in later years.

Evidence for the broad biologic relevance of ROS and RNS in homeostatic signaling grew explosively, yet was met in many quarters with non-acceptance or outright scorn. How could there be any biologic relevance of ROS and RNS in signaling when these reactive molecules are non-specific in their actions? How can something as complex as a living organism rely on non-specific signals? For example, a colleague of mine applied for admission to a graduate program in immunology. Her work was focused on immune cell production of ROS and RNS. She was denied admission to the program on the grounds that immunology is all about specificity, and ROS and RNS are non-specific.

What is "specificity" in biology? The field of immunology was based on the idea of specificity, the understanding that a given lymphocyte or antibody recognizes a particular antigen and not another. That is why we make a different vaccine for each infectious disease. Yet immunologists have no monopoly on specificity. Specificity as an organizing principle in biology runs deeper and broader; it is fundamental to the biochemistry of all living beings.

Consider how we use our genes and pass them on. One strand of DNA pairs with the other because it is made of four different components called nucleotides that are linked in a chain. What earned Watson and Crick a Nobel Prize in 1962 was their recognition in 1953 that once each nucleotide takes its place in the chain, it can bind well to just one of the four others that could face it in a separate chain. That means that a cell can faithfully copy one strand of its DNA by installing at each position in a new strand the one nucleotide that fits opposite the nucleotide on the original strand. Then the cell can use the second strand to do the same thing again and make an exact copy of the first. Because DNA encodes the cell's genetic information, the specificity of nucleotide pairing ultimately allows one cell to give rise to fair copies of itself. The specificity of nucleotide pairing is also what allows a cell to make a fair messenger RNA copy of the DNA in a gene. The sequence of nucleotides in messenger RNA dictates the sequence in which the cell's ribosomes will assemble other building blocks, amino acids, into proteins. Many of those proteins are enzymes. Each enzyme speeds up a particular biochemical reaction by binding with exquisite specificity to the molecules it will modify, called its substrates.

With biochemical specificity as the foundation of life,

what physiologic role could there be for inorganic radical gasses that can attack hundreds of different kinds of molecules? In short, many regarded what I helped discover as an affront to common sense and evolution's elegance.

Whether there's a problem here, or an opportunity for insight, depends on the meaning of "specificity." Eventually I recognized the fallacy of presuming that there must only be one type of specificity.

Infectious agents that can kill us evolve many orders of magnitude faster than we do. They can even evolve a few orders of magnitude faster than we can expand the immune cells in our bodies, cells whose secreted antibodies are specific for the infectious agents' new antigens. We need a way to hit targets in any infectious agent, whether we have encountered that agent before or not, cripple the targets quickly, and disable many at once. Moreover, we need to hit *parts* of their targets that the pathogens can't change by mutation without the targets losing function. Organisms widely distributed across the phyla have evolved a common answer to this challenge: on-demand production of increased amounts of ROS and RNS.

Can biology accommodate more than one kind of specificity? I think the answer is not simply "yes," but "yes, necessarily." When one molecule, like an enzyme, recognizes other molecules, such as its substrates (the molecules that the enzyme modifies), it exhibits *molecular specificity*: selective molecule-to-molecule interaction. ROS and RNS react with many different large molecules, such as enzymes: this is what leads many scientists to call their reactivity "nonspecific." However, a large molecule is made of many atoms. At the levels they attain in cells, ROS only react with certain *atoms* in large molecules. There is a high degree of specificity in which atoms ROS and RNS will preferentially attack within a multi-atom molecule. In other words, the chemistry of preferential reactivity of certain atoms with ROS and RNS allows ROS and RNS to carry a message—to signal—with *atomic specificity*: selective small-molecule-to-atom interaction.

ROS and RNS readily attack the sulfur atom, especially when it has a negative charge. They also attack iron, copper and selenium. However, at most levels in living cells, ROS and RNS spare carbon, nitrogen, oxygen, hydrogen, phosphorus, and other metals—that is, *almost all* the other kinds of atoms and the *vast majority* of all the atoms that large biomolecules contain.

In proteins, sulfur atoms appear mainly on the side chains of the amino acids cysteine and methionine. Only some cysteine sulfurs are negatively charged under the influence of the particular amino acids whose side chains come near them in a protein's structure. Negatively charged cysteine sulfurs—the favored targets of ROS and RNS—contribute to the active sites of many enzymes, such as phosphatases, which remove phosphate groups from proteins. A single human cell can contain hundreds to thousands of reactive sulfurs in cysteine side chains in its proteins. This gives ROS and RNS the potential to coordinately affect a variety of proteins near the places in the cell where small amounts of ROS or RNS are produced.

For example, as mentioned earlier, when the insulin receptor binds insulin, a puff of ROS arises inside the cell near the intracellular portion of the insulin receptor. The ROS come from a superoxide-producing enzyme from a family called NOX, for NADPH oxidase. The ROS transiently inhibit nearby phosphatases. This reveals the otherwise inapparent kinase activity of the receptor itself—that is, its ability to install phosphate groups on tyrosine residues in nearby proteins. By allowing that phosphorylation to proceed, ROS help launch the cell's response to insulin. That is atomic specificity working hand-in-hand with molecular specificity.[24, 25]

Ursula Jakob and colleagues have shown that cysteine-dependent enzymes include histone methyltransferases. Our DNA is organized by being wrapped around proteins called histones. Modifications to the histones affect which genes in the DNA are expressed and which are silenced. If ROS inhibit histone methyltransferases during a cell's response to a stimulus, that can affect the cell's expression of multiple genes for a long time thereafter.

To summarize, ROS and RNS at levels usually encountered in biology are specific for a very small number of targets, when you conceive of their targets as the kinds of *atoms* with which they readily react and the degree of reactivity of those atoms as influenced by other atoms surrounding them. If many of the large molecules in a cell contain one or more of those particular atoms in those particular reactive states, then ROS and RNS can react with many large molecules.

Is this just an inconvenience to living things, or worse, a drastic error on evolution's part? Neither. Think what you may, nature, as it does with everything else, puts the reactivity of ROS and RNS to use. At *low levels* of ROS and RNS, atomic specificity gives a cell a way to simultaneously and transiently coordinate local biochemical events that are otherwise not directly linked. *High levels* of ROS and RNS let a host defense cell alter the function of many molecules in an invading pathogen or cancer cell in a physiologically inappropriate way and for a long time, imposing havoc. Coordination gives way to chaos, and the targeted cell stalls or dies.

Why is there "necessarily" more than one type of specificity? Because the molecular specificity that dominates biological thinking depends on an overall pattern of individual interactions, each of which has atomic specificity— atom-to-atom interactions between some of the atoms in the interacting molecules. Atomic specificity is more fundamental than molecular specificity: it makes molecular specificity possible. The atomic specificity of ROS and RNS is just a special case of the atomic specificities on which the interactions of large molecules and, with them, life, depend.

Two features distinguish the atomic specificity of ROS and RNS from the atomic specificities that control molecular specificity, that is, the interactions of one large molecule with another large molecule, or a large molecule like an enzyme with its substrates of intermediate size. First is the asymmetry in size of the interacting molecules. ROS and RNS contain very few atoms—there are just two atoms in a molecule of superoxide and just two atoms in a molecule of nitric oxide—while the molecules with which they interact can be of any size and contain vastly more atoms. Second is the asymmetry in the number of potentially interacting molecular partners. With molecular specificity, the number of partners for one molecule can be as few as one other molecule. In contrast, for ROS and RNS, the number of interacting molecules is large. It is these unfamiliar asymmetries that gave rise to the misconception that ROS and RNS lack specificity.

There is probably nothing "non-specific" in nature if you look deeply enough. That is nature's startling clarity.

Macrophage Activation: Gearing Up to Kill

MY ENGAGEMENT with paradoxes of specificity began in 1968 when I plunged into research in medical school, taking a year off from coursework to join John David's lab. Recent observations by George Mackaness posed a conceptual challenge for the field of immunology. His findings gripped my imagination then and continue to challenge and excite the field.

Like Lester Grant, Mackaness, an Australian, had been a student of Sir Howard Florey's at Oxford, where he studied the action of antibiotics against *Mycobacterium tuberculosis* in macrophages. From the Dunn School on the edge of the bright green lawns of Oxford University Parks, he moved to the Trudeau Institute on the shores of deep blue Saranac Lake in upstate New York. The institute had been founded by Dr. Edward Trudeau to advance the care and study of tuberculosis at a time when the leading options were sitting in the sun and breathing clean, cold air or having one's infected lung collapsed or cut out. Living in a remote sanatorium probably did little beyond improving the nutrition of some of the patients and restricting the spread of the disease. Between the Dunn and the Trudeau, Mackaness spent a year at the Rockefeller Institute at the urging of René

Dubos, whose interest in tuberculosis had been heightened by his wife's death from the disease.

Mackaness's experiments led to a major shift in our understanding of the immune system. To understand his contribution, we need a quick tour of immunologic history leading up to his work in the early to mid-1960s and beyond.

In 1882, Ilya Metchnikoff, an émigré Russian zoologist fleeing Odessa and soon to be based in Paris, was living in Sicily when he launched the field of immunology with a microscope, a thorn, and a starfish. Seeing cells gather where he punctured the starfish larva with a thorn, he declared that phagocytic cells (cells that eat, later called macrophages or "big eaters") defend the host from invading microbes. In Berlin, the drug-discovering chemist Paul Ehrlich scoffed. He believed that what protects the host from infection are specific, soluble host-derived substances that bind specific, harmful bacterial substances (toxins), rather than host cells that eat bacterial cells. In 1908, Metchnikoff and Ehrlich uncomfortably shared a Nobel Prize.

The Nobel Prize committee had recognized that both were right, but mysteries remained: What are the soluble, immunity-enhancing substances? Are there other host-protective cells besides macrophages? Do soluble factors and host-protective cells interact, and if so, how?

By the 1950s, enough details had been filled in to give a first-draft answer to these questions. The soluble factors are chiefly antibodies and proteins, collectively called complement because they are needed to lyse (break open) cells that antibodies tag for destruction. The immune cells that eat and kill pathogens are macrophages and granulocytes (chiefly neutrophils). Non-phagocytic lymphocytes are somehow critical, too.

As immunologic research expanded, the picture grew more complex. In the mid-1970s, Ralph Steinman distinguished dendritic cells from macrophages. Lloyd Old and his colleagues began denominating lymphocyte subsets, a process that continues today. In the early 1990s, spurred by Charles Janeway, Jr., immunologists came to see the immune system as comprised of two arms, innate and adaptive. Innate immunity, it was proposed, kills pathogens directly. Individual macrophages and granulocytes of the innate immune system are not clonally distinct, so large numbers can be maintained in advance of infection and quickly mobilized to an infected site, but they lack specificity and memory. Adaptive immunity depends on lymphocyte clones (that is, individual cells and their descendants) that proliferate upon encountering a specific antigen for which the individual lymphocyte and its progeny display a specific receptor. Persistence of expanded clones with high-affinity receptors provides memory.

Key to the smooth functioning of this two-armed system is the crosstalk: dendritic cells present an antigen to lymphocytes, along with signals that prepare the lymphocytes to proliferate; lymphocytes, recognizing the antigen, make antibodies that frustrate the attack of the pathogen bearing the antigen or mark the pathogen for destruction by phagocytes or complement, and also somehow instruct macrophages to increase their killing capacity.

It was George Mackaness who first recognized the crosstalk, long before the "innate" and "adaptive" arms were called out and named. At the Trudeau Institute, Mackaness discovered that macrophages taken from mice during an infection with mycobacteria or certain other bacteria, or after a second infection with the same bacterium they had survived the first time, were induced from a state of minimal competence in the control of these bacteria to a state of heightened activity against all of them. In other words, "macrophage activation," as he called it, was specific in its induction, but non-specific in its expression.[26, 28] The importance of this discovery propelled Mackaness to the directorship of the Trudeau Institute, then to election as a Fellow of the Royal Society, and then to presidency of the Squibb Research Institute, the precursor to the research arm of today's Bristol Myers Squibb, a leader in cancer immunotherapy. Nonetheless, the phenomenon was a paradox and its mechanism was a mystery: how could a non-specific response be induced in an immunologically specific way?

In retrospect, the late 1960s marked the transition from the classical phase of immunology launched by two founding fathers of the field of immunology, Metchnikoff and Ehrlich (cells and soluble proteins each do their thing), to the current phase, marked by ever-increasing recognition of the diverse sources of information and means of exchanging it within the immune system; the versatility of means of execution of host-protective functions; the participation by many other cell types in host defense; and the contribution of immune cells to the development and function of the other organs. Mackaness's paradox called out the need to move on from the classical phase.

An example of how far we've come since Mackaness's time is the recent recognition that macrophages can be more readily activated in the future if they or their precursor cells have been activated in the past. This form of memory, called "trained immunity," results primarily from chemical marks placed on or removed from the proteins called histones around which a cell's DNA is wound. The pattern of these extra chemical groups influences which genes are ready to get expressed.

Now we're ready to return to 1968, when I sought a research experience in medical school. I thought the explanation for Mackaness's paradox must lie in cell-to-cell communication, with one type of cell (lymphocytes) responsible for specificity and the other type of cell (macrophages) acting on information that the first type of cell somehow provided. I could best test this hypothesis in a lab that studied both types of cells. Then as now, there were few such labs. Fortunately, one of the best—Professor John David's—was at Harvard Medical School, in the Robert Breck Brigham Hospital atop Boston's Mission Hill. Within the hospital, though, John David's lab was not on top; it was in the basement. The lab upstairs belonged to the department chairman, a world-leading immunologist, Prof. K. Frank Austen.

The two labs, both successful, took different stylistic routes to productivity. Prof. Austen taught that time was important. He periodically marched through the labs with a steel-tipped wooden yardstick to swat us on the butt so we would not be late for seminars. He timed our practice talks with a large, ticking alarm clock, yardstick at the ready. When he felt the time was right, Prof. Austen met with me to explain each project in his lab. He gave me appointments to meet him at intervals for updates, while cautioning me not to discuss the work with members of his lab. They were to work in silence and talk only to him.

Prof. Austen brought me from his office to his lab to show me his kymograph. Based on an invention from 1847, the machine featured an upright, hollow, cylindrical, lampshade-like drum, covered in paper whose surface was smoked with soot, as if it had been held over a fire. As a motor turned the cylinder, a needle on a lever scratched a white trail in the gray, recording the distance the tip traveled up or down and the time course of its excursions, as defined by the rate of rotation of the drum. What caused the needle to swing up was the contraction of a piece of intestine from a guinea pig. The intestinal segment sat in a bath next to the drum, stretched between two fixed posts. By adding substances to the bath that the team collected from antigen-stimulated immune cells, the scientists could tell which purification procedures enriched substances that made the intestine contract. They were discovering key molecular mediators of asthma, a disease in which the airways constrict, and anaphylaxis, a sudden and severe allergic response in which both airways and intestines constrict and blood vessels weep out some of their fluid, which can cause hives, swelling of the lips and tongue, and a fall in blood pressure. Prof. Austen called the active materials "slow-reacting substance of anaphylaxis" (SRS-A). In the years to come he would identify SRS-A as a family of lipids called leukotrienes. In 1997 and 1998, the U. S. Food and Drug Administration approved asthma drugs that work by blocking cells' receptor for leukotrienes. Every day for many years I have taken one of the drugs whose discovery began with the swing of the needle on Prof. Austen's kymograph.

John David's lab had a different feel. Joking was interrupted by singing or cursing, but rarely by silence. Everyone had something to say about everyone else's work. John and his wife, Roberta, who was also his lab manager, invited Amy and me to dinner at their home, where they made sure we became acquainted with Stravinsky on the hi-fi and whatever John was mastering at the grand piano. They sat through the night with us in the medical school dorm common room to watch the Apollo 11 moon landing on TV. John even undertook to cure my naïveté by introducing me to risqué foreign films in a downtown theater. Roberta specialized in getting things done, fast. For example, when the maintenance crew did not react quickly enough to her telephoned complaints that the lab was overheated, she climbed up on a lab bench and swung her hard-heeled shoe to break the glass in a window she could not open.

When I had demonstrated scientific curiosity, experimental tenacity, and the ability to take and make a joke, John and Roberta inducted me into the "Metchnikoff Society." Roberta hired an illuminator who hand-inked heraldic certificates of membership. Membership conferred the privilege to sit in a dingy basement breakroom named "The Metchnikoff," whose couch and chairs nourished mold that seemed to pre-date Metchnikoff himself. Inductees rarely entered the room a second time. Those who earned the right to use it were too busy earning the right. Still, the induction, the certificate, and the special room sent a message that the lab team was a family.

The David lab was given over to the production of a new entity, a "factor," later dubbed a "cytokine," released by lymphocytes in response to an antigen (a foreign substance). "Cytokine" was a neologism with Greek roots that was intended to convey "something that moves (kine) a cell (cyto)" in the literal sense of making a cell move or in the general sense of moving a cell to act differently.

What did the cytokine ("factor") do that the David lab studied? The "factor" made macrophages stop migrating out of the pellets where they had been centrifuged together in the bottom of glass capillary tubes plugged with clay. Whatever persuaded the macrophages to stay put without killing them was called "migration inhibitory factor" (MIF). This was a strange bioassay, yet enormous excitement surrounded the news of the simultaneous discovery of MIF in 1966 by John David,[29] who later chaired the Department of Medicine at the Harvard School of Public Health, and Barry Bloom,[30] who had earned his PhD with Merrill Chase at Rockefeller University and later served as dean of the Harvard School of Public Health. The excitement mounted with the finding by Peter Ward, Heinz Remold, and John David three years later that a lymphocyte factor could have an effect seemingly opposite to MIF's, promoting macrophage chemotaxis (migration up a concentration gradient),[31] and Gale Granger's report, also in 1969, that antigen-stimulated lymphocytes could release a factor he called lymphotoxin that could kill certain cancer-like cells in culture.[32] MIF, chemotactic factor, and lymphotoxin provided the first evidence that lymphocytes could release anything other than antibodies, assuming these factors weren't antibodies—and by so doing affect the behavior of other cells.

Bizarre though it was, the assay to detect a lymphocyte-derived product by its inhibition of macrophage migration was the point of a very big spear, which took the form of a very pointed question: How could cells communicate with each other without using blood-borne hormones like insulin or neurotransmitters like the one discovered by my teachers Kravitz and Potter? Migration inhibition was what we saw, but what else did these messages convey, to what end, and how?

The David lab's version of putting a man on the moon was to purify MIF. We slaved in teams six days a week, immunizing dozens of guinea pigs, harvesting their enlarged lymph nodes, and teasing the tough nodes apart with forceps until our fingers and wrists ached. One of the doctors working in the lab brought his seven-year-old daughter to one of our Saturday workathons. "I hope what you're doing is good for the guinea pigs," she said. Clearly not. What we did led indirectly to better health for many people, but at the time we couldn't know that. We answered her question with a pause in our work that was silent, awkward, and brief.

We added the foreign antigen to the cell suspensions, incubated the cells at body temperature in an artificial medium that models the fluid bathing cells in the human body, collected the medium with whatever the lymphocytes had added to it, and turned it over to the gifted entomologist-turned-biochemist Heinz Remold. Heinz tirelessly applied what could have been called, in retrospect, low-performance column chromatography (a technique to separate molecules based on their size, charge, or other properties by the different times it takes them to percolate through fluid-filled channels surrounding tiny spheres with appropriate surface properties). It emerged later that cytokines work at concentrations far below the capacity of the techniques of the time. It was as if we were trying to reach the moon by linking ladders together.

Heinz fought off hopelessness with humor. When that didn't work, he grunted blues tunes. Perhaps the main reason he left post-war Germany for the US was to collect blues albums; they filled the shelves that lined the walls of his home. The music of sympathy that sustains hope by denying it led Heinz to semi-success: MIF had the properties of a moderately sized glycoprotein distinct from immunoglobulin, the biochemical name for antibody proteins. The complete purification and molecular cloning of MIF lay years in the future with the advent of high-performance column chromatography and other techniques.

After a few months on the production line without a lab bench of my own, I realized my only hope of escape was to set up my own lab within the David lab. I found a little-used storeroom, cleaned it out, built a bench, taped my time-course protocol to the wall, ignored the laughter it provoked, and began asking what the products of antigen-stimulated lymphocytes did to macrophages besides slow their migration. Since precisely measured time was important to Prof. Austen, it would be important to me, too. I set up complex, meticulously controlled experiments that could only be carried off with operations spaced at 30-second intervals. I kept track of the steps with a stopwatch, following flow charts I wrote out on graph paper and pasted up over my bench.

I decided to look for metabolic hallmarks that might be associated with enhanced antimicrobial activity. This idea sprang from something I heard from yet another powerful individual, Prof. Manfred Karnovsky, who lectured to our first-year biochemistry class.

What biochemical processes help a white blood cell kill a bacterium? When the white blood cells called granulocytes or neutrophils eat particles ("phagocytize," from Greek roots for "cell that eats"), they suddenly consume much more oxygen than they do at rest. Karnovksy was a pioneer in analyzing the biochemical basis of this "extra respiration" of phagocytosis. He was just then discovering that phagocytosis triggers a certain biochemical path in the conversion of foods to energy (a process called "intermediary metabolism").[33]

It would later emerge that this path transfers an elec-

tron to a molecule called NADP⁺, converting it to NADPH.
NADPH can donate the electron for the production of the
superoxide radical, the founding member of the family of
molecules called reactive oxygen species (ROS). Also emerging later was the discovery that the enzyme whose function
is lacking in chronic granulomatous disease is responsible
for using NADPH to make superoxide during phagocytosis
without relying on mitochondria, and this "NADPH oxidase" accounts for the "extra respiration" of phagocytosis.
From superoxide, the cell could make other reactive oxygen
species (ROS).[34] It also later became clear that neutrophils
protect themselves from their own enormous quantities
of ROS by neutralizing some of the ROS with a molecule
called glutathione. One of the three amino acids in glutathione is a cysteine that bears an ROS-sensitive sulfur atom.
Regeneration of glutathione in its reduced (un-oxidized)
form also requires NADPH.

To summarize, by using oxygen as part of an enzymatically imperfect program for extracting energy from
food, the mitochondria in most of our cells make small
amounts of reactive oxygen species (ROS). Most scientists
regard these ROS as waste products, but in fact, these small
amounts of ROS help link a cell's behavior to its metabolism. The white blood cells called neutrophils (a form of
granulocytes), which are tasked with defending us from
infection, are equipped with a specialized enzyme system
that can make ROS in far larger amounts. This enzyme
system is normally kept "off." The cell can accomplish this
because the enzyme system is made up of several different
proteins that the cell stores in separate internal compartments, where they do not interact. When the neutrophil
meets a microbe, the cell brings the components of the com-

plex enzyme together. That turns the enzyme "on," and the cell blasts the bacterium with ROS. To kill the bacterium and survive the encounter, the neutrophil uses sugar in the metabolic path that Manfred Karnovsky studied, which provides electrons for two uses—first, to give to oxygen, making ROS; and second, for self-protection, to give, via glutathione, to the ROS that diffuse back into the cell, turning those ROS back into oxygen and water. Karnovsky discovered that phagocytizing neutrophils—neutrophils that engulf particles, such as bacteria—activate that glucose-using, electron-generating pathway.

Macrophages engulf particles, too, I reasoned. Might they operate a similar metabolic pathway? Might "macrophage activation" enhance their capacity to do so? To pursue these questions, I worked for a year in John David's lab, returned to the lab for a few months during the clinical years of medical school when I fled the neurology rotation, and spent my remaining elective time there.

The most important lesson I learned from John David and Manfred Karnovsky in the years 1968–1970 was that science is a bridge. The two professors—one an immigrant from France, the other from South Africa—worked at the same institution, in labs 0.8 miles apart, but had never met. Yet, each gave me a key to his lab. It was my privilege to introduce them to each other. I learned how to measure cellular glucose oxidation in the biochemistry lab and applied the methods in the immunology lab.

Another lesson was to see a third style of management in Prof. Karnovsky's lab to compare with the styles in the Austen and David labs. Prof Karnovsky introduced me to his two postdoctoral fellows. He told me to learn whatever I needed from them and talk to him when my project was done. The fellows showed me what they thought I ought to know. Then conversation was done. I was one of them.

Other lessons were specific to the science. I found another example of what a soluble product of antigen-stimulated lymphocytes could do to another cell: activate intermediary metabolism in macrophages, specifically through a pathway called the hexose monophosphate shunt (HMPS).[35, 36] As Heinz Remold schooled me in protein biochemistry, I learned that "macrophage activation factor" (MAF), like MIF, was a non-immunoglobulin glycoprotein,[37] that is, a protein that was not an antibody and that had sugars hooked onto it. I didn't have time to test the prediction that the enhancement of glucose oxidation through the HMPS was accompanied by enhanced antimicrobial activity, but this was established by a medical student who followed me in the lab, Robert Fowles.[38] This body of work provided the first molecular link to explain the physiologic connection between the adaptive and innate immune systems, between lymphocytes and macrophages.

Did the enhanced metabolic activity of MAF-treated macrophages help drive enhanced ROS production? Did enhanced ROS production contribute to enhanced antimicrobial activity? MIF and MAF co-purified by the techniques of the day, but were they the same? If MAF was a distinct entity, it would check in as a fourth cytokine after MIF, chemotactic factor, and lymphotoxin. If one cytokine could activate macrophages, could another cytokine deactivate them?

Before I could address the questions that arose from my work in the David and Karnovsky labs, there were a few things to attend to—the rest of medical school, internal medicine residency, Public Health Service duty at NIH, oncology fellowship, and a choice: whether to stay at Yale, practice medicine, and do some research on the side, or find a place to pursue research uninterrupted.

Of course, there was no such choice. Nothing in life is uninterrupted. The fork in the road was whether the interruptions would include the immediate needs of cancer patients and their families along with everything else, or just everything else, with the hope of addressing cancer patients' needs in the future. After all, I had just begun to discern a message being sent by one set of cells and received by another. What was the message, exactly, and what exactly did it mean?

What shaped that decision, one of the most important I made, was a string of failures that persuaded me to change direction.

Interferon-gamma
as Messenger

DURING MY ONCOLOGY fellowship at Yale in the Division of
Hematology and Oncology, I learned that the training program was funded in part by an outlying community hospital. The funding arrangement required that I work there for
three months. When I arrived, the lone oncologist on staff
seemed overwhelmed. Perhaps he sized me up and decided
it would be too hard to train me how to administer potentially lethal drugs. Perhaps he couldn't bear it that many of
the people waiting outside his office for those drugs were in
their teens and twenties and would not be getting older. In
any event, on my fifth day in the post, he pulled up a station
wagon to a side door, cleaned out his desk, and drove away.

I felt it would be irresponsible for me to manage the
patients on my own. I petitioned the department to send a
board-certified oncologist to the outlying hospital or advise
the hospital to send their patients to the medical center.
The department refused. In turn, I refused to continue the
rotation. I was about to be expelled from my fellowship for
insubordination when the program director made an offer.
I could remain in the program, but only if I retrieved all
copies of my letter of protest, tore them up in his presence,
and spent the rest of the rotation out of his sight.

Thus my inglorious entry to the lab of Yale faculty member Dr. Richard Root in the Division of Infectious Disease, a safe physical and administrative distance from the Division of Hematology and Oncology. Dick was an inspiring mentor. Although I was from an alien and troublesome tribe—oncologists whose toxic drugs suppressed patients' neutrophil counts, leading to difficult-to-treat, life-threatening infections—he included me in Infectious Disease Division's picnics and softball games. I missed every pitch but caught every glance he gave his beloved wife, Marilyn. She clearly knocked Dick out of the park, along with socking doubles and triples.

In the years to come, Dick went on to chair the Departments of Medicine at the University of California San Francisco and University of Washington. He was crushed when Marilyn died of amyotrophic lateral sclerosis. Five years later, he was remarried and back in full swing. Sadly, his swing was checked forever during a visiting professorship in Botswana. He was canoeing on the Limpopo when a crocodile lunged from under, snatched him, and dispatched him.

There are many versions of an ALS-like death, a death you know is coming once you have a diagnosis. At least Marilyn could say goodbye. There are many versions of the crocodile, a death that strikes without warning from beneath the surface. At least the way Dick lived left nothing else unsaid when he lost his chance to say farewell.

Under Dick's tutelage at Yale, I learned to measure the respiratory burst of neutrophils. The respiratory burst—the abrupt, large-scale addition of an electron ("reduction") to oxygen to produce ROS in a cell without the involvement of mitochondria—was just then emerging as the first molecularly defined antimicrobial mechanism of the innate immune system.[25] I saw my chance to return to unfinished business with activated macrophages. I soon found that macrophages were the second kind of cell capable of releasing large amounts of ROS. In contrast to neutrophils, however, macrophages had to be immunologically activated.[39]

Almost every scientific discovery requires or affords an opportunity for self-discovery. I was devoted to medical oncology, despite certain inconveniences that may have stemmed from my status as a misfit and rebel. For example, I was frequently on call during those two years, but the oncology division never gave me access to an on-call room. If the security guards forgot to lock up the clinic, I could sleep fitfully on an examining table, using sheets I stole from linen carts on the wards. When the clinic was locked, I could sometimes cadge a sympathetic secretary to lend me a key to the Hematology-Oncology library, which had a couch. No matter—I could cope with the frustrations of round-the-clock living in a hospital. But when I had found time to work in Dick Root's lab and had begun assays on multiple populations of macrophages in head-to-head comparisons, and my beeper summoned me to the emergency room, and I returned hours later, the macrophages had to be poured down the drain. That was frustration of another order.

My response was a double departure: from Yale and from the practice of medicine in favor of full-time research. The move to Zanvil Cohn's Laboratory of Cellular Physiology at Rockefeller University afforded an extraordinary educational opportunity. René Dubos occupied the office across the hall and would occasionally discuss articles with me, including mine. Dubos discovered the first antibiotics made by organisms in the soil. He interpreted them as chemical messages helping to regulate an ecosystem. Enlarging that thought, he became the first environmentalist after Alexander von Humboldt, a century before, had introduced the concept that geographically varied physical surroundings should be objects of study, because they shape plant and animal biology and human society. Dubos famously taught us, "Think globally, act locally."

Down the hall from Dubos, Ralph Steinman had just discovered dendritic cells,[40] for which he would be awarded a Nobel Prize in 2011 (Ralph died on Friday, September 30, 2011, but his death, which would have precluded the award, had not been reported by the time of the announcement on the morning of Monday, October 3). Sam Silverstein, having been the first to climb peaks in Antarctica that would later be named for him, had just launched the field of cell biologic studies of phagocytosis.[41] Andy Luster, an MD-PhD student working with Jay Unkeless, teamed up with Jeff Ravetch to discover the first member of a large family of important cytokines called chemokines.[42] Bill Muller and Michel Nussenzweig, two more MD-PhD students, would later join me as editors of The Journal of Experimental Medicine. Michel, who worked on dendritic cells with Ralph, went to Stockholm to receive Ralph's posthumous award, and deserves to return for his own.

Also at Rockefeller was an inspiring and creative biochemist, Anthony Cerami. From his beginnings on a chicken farm in New Jersey, Tony became a lab head and dean of students at Rockefeller. His work epitomized the idea that biochemistry offered a powerful approach to understanding infection biology. His trainees included Kevin Tracey and Bruce Beutler. Kevin, a brilliant neurosurgeon, researcher, inventor, and author, would become president of the Feinstein Institute for Medical Research at Northwell Health on Long Island. Bruce would share the 2011 Nobel Prize with Steinman and Jules Hoffman. As with many others at Rockefeller, Tony Cerami's approach refuted a prevalent notion, that basic scientists should leave questions posed by disease to physicians and physician-scientists, along with any medical applications of what they learned.

The consummate physician-scientist was the great, kind, and good Maclyn McCarty, another editor of the *Journal of Experimental Medicine*, whose office was a few floors above my lab. Mac, a pediatrician, had discovered that DNA is the hereditary substance, as he reported with Oswald Avery and Colin MacLeod in the *Journal of Experimental Medicine* in 1944. Mac's modesty, his discovery's refutation of alternative explanations for heredity favored by others more vocal, and Avery's death eleven years later combined to deprive Mac of what would have been the twentieth century's best-deserved Nobel Prize in Physiology or Medicine. Today, the approaches that Tony and Mac took to basic science are called "molecular medicine" or "translational medicine," that is, the effort to turn basic discoveries into means to prevent, diagnose, or treat disease.

With the opportunity to set up my own lab, I reflected on my experiences in the labs of Profs. Austen, David, Karnovsky, and Root. I decided to combine features of each with my experience as an intern and resident in organizing a patient-care team. As I did in the hospital, I would recruit people from different disciplines. Multi-disciplinarity was consonant with the environment in the Laboratory of Cellular Physiology. As in the David lab, there would be no intellectual hierarchy. Each person would be encouraged to contribute to others' efforts, yet all trainees would be secure in their roles as leaders of given projects. We could talk, joke, and sing, but not a lot. As in the Austen, Karnosky, and Root labs, we would focus. We would give ourselves the chance to enter a zone of serenity, the one reward a scientist doing benchwork can aspire to daily. After all, the thrill of discovery and the joy of sharing what you've found take years to come, if they come at all.

Building on my experiences with all four professors, I would bring a biochemical perspective to immunobiological questions. I used much of my start-up funds to buy two major items of equipment—a temperature-controlled fluorimeter and a dual-wavelength scanning spectrophotometer. I arrived with the first known functionally relevant biochemical assay for macrophage activation—the enhanced capacity to produce ROS, as I discovered in Dick Root's lab—and used it as a read-out to return to the question from my time in John David's lab—which glycoprotein is the macrophage activation factor?

It proved to be a blessing that years of medical residency and fellowship had delayed my return to this problem. The intervening years brought advances in column chromatography for protein purification and the advent of monoclonal antibody and recombinant protein technologies. With my assay and these three new sets of tools, I was finally able to identify the major lymphocyte-derived macrophage activation factor (MAF). It was not MIF after all. Its identity was completely unexpected: interferon-gamma (IFN-γ).[20] Together with macrophages' enhanced ROS-releasing capacity, my Cornell colleague Henry Murray showed that interferon-gamma improved the ability of macrophages to control two protozoal pathogens—*Toxoplasma gondii*,[20] a cause of miscarriages, stillbirths, mental disability, and other ailments around the world, and *Leishmania donovani*,[43] a parasite that causes visceral leishmaniasis, a debilitating and often fatal infection found in regions with tropical climates. It was Henry Murray who later saved my life when I developed septic shock.

My first evidence for interferon-gamma's ability to activate macrophages was with macrophages that developed from human blood monocytes cultured in vitro ("in glass," meaning in laboratory vessels).[20] I was eager to test the idea in vivo—"in life," meaning, in a host organism—and not just in mice, but in people. The next step was to pick a disease whose victims appear to be suffering from inadequate activation of their macrophages.

Rockefeller University and its next-door neighbor, Cornell University Medical College, were pioneers in what is now called "global health." At Cornell, Prof. Walsh McDermott, who had helped introduce penicillin into clinical practice during World War II, went on to help pioneer the treatment of tuberculosis. He would receive the Albert Lasker Award in 1955 for introducing isoniazid, one of the first TB drugs, in the United States. Another Cornell professor, Benjamin Kean, was a leader in what was then called "tropical medicine." At Rockefeller, René Dubos, whose former student Bernard Davis went on to teach me microbiology at Harvard Medical School, had been the world leader in studying *Mycobacterium tuberculosis* in the laboratory. Tony Cerami and George Cross were working on African trypanosomiasis, also called "sleeping sickness." Rockefeller scientists William Trager and James Jensen had just discovered how to grow malaria parasites in red blood cells. No wonder various members of Zanvil Cohn's group turned to additional diseases of the global south with their understudied biologies and inadequate therapies: leishmaniasis, South American trypanosomiasis (Chagas disease), and leprosy.

Leprosy is caused by a bacterium, *Mycobacterium leprae*, a cousin of *Mycobacterium tuberculosis*, the bacterium that causes tuberculosis. The term "mycobacteria" comes from the Greek for "fungus," reflecting historical confusion over the nature of these slow-growing bacteria. Some people's macrophages kill the leprosy bacteria so effectively that only a few bacteria remain, although the strong immune reaction against them can damage tissue. In that form of the disease, the patients' immune system vigorously attacks infected Schwann cells, cells that surround and insulate nerve fibers. As a result, the nerves lose their ability to conduct electrical signals alerting the brain to pain. Lacking sensation, patients traumatize their hands and feet and begin to lose fingers and toes. At the same time, their macrophages are activated and keep the number of leprosy bacteria vanishingly small in the skin, where biopsies are taken to monitor treatment. However, in other people with leprosy, the macrophages seem clueless and allow the leprosy bacteria to proliferate within them. This form of the disease is called "lepromatous" for its potentially disfiguring swellings. Here, the patients' lymphocytes fail to recognize the leprosy bacteria, their macrophages are not activated, and the skin becomes bloated by accumulations of ineffectual macrophages stuffed with leprosy bacteria.

Cohn, Wes van Voorhis, Gilla Kaplan, Ralph Steinman, and their colleagues were studying the "lepromatous" form of leprosy. They were characterizing lepromatous leprosy as a failure of macrophages to become activated in response to the bacteria.[44] Given my finding that interferon-gamma was the principal macrophage-activating factor, they asked whether lymphocytes of patients with lepromatous leprosy, unlike those with the type of leprosy that involves very few leprosy bacteria, fail to produce interferon-gamma in response to the bacillus. The answer in vitro was "yes." Where better, then, to test if interferon-gamma would work as a macrophage activating factor in vivo, than in patients with that disease?

First, I needed to secure a suitable supply of interferon-gamma and permission to give it to people. Then I needed volunteers with lepromatous leprosy.

It was feasible to conduct a clinical trial with interferon-gamma only because of recent discoveries by Stanford professor Stanley Cohen, University of California-San Francisco professor Herbert Boyer, and their colleagues. In 1973, they stunned the scientific world with the demonstration that they could take two different genes from a bacterium, cut them up, recombine their parts, put the synthetic gene back in a bacterium and get the bacterium to make a new, "recombinant" protein. In 1974, they went a key step further and showed they could take a gene from one species of bacterium, put it in another species of bacterium, and get the second species to produce large amounts of the protein that the foreign gene encoded. The same method allowed bacteria to express a biomedically useful protein from an animal's gene. So began the recombinant DNA revolution, with its twin potentials: to make proteins whose sequences could be modified as desired, including by putting "tags" on them to make them easy to pull out from a complex mixture; and to make potentially unlimited amounts of any given protein without having to obtain it from its natural source. Rather than collecting human or animal tissues in order to purify proteins from them, as we struggled to do in John David's lab to get tiny amounts of MIF from the lymph node cells of guinea pigs, scientists could produce the same proteins in bacteria grown at industrial scale.

Within two years—in April 1976—the biotechnology industry was born when Boyer and an investor named Robert Swanson each ponied up $500 to launch a firm they called Genentech. The third member of the firm was molecular biologist David Goeddel. By 1978, his team produced the first biotechnology drug, recombinant insulin. No longer need insulin be laboriously purified from pancreases of animals; it could be farmed from vats of bacteria.

By 1982, David Goeddel and his Genentech associate Patrick Gray had produced recombinant interferon-gamma. Years later, I collaborated with Stanley Cohen to identify genes that restrict the ability of macrophages to kill mycobacteria. But long before that, the leprosy quest introduced me to Pat Gray and David Goeddel.

Another of Genentech's early hires was Costa Sevastopoulos. Although trained as a physicist, he had oversight over the fledgling firm's clinical research collaborations. In 1984, with Costa's enthusiastic support, I wrote an Investigational New Drug Application to the Food and Drug Administration. Today, collecting the data and preparing the application would be an effort for a large group. Then, I made a presentation to the Rockefeller University Institutional Review Board, chaired by Maclyn McCarty, who gave their approval as well.

With pure, sterile, quality-controlled, recombinant interferon-gamma from Genentech in hand and permission to use it from the FDA and Rockefeller, all I needed were volunteers with lepromatous leprosy. I teamed up with New York City-based leprologist William Levis, whose Staten Island clinic took care of most of New York City's hundreds of leprosy patients. We recruited some of them to take part in a clinical trial we conducted at the Rockefeller University Hospital. One volunteer worked as a nanny for a newborn baby in a wealthy Connecticut suburb. Another assisted in a hospital operating room. A third was a cook in a restaurant. None had yet been disfigured or disabled by the disease, but each lived in fear that in time it could cost them their jobs and turn them from providers to dependents.

Because no one knew how to grow the leprosy bacillus in the laboratory, progress in treating the disease was measured by scoring skin biopsies for the reduction in bacterial numbers. This was judged by counting bacteria in thinly sliced pieces of the biopsied skin that were mounted on glass slides, stained, and viewed through a microscope. To my astonishment, jet-gun injection of one thousandth of a gram of interferon-gamma into the skin of the study subjects led to rapid clearance of most of the bacteria from the vicinity of the injection site.[21] The clearance of bacteria was much faster than could be achieved by existing drugs—ten days versus six months or more. Moreover, I found that the monocytes taken from the leprosy patients' blood released abnormally small amounts of the antibacterial product hydrogen peroxide when ingesting leprosy bacteria in vitro. The injection of those tiny amounts of interferon-gamma in their skin restored the ability of the monocytes circulating in their blood to produce hydrogen peroxide, even though the concentrations of interferon-gamma reaching the blood must have been extremely small. This experiment established that interferon-gamma is a physiological macrophage activating factor—it can convert macrophages in a living host from harboring infectious agents to snuffing them out. Moreover, this was the first time that a cytokine—a non-antibody host protein used by cells to signal each other—was used to treat a non-viral infection in humans or to correct an immunological deficiency.

After I moved to Cornell University Medical College in 1986, I found that intradermal injection of that same tiny amount of interferon-gamma on one side of the patient led to rapid activation of macrophages and lymphocytes in leprosy lesions on the other side of the patient as well.[45]

When the first results were published in 1986 in the *New England Journal of Medicine*,[21] Patrick Gray invited me to come to South San Francisco to visit Genentech and give a seminar about the work that his cloning of interferon-gamma had made possible. I flew out, toured the facility, met scientists throughout the day, and gave my talk toward the end of the afternoon, a Friday. I was surprised that Dave Goeddel did not attend, but I appreciated that he had more important things to do. Near the end of the talk, I began to hear noises from above the ceiling tiles. They grew louder as I wrapped up and congratulated Genentech on enabling such path-breaking studies.

Applause was spotty, tepid, and brief. Worse, there was only one question. Pat Gray raised his hand. "What is leprosy?" he asked. My heart sank.

I had no idea that the gulf separating this room full of talented "gene jockeys" from the world of medicine they were revolutionizing was so wide that they had not heard of this Biblical disease. I was saddened that they could scarcely appreciate what they had done. I was frightened by that, too.

While I launched into an explanation, it became clear that the audience was more interested in the ruckus over my head. It was my turn to ask a question. "Pat, what is that noise?" I asked. "That's Dave Goeddel up there," he answered. "It's his way of reminding us that Friday afternoon is time for fun and beer." I ended my visit to the future by drinking alone in an ebullient crowd of scientists even younger than I.

Others took note, however. As mentioned, treating leprosy patients with recombinant interferon-gamma was the first example of what is now called "host-directed therapy of infectious disease" for a non-viral infection. It soon led to the second example, this time for a protozoal rather than a bacterial infection.

Late one Saturday afternoon in 1988, two years after publication of the leprosy report, I was mowing the lawn when Amy called me to the phone. The caller introduced himself as head of the Institutional Review Board at Memorial Sloan Kettering Cancer Center. He quizzed me about the safety profile of interferon-gamma, what I understood about its mechanism of action, and whether I had any unopened vials in my lab. He said he would explain his call later. That evening, he called back. The Institutional Review Board had met, considered my responses, and approved a request from their medical staff to seek a compassionate use exemption from the Food and Drug Administration to give interferon-gamma to a little girl in Memorial Hospital who was near death. At age ten, she had apparently been cured of Hodgkin's disease, a form of lymphoma, when her doctors removed her spleen and gave her radiotherapy and chemotherapy. Now eleven, she had returned to the hospital with a fever. Her condition rapidly worsened; she seemed to have meningoencephalitis, inflammation of the brain and the membrane lining it. When no diagnostic test revealed the cause, the physicians assumed that the lymphoma was back. They gave her more chemotherapy. A technician examining a sample of her blood under a microscope reported to her supervisor that she saw something moving. The team summoned Herbert Tanowitz, a parasitologist at Albert Einstein College of Medicine. "Those are trypanosomes," he told them.

Trypanosoma cruzi is the protozoal parasite that causes Chagas disease, rarely found outside of South America. The girl had been born and raised in the Bronx. She had never traveled beyond the northeast US. During her lymphoma treatment, she had received transfusions of platelets, cells in the blood that promote clotting at sites of injury. Hospital records showed that platelets had come from six different donors. One of them was a seventy-year-old woman in good health who had immigrated to the United States from Bolivia sixteen years before donating platelets. Presumably this generous woman unknowingly brought the parasites with her. The donor's healthy immune system kept the trypanosomes in check, but the recipient's immunosuppressed state allowed them to flourish.

The treatment for Chagas disease was a drug called nifurtimox. Remarkably, the compound contains a nitro group, which might be released as nitric oxide or a compound related to nitric oxide, the product of an interferon-gamma-inducible enzyme that my lab would purify the following year. The Centers for Disease Control and Prevention in Atlanta flew a supply of nifurtimox to New York. On the third day of using the drug, the girl's blood pressure plummeted. Fluid had accumulated in the sac surrounding her heart, compressing it. Her doctors drained the fluid. A pathologist examining the fluid under the microscope saw more of the wriggling, worm-like organisms. On the fourth day, the team urgently sought another option. That's when my lawn-mowing was interrupted by a call. The team knew about my work with interferon-gamma not only from my report on its use in leprosy, but from three other studies that I coauthored in 1986 with Memorial Sloan Kettering Cancer Center investigators on the use of interferon-gamma in patients with cancer.

Now, my task was to clear the regulatory path for giving the girl interferon-gamma to compensate for her deficient immunity. Although it was now Saturday evening, I telephoned the Food and Drug Administration. I convinced the operator that the call was urgent and she should give me the home number of the officer on duty. A babysitter answered; the officer and his wife were at a dinner party. I phoned the home of their hosts and secured the officer's permission. I called Genentech and got their permission as well. Sunday morning, the fifth day of nifurtimox treatment, I retrieved a box of vials of interferon-gamma from a refrigerator in my lab and crossed York Avenue to Memorial Hospital.

The girl had developed seizures and gone back into shock. I recommended a daily dose and watched the interferon-gamma being injected. Within three more days, the parasites had disappeared from her blood and her condition was greatly improved. On day 23, she went home. I saw her once more, on a follow-up visit. She was fine.

I continued to encounter the disheartening gap that sometimes yawns between translational scientists, who put basic
science to medical use, and basic scientists, most of whom
have had limited exposure to medical biology, including basic scientists successful enough to attend Gordon
Research Conferences. These are highly prized meetings
of about 100 researchers who come together from around
the world for nearly a week to share their latest findings
on a single topic. After chairing Gordon Research Conferences on two different topics ("Cancer" and "Phagocytes"),
I served on the Gordon Research Conference Scheduling
and Selection Committee and the Gordon Research Conferences' governing council. Those credentials assured my
admission to any of these conferences to which I applied, no
matter the topic. Attendance was otherwise limited to leaders and up-and-comers in the specific topic of the conference. I indulged in this opportunity to broaden my horizons
by attending a wide range of Gordon Research Conferences,
such as "Bioorganic Chemistry" and "Phosphorylation and
G-Protein Mediated Signaling," besides the continuations of
the ones I had chaired. At those meetings I generally knew
no one, except by reputation.

Gordon Conference attendees are encouraged to mix at
meals. The man who put his tray down next to mine at the
first dinner at "Phosphorylation and G-Protein Mediated
Signaling" was an eminent discoverer of tyrosine kinases,
a class of enzymes that includes the receptor for insulin. He
asked what I was working on. There was no sign of recognition when I started talking about macrophages and lymphocytes, so I moved on to neutrophils. He still had no idea what
I was talking about. I got him to acknowledge that he was
familiar with the formation of pus at the site of an infec-

tion. He was astonished to learn that pus consists mostly of neutrophils that have died fighting bacteria and that its green cast comes from iron in the enzyme that the cells use to make their own version of Clorox®. After absorbing this information, he looked uncomfortable, rose with his tray in hand, said he wanted to get more to eat, and did not return.

Lessons:

1. Same as at Genentech. There is a key need for the biomedically bilingual—people who can speak the language of basic science along with the language of medicine. If even high-powered PhD's are cut off from this appreciation, what about the public? Is there a way to explain such things in story-like form and keep it true?

2. Many people you meet can markedly change your outlook or your path—among them in my case, Lester Grant, Roger Revelle, John Fairbank, Judy Sulzberger, Hermann Lisco, John David, Richard Root and Ralph Steinman, along with Michael Sporn, Philip Davies, and Lloyd Old, about whom more in coming pages. Yet one meets others, equally influential, who have little impact. Whether meeting someone makes an impact, and how that impact alters your course, may be determined within minutes of meeting, but the reasons are obscure. This can make a life-path feel chaotic. There is pattern, but it takes reflection to resolve.

3. Dinners are liable to be lonely if you must discuss pus.

On my return from Genentech in 1986, a series of studies I conducted, collaborated in, or helped design soon showed

that administration of interferon-gamma not only activated monocytes (cells that mature into macrophages) in
the blood of cancer patients,[46] but also reduced the incidence of serious infections in people with chronic granulomatous disease,[22] the disorder in which white blood cells
make too little ROS and struggle to kill infectious agents,
and also led to resolution of the parasitic disease visceral
leishmaniasis.[47] By then, Genentech had sold the rights to
recombinant interferon-gamma to a European firm. The
new owners denied my request for access to interferon-
gamma for further studies in leprosy. By and large, people
with leprosy are among the poorest on our planet. You can
connect the dots. Interferon-gamma could be a standard
treatment for lepromatous leprosy, but it is not.

Our discovery that interferon-gamma could activate
macrophages in vivo in mice[48] was followed by evidence
from others that knocking out interferon-gamma or its
receptor made mice extremely susceptible to other mycobacteria besides the agent of leprosy, namely, bacteria that
cause tuberculosis and bacteria related to those (e.g.,[49]). My
future colleague and now *Journal of Experimental Medicine*
co-editor Jean-Laurent Casanova discovered that the same
was true in people who have genetic deficiencies in the production of interferon-gamma or in their cells' ability to
respond to it (e.g.,[50]). Interferon-gamma-releasing capacity
in response to mycobacterial antigens became a clinical test
for infection by *Mycobacterium tuberculosis* and a biomarker
used to monitor trials of tuberculosis vaccines. Adminis-
tering interferon-gamma became a treatment for infected
patients with genetic or acquired defects affecting their
ability to produce it. Inhaled nitric oxide became an experi-

mental treatment for difficult-to-treat infections of the airways, including by so-called non-tuberculous mycobacteria.

These findings contributed to a growing impression of universality involving the functions of activated macrophages in different species and for different functions. The next big twist in my path arose when that idea collided with results of our studies on tumor cells.

But first, more life lessons.

Home Invasion

ON THE COLD, sunny morning of December 9, 1983, I walked the few hundred yards from the maternity ward at New York Hospital to my lab at Rockefeller University. There, my lab mates greeted me with champagne and croissants to celebrate Amy's delivery of our first child, Eric, the afternoon before. Joining three PhD students and two postdoctoral fellows in raising a plastic glass was the visiting chair of the department of pediatrics at National Jewish Hospital in Denver, Richard Johnston. Eric's first mark of distinction was that Dick Johnston volunteered to be his first babysitter.

Soon immunity intruded, bestowing on Eric another distinction rare at the time: severe food allergies. Conventional baby formula made Eric vomit. The pediatrician said he would outgrow it. Then Eric developed asthma. Was it connected to the formula? We didn't know. We administered bronchodilators (drugs that help relax constricted airways) by dissolving the medication in apple sauce or in a nebulizer. Episodes of shortness of breath became increasingly severe, but the pediatrician denied my request that he prescribe a vial of epinephrine for me to keep on hand. Epinephrine is the medicine most often used to relieve a severe asthma attack. Epinephrine counters the effect of substances released by immune cells that make airways constrict and blood vessels leak fluid into the tissues, like Professor Austen's "slow-reacting substance of anaphylaxis." It was epinephrine that revived me as a child of eight who could scarcely breathe.

Few pediatricians back then had seen children with severe food allergies. Our pediatrician seemed to consider the problem a fictional projection of parental anxiety. More sympathetic was a colleague who joined a lab near mine after completing his pediatric residency. He helped me cadge epinephrine and a syringe from the Rockefeller University Hospital. Amy and I took them with us wherever Eric went.

We stopped giving Eric dairy products but didn't scrub them from our home. Like most people in the early 1980s, we did not grasp the magnitude of the threat. By the time Eric was two, we had moved to the suburbs. One evening, Amy and I brought him with us to a gathering of Rockefeller scientists in another town. We asked the host, who came from India, if the bread called naan that he served was dairy free. He said it was, but in fact, naan is usually made with yogurt and milk. Eric chewed some. Before we could stop her, one of the guests, despite knowing of Eric's milk allergy, slipped him a bite from her plate, which held a yogurt-based dish. Concerned, we left the party. On the way out, Eric began to struggle for breath. As we neared the car, he retched, wheezed, and grayed. Then his face ballooned.

The host, who had walked us out, offered to drive us to the local hospital. I snatched the epinephrine and the syringe from the trunk and jumped in the back with Amy and Eric. As Eric turned blue, I cracked the vial, filled the syringe, and injected his thigh. Quickly, he pinked.

When we reached the emergency room, the doctor on call was unfamiliar with the term "anaphylaxis" (from the Greek for "guarding again"). He did not know that epinephrine was the major remedy, nor that the symptoms could return in the following hours and require a second dose. We called our new pediatrician. He urged the emergency room doctor to keep Eric under observation for several hours. We waited. Eric dozed off, breathing easily. A few hours later, we drove home.

Within days we were in the office of a pediatric allergist. He confirmed that Eric had severe skin-prick reactivity to dairy products, and also to hen's egg, peanut, corn, and soy. When the blood tests came back, they revealed high levels of immunoglobulin E (IgE) antibodies against each. We began to appreciate the level of vigilance this required when Amy, having had ice cream about half an hour before, returned home and kissed Eric on his cheek. Moments later, a hive rose there in the shape of her mouth. The allergist advised a campaign of scrupulous avoidance of the offending foods. He prescribed Epipens—spring-activated syringes pre-loaded with epinephrine. When Eric reached his teens, wherever he went, one pocket bulged in his pants. There he kept not one Epipen, but two.

The childhood years brought more frightening episodes. When Eric was a toddler, his lips swelled and his airways constricted when we carried him to a New Year's Day party, where eggnog simmered in a chafing dish. His eyes itched and his lips and tongue tingled as they began to swell when we walked past a pizzeria whose exhaust fan hummed over the door. Visits to other children's homes were dangerous experiments.

Eric's upbringing meant navigating a maze. Prepared

foods like bread with no dairy products among the intended ingredients still caused reactions if they had been made in equipment used at other times for foods containing milk, butter, or cheese. Standing in grocery store aisles scrutinizing labels was just a first step; next were phone calls to manufacturers to learn how they separated and cleaned their production lines. Keeping a dairy product in the refrigerator for one member of the family was like leaving cyanide out for another.

When Eric was in junior high and attending state-wide music competitions in Rochester, or a program at Eastman School of Music there, Amy or I traveled with him with a pasta pot and an electric griddle. In time, Amy discovered a firm that made pre-packaged, dairy-free rations for the U. S. military under halal supervision. These solved some problems but not all. When Eric traveled by plane as an adult, the post-9/11 approach to airport security sometimes required that he open each packaged meal. Then he would have to toss them all.

When Eric was seventeen, the *New York Times* reached us through our membership in the Food Allergy Research and Education (FARE) network to ask if we would share Eric's story. Eric agreed. Susan Dominus's feature, "The Allergy Prison," appeared in the *New York Times* Sunday magazine on June 10, 2001. Eric's story was recounted alongside others. In the years that followed, parents, pediatricians, and educators became aware that severe food allergies are a real and growing problem. Scientists speculate about the cause. There is evidence that that over-use of antibiotics in the food industry and medical practice has reduced the diversity of helpful microbes in our intestinal tracts, confusing our immune systems.

A chronic immune disorder in one member of a family can affect the others in many ways. For example, when the sorely needed individual attention for Eric's younger brother Noah included a trip outside the home for a dairy-containing treat, we had to make Noah wash his face and hands and change his clothes when he got home. Little wonder that whatever Amy made for dinner, Noah demanded that his be something else. How distracted were his parents? For the first few years, we forgot to pay for auto insurance, risking financial ruin.

I faced death from asthma as a child. In years to come, I would undergo septic shock, where I faced a nearly even chance of dying or surviving. During those illnesses, I did not fear for my life. Perhaps I was pre-occupied by the struggle to breathe or the struggle to think when my blood pressure fell. Perhaps optimism during one's own illness is an evolved effort to rally.

In contrast, a parent's fear for the life of their child is ever-present. It escalates when the potential cause of death is nearly ubiquitous and potentially unseen. With its constriction of airways and vascular leak, anaphylaxis combines the worst features of asthma and sepsis and can kill faster than either.

An increasing number of families now experience immunity's home invasion, and not just from anaphylactic allergies. Aberrant immune reactions against self-antigens—natural components of one's own body—underlie rheumatoid arthritis, systemic lupus erythematosus, multiple sclerosis, psoriasis, insulin-dependent diabetes, and many other disorders.

Happily, Eric and Noah became fast friends. Moreover, by his mid-thirties, Eric's allergies were gone (while immunologists do not fully understand how allergies form, they know even less about why they sometimes disappear). For the first time in Eric's life, he tasted cheeses, ice creams, chocolates, and pizzas. His joy was indescribable.

Lessons:

1. Immunity is the only bodily system licensed to kill. When we encounter alien genomes in our body (viruses, bacteria, fungi, protozoa, or worms) or our own cells with altered genomes (cancer), immunity is our most effective protagonist. Yet, in countless situations, immunity can be a potentially lethal antagonist.
2. You can spend your life studying immunity without learning how to stop it from hurting a person you love. That's no reason not to try.
3. If you like what you're eating, savor the sensation.

Holding Back
and Falling Down

NOTHING IN THE immune system goes unregulated. Destructive power must not only be inducible; it must be suppressible as well. Realizing this led me to study the counter-regulation of macrophage activation. During those years, the theme of holding back in the immune system was mirrored by a series of instructive failures in research—mine and others'—linking these two themes in memory.

Initially, my studies of macrophage actions on tumor cells progressed in parallel with studies, done by my lab and others, of their actions on protozoal parasites and bacteria. Activated macrophages could kill mouse tumor cells in vitro using ROS.[51-58] Artificial macrophages that could produce nothing but ROS could protect mice from otherwise lethal inoculations of tumor cells.[56] For their part, tumor cells went to the trouble of releasing a factor that could antagonize or even reverse interferon-gamma-induced macrophage activation.[59] We eventually purified this macrophage deactivation factor[60] but were never able to clone it—that is, to isolate the gene encoding it. Descartes wrote, "Je pense, donc je suis" ("I think, therefore I am"); contemporary biologists are more likely to say, "It's been cloned; therefore it exists," with the corollary, "If hasn't been cloned, don't bother me." In other words, it had become standard to doubt the identity or even the existence of a protein until the gene encoding it was isolated.

The molecular identity of this first-found macrophage deactivation factor is unfinished business. What stopped me from working on it was the first of three failures related to protein purification.

Why keep talking about failures? Failures are full of lessons. In science, the "failure" of a gene because of its mutation or experimental deletion ("knock-out") helps reveal its function from the change in the host's phenotype—the constellation of its properties. Likewise, failures in interpersonal interactions can teach us more about their functions.

Subita Srimal was a postdoctoral fellow in my lab who purified macrophage deactivation factor. When Subita returned to India, another lab member picked up the project at a time when she was facing major stresses at home. She told me about them, but I failed to recognize their gravity and offered nothing more than sympathy. To meet my expectation that she make quick work of repeating the purification, she tried a shortcut so sure to fail that in retrospect I see it as another call for help. Proof came back from protein sequencing that the product was an irrelevant protein commonly used as a molecular standard. The stuff was sitting in a bottle on the shelf above her bench. She must have heavily spiked our sample with it, despite knowing that sequencing would reveal the contamination. She quit, and our funding ended. I had to put the project aside.

Such setbacks are not reserved for junior scientists. A few years later a senior scientist called with great excitement. He had taken a year off from his duties as a department chair at an eminent institution to continue his research on a protein of immunologic interest. He finally had the recombinant protein, though it was not yet pure. It had remarkable properties, which he had described in several recent publications, and he was sending me some of the crude preparation to test while purification was underway. I found that the preparation he sent induced the enzyme "iNOS" in human macrophages cultured from healthy volunteers, something I had otherwise been unable to do in over 50 experiments, even when following procedures published by others. Four experiments in a row with this brew had worked. I was in the midst of the fifth such experiment, which used up the last of the material, when he called again. This time he was in tears. His now purified material had just been identified by peptide mass fingerprinting. It was a commercially available plant protein commonly used in immunology labs for its ability to activate human lymphocytes. A research assistant explained that when purifying the potentially medically useful human protein proved too difficult, she had added this unrelated and medically useless plant protein to his preparations, because she expected some of its properties would mimic those he expected to see. The professor retracted the papers he had just published. I tried to reproduce the iNOS-inducing effect with the commercial reagent but could not. I was never able to figure out why; I suspect that she had added something else, too. Soon thereafter, the professor retired.

The third experience with protein purification involved contamination of another sort. People in my lab purified a new antibacterial protein from neutrophils, along with the ones that were already known. A company proposed to work with us to see if any of these proteins might be clinically useful as antibiotics. They sent their scientists to my lab to learn the purification technique and work alongside us. Around 1991, their CEO invited two of us to St. Louis. He met us at the airport in his Mercedes and made room for our luggage among his golf clubs in the trunk. He took us to an enormous factory the company had bought to produce the proteins, then to a spacious, nearly vacant suite of offices, where he introduced us to someone he had just hired as director of marketing. "You are getting far ahead of yourselves," I said. They shrugged. Some months later a friend at Merck called my attention to a paper published by the company's scientists identifying another neutrophil protein they must have purified while working with us. We were neither informed nor acknowledged. The company collapsed soon after that when it emerged that the CEO had embezzled its funds. I heard that when he got out of jail, he found work helping to manage a golf course.

Lots of lessons, from science to psychology.

1. Identification of new proteins can be of biological and commercial significance, but their purification can be elusive when monitored by biological activity. For example, purification can destroy the activity by changing how the protein folds or by removing a component with which it needs to interact.
2. When people under pressure think what's hard ought not to be, beware deception.
3. Money is like oxygen, water, and salt. We need a certain amount. Beyond that, it can ruin you.

The original macrophage deactivation factor faded from view. There was far greater impact in 1988 when we identified a cytokine that others had already cloned—trans-

forming growth factor-beta (TGF-β)—as a host protein that
prevents and reverses macrophage activation.[61] In 1991, we
and others identified interleukin-10 (IL-10) as the second
cloned cytokine that could do the same.[62] This work introduced a phenotype overlapping with what is now called
"alternative macrophage activation" that contributes to the
tumor-supporting properties of tumor-associated macrophages, a topic of widespread current research.

Michael Sporn's discovery of transforming growth factor-beta in 1981 followed his discovery of the cancer-preventing effect of retinoids and his introduction of the
concept of cancer chemoprevention—the ability of certain
chemicals to prevent cancer from arising. In 1988, our collaborative demonstration that transforming growth factor-
beta had pronounced actions on macrophages, a major cell
type in the immune system,[61] was contemporaneous with
Anthony Fauci's demonstration of its impact on lymphocytes. Until then, transforming growth factor-beta had only
been of interest to cell biologists and tumor biologists, and
it was an era when those scientists and immunologists had
little to do with each other.

I met Mike Sporn in New Hampshire at a series of Gordon Research Conferences on Cancer in 1982, 1983, and
1984. By 1982, the discovery of oncogenes—cancer-caus-
ing genes—by Vogt, Duesberg, Bishop, Varmus, and others, beginning in the 1970s, had so galvanized the field of
oncology with fresh ideas and new leaders that the attendees could not agree on a single oncogene-discoverer to help
organize the 1983 conference as its vice chair, a position that
would lead to serving as chair for the 1984 conference. They
split their votes so badly that I ended up being elected.

In 1984, as I chaired my first international conference,

the Gordon Research Conference on Cancer, the first person scheduled to speak on the first morning of that conference, Peter Duesberg, did not show up. I had confirmed his attendance the day before. I had secured grants to cover the cost of his travel from Berkeley to New Hampshire. I find this hard to separate in my mind from events three years later, when he began denying that AIDS is caused by HIV. What could have been a debacle was rescued by a biochemically rigorous presentation by Michael Sporn, a wiry physician-scientist who spoke with economy and precision at a measured pace. Mike's talk launched a friendship that entered its fourth decade; sadly, Mike died shortly before this book went to press. Our scientific collaborations started with inflammation and Alzheimer's disease and briefly included tuberculosis, a disease that Mike survived in medical school and that transforming growth factor-beta promotes through its suppression of lymphocyte function and macrophage activation.

In 1995, when Mike and his beloved wife, Kitte, a cancer nurse, left the National Cancer Institute in Bethesda, Maryland, for Dartmouth in Hanover, New Hampshire, they set up house on a mountainside in Vermont. Their house sat on a large, sloping meadow topped by acres of forest. Mike sought to invigorate the local economy by launching a new industry, bison farming. He imported a herd. The huge beasts lumbered alongside his pickup truck as it bounced about in low gear, cab empty, Mike standing in the back, forking hay over the side. Only an electrified fence protected his house from the horde.

Mike ventured on foot into the meadow to inspect the irises ringing the buffaloes' watering hole. Soon he and his colleague Gordon Gribble had extracted oleanoic acids from the flowers' bulbs. Sporn and Gribble embarked on the synthesis of potent variants of these compounds, collectively called triterpenoids, that have anti-inflammatory and cancer-preventing properties.

Mike's triterpenoids do diverse things by interacting with more than one target. They do some things particularly well for the same reason, including cancer chemoprevention. That ran them afoul of the pharmaceutical industry's version of the dogma of specificity. Mike's anticancer compounds were not approved drugs by the time Kitte succumbed to the disease she had spent her professional life combatting. Mike threw himself even more intensively into his two other loves—science and classical music. Both forms of communication connected us until Mike's passing.

Nitric Oxide Synthase

GIVEN THE ABILITY of interferon-gamma-activated macrophages to kill mouse tumor cells with ROS, I was astonished to discover in 1985 that the human tumor cells we tested were about two orders of magnitude more resistant to hydrogen peroxide (a major form of ROS) than mouse tumor cells.[63] Investigation into the basis for this led to two important findings. Many human tumor cells produce as much ROS as activated macrophages do,[64] and in some cases this contributes to their autonomous growth, that is, their ability to proliferate without waiting for other cells to instruct them to do so. They are protected from ROS by up to six enzymes called peroxiredoxins, among other antioxidant defenses.[65] It was becoming clear that not all the tumoricidal (tumor-killing) or microbicidal (bacteria-killing) actions of activated macrophages could be attributed to ROS. The next big question: What other chemistries were involved?

By 1987, John Hibbs, working in Salt Lake City, had discovered a macrophage-mediated tumoricidal process dependent on the amino acid L-arginine and associated with production of a simple inorganic molecule, nitrite. As an anonymous reviewer of the paper that John submitted to *Science*, I suggested that he test whether nitrite itself was tumoricidal. It was not, nor was it microbicidal.[66] The burn-

ing questions were the identity of the cytotoxic (cell-harm-
ing) substance associated with production of nitrite and the
enzymatic process by which mammalian cells could generate it.

In 1989–1991, postdoctoral fellows Dennis Stuehr and
Nyoun-Soo Kwon, MD-PhD student Hearn Cho, and I identified a cytokine-induced enzyme in macrophages that produced nitric oxide, earning it designation as a nitric oxide
synthase (a synthase is an enzyme that makes—synthesizes—the product named).

We found that the enzyme accomplished this feat by
combining an atom of oxygen with an atom of nitrogen har-
vested from the amino acid arginine, and we identified an
intermediate in the reaction. We also identified the molecule NADPH as a second substrate, along with the first-
identified substrate, arginine. This allowed us to apply a
NADPH-based method of affinity chromatography for
purification of the enzyme—that is, we could attach a compound related to NADPH to inert beads packed in a glass
column, and the enzyme would bind to the beads while we
washed other proteins away.[67] Next, we discovered a third
molecule called tetrahydrobiopterin that is also required
for the enzyme to act.[68] Michael Marletta's lab at MIT made
the same discovery at the same time.[69]

Armed with this information, we could add arginine,
NADPH, and tetrahydrobiopterin to each chromatographic
fraction and monitor nitric oxide synthase activity as we
separated individual proteins from activated macrophages.
When we purified[70] and cloned[71] the enzyme from macrophages, we could demonstrate its transcriptional induction,
that is, the biochemical "reading" of its gene to make messenger RNA, which in turn directs the production of the

protein. We found that cytokines and microbial products interacted synergistically to induce iNOS.[70-73] We also discovered that the enzyme had no need for elevated levels of calcium. The importance of that observation emerged when efforts from around the world revealed that there are three different mammalian NOSs. The inducibility and calcium-independence of the macrophage NOS distinguished it from the NOS that had been cloned earlier (neuronal NOS)[74] and the NOS that was cloned later (endothelial NOS).

It stunned the world of science to learn that mice, people, and, as emerged later, many other organisms can make a tiny gaseous molecule—nitric oxide—that has a free electron and is therefore quick to react with other molecules. Scientists were only starting to get over their surprise that cells can make superoxide, another tiny gaseous molecule with an unpaired electron that is looking to bond. It was equally baffling that evolution equipped mammals with three different enzymes that make nitric oxide. Curiously, evolution treated one of the three with kid gloves: cells do not express this nitric oxide-producing enzyme until they sense infection or inflammation. This is the form of NOS we discovered. Because it was the second NOS to be purified and cloned, it is sometimes called NOS2. We showed that NOS2 accounted for much of the anti-tumor activity of activated mouse macrophages.[75-78]

The enzyme also bears the name I gave it, "iNOS," for NOS *induced* in response to *immunologic* and *inflammatory* stimuli and *independent* of elevated *intracellular* calcium.[71] This was followed a few months later by the enshrinement of nitric oxide as "molecule of the year" by *Science*. There ensued a torrent of iMacs, iPods, iPads, and iPhones, and in biologic circles, iPS cells, iNKT cells, and iTregs. Whether "iNOS" set off this naming frenzy can be left to linguistic historians.

Not only is iNOS one of three mammalian NOS's, but there are related enzymes in birds, fish, mollusks, sea squirts, sponges, insects, molds, and bacteria. Mosquitoes and ticks use nitric oxide both to suppress the parasites that infect them and to keep our blood flowing when they bite us. The family of enzymes whose primary product is the nitric oxide radical ($\cdot$NO) evolved independently of the family of enzymes whose primary product is the superoxide radical ($O_2{}^{\cdot-}$). Yet both enzyme families converged on producing tiny, inorganic radical gasses as biologically critical components of homeostatic signaling and host defense in diverse organisms.

Evolution held another surprise in the form of another convergence between two independently evolved enzymes, mammalian iNOS (NOS2), which can kill bacteria, and a bacterial enzyme that can kill us. But first, more background.

When the neuronal NOS (nNOS, or NOS1) and the endothelial NOS (eNOS, or NOS3) were studied as purified proteins, they were inactive without the addition of calcium ions (Ca^{2+}) and the protein calmodulin. Calmodulin changes shape when it binds Ca^{2+}, and in this "activated" form it can attach to other proteins to change their shape in turn, activating them. The level of Ca^{2+} required to activate calmodulin and all calmodulin-dependent enzymes known by the early 1990s is only achieved in the cytosol (the intracellular space where most calmodulin-dependent enzymes reside) for a brief period after a stimulus to the cell that allows Ca^{2+} to come rushing out of intracellular storage vesicles. Those vesicles quickly refill by taking Ca^{2+} back in. Calmodulin then reverts to its inactive form and lets go of enzymes it was embracing. The calmodulin-dependent enzymes then return to their resting state. The Ca^{2+}- and calmodulin-dependence of a nitric oxide synthase was first noted by David Bredt and Solomon Snyder at Johns Hopkins Medical School en route to purifying nNOS (NOS1).[74] Because nNOS is expressed chiefly in neurons, its calmodulin-dependence implied that it is activated when a neuron binds a neurotransmitter, that is, the neuron receives a Ca^{2+}-elevating signal from another neuron with which it shares a synapse. Similarly, the calmodulin-dependence of eNOS, which is expressed chiefly in endothelial cells lining blood vessels, explained how eNOS is activated by each pulse of the blood, because an increase in pressure transiently elevates Ca^{2+} in endothelial cells.

How could iNOS dispense with the requirement for elevated Ca^{2+} and added calmodulin? And why does iNOS in activated macrophages produce orders of magnitude more nitric oxide than nNOS in neurons and eNOS in endothelial cells?

With the help of colleagues at Merck Research Laboratories, in 1992 we discovered that our purified iNOS included calmodulin as a tightly bound subunit without requiring that calmodulin bind Ca^{2+}.[79] Once the gene encoding iNOS is transcribed and the protein is made, iNOS can stay on unless it runs out of substrates or encounters an inhibitor. Using recombinant proteins with parts cobbled together from different NOS isoforms, MD-PhD student Jia Ruan in my lab demonstrated that specific regions of iNOS conferred this unprecedented property,[80] endowing iNOS with the high output phenotype that gives it antitumor and antimicrobial potential.

Apparently, evolution learned that it is safe for the body to express two of its three NOS isoforms all the time, because they only make nitric oxide in response to a signal that lasts a very short time, the result being production of nitric oxide briefly and in tiny amounts. In contrast, iNOS is rambunctious; it ignores the signal that controls its siblings. Cells only express iNOS when the host senses trouble. Interferon-gamma is a powerful inducer of iNOS expression. The copious amounts of nitric oxide produced by iNOS can be destructive for cancer cells, bacteria, and other infectious agents, sometimes at a cost to the host.

In October 2001, I was walking to work when a bevy of news vans and police cruisers blocked me from passing by the Manhattan Eye, Ear and Throat Hospital on East 64th Street. A stockroom worker there, Kathy Nguyen, had contracted anthrax. She was one of seventeen people infected and one of the five who would die from contact with anthrax spores mailed by a domestic terrorist, an employee at the National Institute of Health's Fort Detrick facility in Maryland.

What gives this bacillus such lethal power? Four years later, it was discovered that anthrax cripples host phagocytes through the remarkable biochemical behavior of its form of an enzyme called adenylyl cyclase. Many organisms, including humans, have adenylyl cyclases. All other adenylyl cyclases are signaling enzymes that help cells maintain homeostasis. Most members of the adenylyl cyclase family are calcium- and calmodulin-dependent. In contrast, the adenylyl cyclase of the anthrax bacterium, *Bacillus anthracis*, turns itself on inside host cells by attaching the host cells' own calmodulin without a need for elevated intracellular calcium.[81] Shortly after the bacterium injects its adenylyl cyclase into host cells, the product of the bacterial adenylyl cyclase, called cyclic adenosine monophosphate, rises to levels so high that it freezes in place the white blood cells that would otherwise engulf and kill the anthrax bacterium. That explains the chilling scene in a photograph taken through a microscope and published in the *New England Journal of Medicine*, depicting a sample of cerebrospinal fluid taken from the first victim of the anthrax attack.[82] The fluid was teeming with anthrax bacteria and crowded with neutrophils, but none of the neutrophils had ingested any of the bacteria.

In a striking example of evolutionary convergence, the anthrax bacterium evolved the ability to commandeer a host protein, calmodulin, to help the bacterium impose inappropriately strong and sustained signaling on host immune cells, paralyzing them. Host immune cells evolved the same calmodulin trick to put iNOS, one of its own signaling enzymes, into overdrive, imposing inappropriately strong and sustained signaling on bacteria, paralyzing *them*.

To my knowledge, iNOS and the adenylyl cyclase of anthrax are the only known examples in biology where one member of an enzyme family has found this same way to escape the regulatory signal that controls the other members of the family. We and anthrax have each taken a similar route to harming the other: by co-opting calmodulin, we make too much nitric oxide for the bacteria, while the bacteria use the same maneuver to make too much cyclic adenosine phosphate for us.

The years I devoted to iNOS from 1988 on afforded another instance where discoveries about the question under study went arm-in-arm with self-discovery. I found myself powerfully attracted to the effectiveness of working with a diverse team of outstanding scientists in a well-equipped and well-resourced drug company on an academic, collaborative basis. That experience profoundly affected my thoughts, and beginning about fifteen years later, my actions.

Purification and characterization of iNOS were the fruits of an extraordinary, unfunded collaboration with Merck Research Laboratories that began in 1991. Philip Davies, Executive Director of Immunology and Rheumatology Research at Merck, invited my student, Hearn Cho, to stay with him in his home near the Rahway, New Jersey, campus, where he gave Hearn access to a 250-liter mammalian cell fermenter. Hearn returned to the lab at Cornell with grapefruit-sized pellets of macrophages packed together at the bottom of tubes by centrifuging the fluid in which they had been growing. The macrophages had been activated by interferon-gamma and bacterial endotoxin (also called lipopolysaccharide, or LPS). Now they served as the starting material for purification. Richard Mumford, an ace biochemist at Merck, encouraged me to rent a pickup truck and drive up to a side entrance of the Rahway facility. Richard distracted the guards while we borrowed several chromatography workstations to supplement the single unit we had in our lab. At Cornell we worked in shifts to purify the protein. I then drove a truck back to Merck. Richard distracted the guards again while we returned the equipment.

We used the protein to raise antibody by injecting it repeatedly into rabbits and collecting some of their blood several weeks later. Qiao-wen Xie in my lab used the antibody to isolate phages (viruses that can infect bacteria) that expressed the gene in the form called a complementary

DNA (cDNA). We sequenced the cDNA by hand, using a now obsolete process in which short strands of DNA were synthesized in four separate reactions, each of them containing all four building blocks of DNA. Each tube also received a different one of the four building blocks that was modified so as to prevent the addition of the next link in the chain and was tagged with radioactivity. The synthesized fragments were then separated from each other in a gel subjected to an electrical field. When we placed a radiation-sensitive film over the gel, we could tell which building block had terminated each fragment. The distance that the fragment had migrated in the gel reported its relative length. We took turns "reading" the gels and calling out the inferred sequence. We then took samples of the purified protein and digested them with an enzyme called trypsin that cuts proteins into fragments called peptides by breaking the bond between the amino acids arginine or lysine and whatever amino acid follows. When we had electrospray ionization mass spectrometric evidence of the masses of the individual tryptic peptides, we sat at Richard's kitchen table with a slide rule trying to match measured masses to the masses predicted from the cDNA, taking natural isotope abundance into account. What we labored at in 1992 was one of the earliest examples of a technique called peptide mass fingerprinting that is now a computerized routine.

Soon another of my students, John MacMicking, moved in temporarily with Phil Davies at his home and worked with another star at Merck, mouse geneticist John Mudgett. By 1995, they had produced iNOS knock-out mice, mice in which the gene encoding iNOS was disrupted. We tested the mice first in models of shock caused by endotoxin

(LPS), a profoundly inflammatory substance shed by one major class of bacteria, and listeriosis, an infection caused by bacteria from another major class. Gary Hom, a physiologist at Merck, slipped a catheter into the carotid artery in the necks of wild type (normal) and knock-out mice to measure their blood pressure. We found that iNOS mediates the severe hypotension—the collapse of blood pressure, or "shock"—in mice responding to endotoxin, a model of septic shock, that is, shock caused by infection.

Shortly after that, during a course of high-dose steroids for asthma, I developed septic shock myself, as described earlier. When I was moved out of the intensive care unit to a regular hospital bed, my lab mates brought me a laptop and a stack of relevant articles from the scientific literature and I finished writing our manuscript on iNOS knock-out mice.[83] This contributed to the impression that it takes a near-death experience to write papers that are readily accepted at the journal *Cell*.

John Mudgett and our lab shared the iNOS knock-out mice with over 100 labs. Jackson Labs in Bar Harbor, Maine, distributed iNOS knock-out mice that had been generated independently by Victor Laubach and Oliver Smithies.[84] The ensuing worldwide effort revealed that iNOS plays an important, complex role in infection, inflammation and cancer. Our own contributions focused on tuberculosis,[85] viral infections,[86] and Alzheimer's disease,[87] while others addressed conditions ranging from obesity-dependent insulin resistance[88] to chronic obstructive pulmonary disease, to name a few.[89, 90] Soon, high output production of reactive nitrogen species (RNS) took its place alongside high output production of reactive oxygen species (ROS) as a cardinal feature of "classical" macrophage activation and a principal effector of the enhanced antitumor activity, antimicrobial activity, and host toxicity of macrophages, although both sets of signaling molecules have diverse roles in many other cells (e.g.[5, 17, 24, 25]).

Continuing John MacMicking's work, an MD-PhD student, Michael Shiloh, studied mice lacking both iNOS and phagocyte oxidase ("phox"), the enzyme that generates most of the ROS in activated macrophages. Surprisingly, by 1999 he found that the two enzymes were mutually partly redundant and collectively indispensable for host defense.[91] The singly deficient mice were susceptible to separate sets of specific pathogens, as long as the mice were inoculated with the infectious agents. In contrast, the doubly deficient mice all died from spontaneous infections by their own microbiota (the bacteria that reside normally in the gastrointestinal tract, on the skin and at other body surfaces). We learned how to keep most of these "double knock-out" mice alive by continuous administration of antibiotics and antifungal agents, but even with this treatment, many of the mice developed massive abscesses filled with neutrophils and monocytes. This is the most severe infectious disease phenotype reported for a mouse with normal numbers of white blood cells that mobilize to infectious sites. Apparently, nothing else in the immune system's armamentarium suffices to protect mice from their own microbiota if the mice lack both iNOS and phox.

It took another two decades to identify the first human being whose iNOS-encoding genes were mutated in both copies in such a way as to inactivate the enzyme's function.[92] The discovery, by Scott Drutman and colleagues in Jean-Laurent Casanova's lab, with a little help from mine, explained why this man died of a virus infection. What was harder to understand was how he had survived to adult-hood. A survey of all available human genomic sequences revealed no other example of people with loss-of-function ("knock-out") mutations in the gene encoding iNOS. Sta-tistical analysis suggested that such mutations would have been detected in some of the sequenced genomes if the loss of function of human iNOS did not greatly endanger survival.

Efforts continue today to exploit nitric oxide biology for medical benefit. Best established is the administration of small amounts of nitric oxide gas to patients whose lung arteries are constricted, such as newborns with a disor-der called persistent pulmonary hypertension. Still under study is the administration of chemical compounds that inhibit iNOS in diseases ranging from Alzheimer's to chronic obstructive pulmonary disease to cancer,[93] where iNOS's ability to kill cancer cells[78] can be outmatched by its ability to inactivate proteins that attract cancer-killing lymphocytes into tumors.[94]

The Immune System Needs *Us*

WE ALL KNOW why we need the immune system: to protect us from infection. I've come to realize that the immune system needs *us*, too, and for the same reason.[95] "Us" means people in a society who work together to create, apply, and preserve measures that compensate for what the immune system does not do well enough.

For all its power, the immune system is the one organ system that most often fails before old age. A cardiologist dropping her kids off at school on the way to her office would never expect almost all the people she sees en route to miss school or work during their childhood, youth, or middle years because their heart had failed. Yet almost all the children, teachers, parents, and passers-by she sees that day will have had or will have one or more infections that keep them home for a day or more. Each such episode represents a failure of the immune system.

In the pre-societal, pre-medicine wild, being laid low by infection would have been a bigger threat than it is today, magnifying the risk of death from exposure, predation, or starvation. Today, most of us recover promptly from infections and just as quickly forget them. However, we must not forget those whose immune systems failed them fatally: the more than 6 million who had died from COVID-19 when these words were written, along with the annual deaths of

245

1.7 million people from fungal infections; 1.5 million from tuberculosis; 1 million from HIV; 808,000 from pneumonia; 650,000 from influenza; 600,000 from shigellosis; 409,000 from malaria; 300,000 from bacterial meningitis; 200,000 from reovirus; 155,000 from salmonellosis; 50,000 or more from African trypanosomiasis ("sleeping sickness"); 50,000 from visceral leishmaniasis ("kala-azar"); and so on. Over 1 million people now die each year from bacterial infections that were once curable but are now resistant to the antibiotics available. COVID-19 deaths have been skewed toward the elderly, but a very high proportion of the other people we lose each year to infection are children and young adults whose immune systems were normal when they got sick, yet failed them in their time of need.

What accounts for the routine failure of a bodily system so richly endowed with mobility, memory, and weaponry? Protecting us from infection is a complicated job. It's not just about killing invaders; it's about deciding what to kill and when, coordinating means of attack, fending off counterattack, minimizing bystander damage, and helping heal battle sites. But then, the job of every organ system is complicated. *What's immunity's problem?*

The answer has to do with the number of genomes whose information the immune system monitors. The human genome—the full set of genes within us that affect who we are and how we are—is actually a metagenome made up of four genomes, or five in someone who's pregnant. The genome we contribute to our descendants is contained in our germ cells—ova or sperm. This germ-line genome is what most people mean when they speak of "the human genome." However, the genome in all our other cells—the somatic genome—differs from the genomes our parents gave us by virtue of mutations we acquire as we go through life. Some mutations arise from biochemical imperfections in the process of copying DNA when cells divide as we replace them or add more of them. Some arise when our DNA encounters reactive oxygen species or reactive nitrogen species from within or toxic chemicals from without. Mutations arise normally in our lymphocytes' antigen receptors and antibodies when the cells diversify their receptors and antibodies to select those that bind better to a pathogen than the ones encoded by the genes our parents gave us. A third human genome is encoded in our mitochondria, the energy-producing organelles within most of our cells. Mitochondria arose in evolution when a bacterium fused with a single-celled organism whose own genes were confined in its nucleus. Sperm inject their nuclear DNA into a fertilized ovum; the ovum contributes both its nuclear DNA and its mitochondria, so we inherit the mitochondrial genome from our mothers.

The immune system deals not only with those three genomes but with a fourth as well: all the information and action generated by all the genes in all the microbes that occupy our bodies, chronically or transiently, on our skin, in our airways, and in our genitourinary and gastrointestinal tracts—viruses, bacteria, bacteria-like cells called archaea, and fungi. All of us house some members of all these groups all the time. Some of us also host protozoa and worms.

Our hearts, brains, bones, and muscles represent solutions to the challenges posed by longstanding features of the environments in which our ancestors evolved. These solutions have approached an ideal within constraints imposed by those environments, by the germ-line gene pool, and by solutions that were selected earlier. The immune system cannot approach such an ideal, because when it controls infectious agents, some of them evolve to evade control, and they evolve many orders of magnitude faster than we do. In effect, the immune system's solutions to problems of infection impose selection on the problem, and the problem evolves faster than the host.

By the time a human being reaches reproductive age, his or her immune system has learned a great deal from the recovery from each infection. That new knowledge is encoded in the somatic genome—in lymphocytes' new antigen receptors and antibodies. This wisdom does not enter the germ-line genome. Our offspring start fighting their own infectious battles using genes for antigen receptors and antibodies that we got from our parents and they get from theirs.

Not so the bacteria. When their own mutations lead to a change in their antigens or a higher level of resistance, they pass the modified genes to their descendants. Moreover, they often share genes with their neighbors. That means that the adaptability of pathogens can be both heritable and communal. Our adaptability is not heritable, but it can be communal if we make it so.

Immunologists view the human immune system as having two branches, innate and adaptive. In the last century and a half, humans have collectively constructed another immune system that I call "adopted,"[95] because it is volitional. Human society has adopted a highly effective, collective approach to immunity only within the past several generations. "Adopted immunity" is estimated to have reduced infectious disease deaths in the US by 96% in the 1900s. Shockingly, we are in the process of de-acquiring some of our adopted defenses because of polarized politics that amplify vaccine resistance and misaligned business models that waste antibiotics and kneecap their development.

The adopted immune system has four branches of its own that compensate for the inherent limitations of innate and adaptive immune systems. The first branch is sanitation, using the term in a broad sense to include not just waste collection but potable water, clean air, and shelter. The second branch, nutrition, offers the infection-fighting power of vitamins, minerals, essential amino acids, and the right levels and sources of calories. The third branch is vaccination—the induction of our own adaptive immune response in advance of encountering the pathogen. The fourth branch was adopted most recently, when we learned how to take or mimic elements of the immune systems of other species—bacteria, fungi, corals, and plants—for use as anti-infectives.

Most antibiotics are derived from or modeled on compounds that bacteria and fungi make as an evolved system of communication and competition in terrestrial and aquatic environments. The post-World War II industrialization of antibiotics has created a tragedy of the commons by depleting this precious communal resource through mis-use, over-use, and a broad retreat from research in a market perceived as low-reward, because prompt cures mean brief use, hence less profit. Most of the world's antibiotic tonnage is not used to save lives; it is used to spur the growth of healthy food animals, spreading vast quantities of the drugs through the environment and hastening the spread of resistance.

These thoughts launched me on one of the current legs of my journey, opened my eyes to challenges facing science and society in antibiotic research and development, and gave me reason to draw on the collaborative experience with Merck in the early days of characterizing iNOS to ponder how academics and drug companies might restructure their relationships to improve our chances of coping.[1, 7, 96–105]

In 2004, I wrote a commentary in *Nature* calling for "open labs" where discovery scientists from academia could work shoulder-to-shoulder with drug development scientists from industry.[7] Six years later, that vision became reality. A Spanish campus of the pharmaceutical company GlaxoSmithKline (now called GSK) opened its doors to academic collaborators with the support of a charity, the Tres Cantos Open Lab Foundation. GSK funded the charity but left its control to a Board of Directors-Trustees with one GSK member. I joined the foundation's Board of Governors and later its Board of Directors-Trustees, and I serve as chair of each as this is written. The Foundation awards grants to scientists who come to Spain to work inside the company for up to a year. They have access to GSK's resources and work together with GSK scientists to develop treatments for tuberculosis, malaria, other parasitic infections, and infectious diarrheal diseases. New intellectual property is governed by the royalty-free sharing principles of the World Intellectual Property Organization. Results are published. New compounds are shared with those who request them. Any resulting pharmaceuticals must be affordable to those in need.[96]

Buoyed by the success of the Open Lab, I spent much of 2011–2013 leading a planning team for the reciprocal experiment—bringing drug company scientists into the research environment of academic institutions. I became a founding member of the Board of Directors of the Sanders Tri-institutional Therapeutics Discovery Institute ("Tri-I TDI"), a not-for-profit corporation owned by Rockefeller University, Memorial Sloan Kettering Cancer Center, and Weill Cornell Medicine. In Tri-I TDI's ninth year, I became chair of its board. The joint action and close cooperation of the three institutions mirrors what they achieved in the Tri-Institutional MD-PhD program that I helped to launch two decades earlier.

Some of the companies I came to work with seemed to have conflictual corporate halves—a dominant business, legal, and marketing side, and a subordinate scientific side. The business side was sometimes tarnished by practices I considered rapacious, unethical, or neglectful of society's medical needs. Pharma's dual personality was on full display in 2012, when the same major pharmaceutical company that has consistently been ranked highest for social responsibility paid a $3 billion fine for promoting drugs for unapproved uses, hiding safety information, and bribing prescribers. I have never met the marketers at these companies, just the scientists. I found most of the scientists to be altruists who are skilled in sharing understanding in verifiable ways.

The science of drug development attracted me not only for its potential to improve health but also for its multidisciplinarity, and even for its extraordinary difficulty— the disproportion between the quantity and quality of resources applied and the low rate of success. This holds a mirror to society at large in its struggle to overcome its major maladies. Perhaps learning how to work together to rescue antibiotics as a key arm of adopted immunity can illustrate approaches to other global problems.[101]

Antibiotics rescued me from septic shock. Not so fortunate are the many hundreds of thousands of people with drug-resistant infections. The spread of antibiotic resistance is outpacing our dwindling success in finding new antibiotics. One solution on the scientific side is to seek new antibiotics by thinking of them as means of intervening in the struggle between the host and its bacterial invaders, rather than as compounds that kill bacteria in culture under conditions that are largely irrelevant to what the bacteria experience in the host. Potential solutions on the organizational and societal side will require more than venues for academic-industrial cooperation, though those are important. A fundamental fix will require a different business model, one that realigns incentives with innovation and access.[1, 97]

As this is written, my lab is working on tuberculosis drug development with multiple drug companies on an "open access" basis, and some of them are working with each other, in an innovative organizational scheme set up by the Bill and Melinda Gates Foundation and called the TB Drug Accelerator. Its success has led to similar intersector, multi-party Drug Accelerators for other infectious diseases.[102]

Working with industry professionals in drug development—medicinal chemists, enzymologists, structural biologists, molecular modelers, and pharmacologists—gives me an opportunity to foster frameworks in which otherwise competing groups collaborate. Prototype organizations like the Tres Cantos Open Lab Foundation, the Tri-Institutional Therapeutics Discovery Institute, and the TB Drug Accelerator bring together discovery scientists and drug development scientists. The TB Drug Accelerator brings together scientists from multiple institutions of each type. The Open Lab Foundation and the Drug Accelerator focus on infectious diseases in part because of unmet need, and perhaps in part because the anti-infective agents are relatively unprofitable, meaning that the sums the participating institutions might forego by sharing ownership are minimized. Nonetheless, the success of these prototype research collaboratives has begun to encourage academia, foundations like the Cancer Research Institute, and even the pharmaceutical industry to collaborate in advancing the immunologic control of cancer as well.

Promoting macrophage activation for better host defense against infections and interfering with bacterial defenses against host immunity amount to a pincer movement, a classical tactic in a war with one of our oldest enemies. It has taken nearly fifty years to advance this strategy. An analogous strategy that takes a holistic view of the host immune system is emerging to control cancer.

On December 15, 2021, scientists reported that an inhibitor of iNOS improved the response of women receiving chemotherapy for the most aggressive form of breast cancer.[93] The chemotherapeutic agent was taxane, a type of drug that my colleagues and I showed in 1990 triggers release of tumor necrosis factor,[106] a powerful macrophage-activating cytokine discovered independently by the labs of Lloyd Old and Tony Cerami. The inhibitor of iNOS, an enzyme my lab discovered, and taxane, a drug whose immunologic action my lab discovered, may have acted together to frustrate the tumor's subversion of host immunity. I learned of that report on December 22, 2021, fifty-five years to the day since my mother died. Perhaps I did not fail her after all.

PART FOUR
A Gift

All the Difference

AS ROBERT FROST put it in "The Road Not Taken," I "took the other, as just as fair / And having perhaps the better claim, / Because it was grassy and wanted wear." After pledging to fight cancer, accepting Hermann Lisco's advice to use the immune system to do it, and chairing the National Cancer Institute's Tumor Immunology Committee in 1979 and 1980, following the path of my "emotional logic" meant pulling myself off the then grievously under-powered track of "tumor immunology" to take my own indirect route to the same goal.

What greatly helped me to overcome self-doubt in doing so was the support of Lloyd J. Old, a foundational figure in tumor immunology. In 1959, working with Baruj Benacerraf, Lloyd Old was the first to show that a mycobacterium could stimulate anti-tumor immunity. This laid a foundation for the belief that studying immunity to mycobacteria is relevant to tumor immunology. Lloyd's 1959 experiment in turn rested on the foundation laid by a Cornell surgeon, William Coley, who discovered that surgical wound infections were sometimes followed by regression of the cancers he had been unable to remove in their entirety. Coley went on to inject bacteria into tumors he considered inoperable. After his death, his daughter, Helen Coley Nauts, tracked down many of those patients and documented that some of

257

them were indeed cured. Pursuing the mechanism, Lloyd Old and his associate Elizabeth Carswell discovered "tumor necrosis factor" as a product of macrophages responding to bacterial products. Helen Coley Nauts launched the Cancer Research Institute in 1953 and asked Lloyd Old to direct it.

One day in 1985 the phone in my lab rang. It was a warm "cold call" from the Vice President and Associate Director of Scientific Development of Memorial Hospital, across the street and one block down from Cornell University Medical College, where I had just moved from Rockefeller. He introduced himself only as "Your neighbor, Lloyd." A long, rambling near-monologue followed. Lloyd expressed wonderment at the latest discoveries in immunology and praised the people responsible, interspersing these remarks with discourses on classical music. He paused periodically to ask me what I thought. If he approved of my reply, he would go "Ah!" and bring the discussion to a deeper level. If he disapproved, there would be a silence whose length seemed to be proportionate to his disappointment. The longest pause followed my expressing interest in the music of Ligeti. Over the years there were many of these calls, each usually lasting thirty minutes or more. Sometimes there were lunches at his office at Memorial Sloan Kettering Cancer Center or his Sixth Avenue offices at the Ludwig Institute for Cancer Research, which he directed.

The first call from Lloyd, much like my medical school admission interview with Dr. Funkenstein, proved to be an audition in the form of a listening test. Despite the Ligeti liability, I passed, because the conversation ended with an invitation to join the Scientific Advisory Board of the Cancer Research Institute (CRI). Lloyd's unflagging interest and kindness told me that he saw that we shared the same goals, even though I was taking a different route. I joined CRI thirty-seven years ago. I have been its associate scientific director since 1989 and chaired its fellowship committee from 1989 to 2003. This gave me an opportunity to help hundreds of young scientists launch careers in fundamental immunology and, as the field grew in strength, tumor immunology. Today I help keep Lloyd's memory alive by chairing CRI's Lloyd J. Old STAR Program—Scientists Taking Risks—for mid-career scientists exploring innovative approaches to cancer immunotherapy.

Around 2009, I visited Lloyd in the hospital after he underwent cancer surgery. Late in November 2011, he stood erect but pale, unsteady, and clearly in pain on the sidewalk of 68th Street outside Memorial Hospital. We shook hands and said our goodbyes. A few days later, Lloyd died.

Eight months before Lloyd's death, the FDA approved the first immunotherapeutic cure for melanoma, based on an antibody pioneered by Lloyd's colleague at Sloan Kettering Institute, Jim Allison, who would win a Nobel Prize for that discovery, and with whom I co-chaired the PhD-granting program in immunology that Weill Cornell shares with Sloan Kettering Institute. Two months before Lloyd's death, Ralph Steinman, our neighbor at Rockefeller University, died of cancer on the eve of winning a Nobel Prize for work that has also helped drive cancer immunotherapy to the forefront of biomedicine.

An African proverb advises, "If you want to go fast, go alone; if you want to go far, go together." Lloyd was one of many who provided support on my less-traveled road. His death re-awakened memories of Lester Grant, who introduced me to science. As mentioned earlier, Sir Howard Florey, head of Oxford's Dunn School in Lester's day, worked with Fleming, Chain, and Heatley to give the world penicillin, then went on to study the role of leukocytes in inflammation. My own career has crossed the same bridge in the other direction—from leukocytes and inflammation to antibacterial chemotherapy. When I was invited to Oxford in 2006 to visit the Dunn School and give the Norman Heatley lecture, I was moved by a vivid reminder that my mentor had walked those halls: I found Lester's framed photo among those on the wall. Non-scientists also helped me do science, beginning with Judy Sulzberger. Decades later, along came Kevin Brine, an Overseer at Weill Cornell. His philanthropic support allowed me to recruit a chemist to my lab, Gang Lin, fueling a transformation in the lab's outlook. Then the transformative generosity of Abby and Howard Milstein enabled our search for new chemotherapeutic approaches to infectious disease.

Telling a story centered on oneself is as misleading as trying to understand a tapestry by tracing one fiber. The story I would have told if I had the skill and the space and if I had carried the story closer to the present day is woven from the efforts of extraordinary students, fellows, research assistants, collaborators, and colleagues who shared their knowledge, enthusiasm, and creativity. I'll let one represent all: Aihao Ding.

One of the first students to be allowed out of the People's Republic of China to pursue a PhD in the West, Aihao Ding arrived at SUNY Downstate. She chose SUNY because a visitor to China had given her its brochure and she did not know the name of any other American biomedical institution. When she got to Brooklyn, she rented a television, locked herself in her apartment, and taught herself English. When the time came for thesis research, she worked in the lab of the dean. Upon winning her PhD, she applied to my lab for a postdoctoral fellowship. The dean sent a two-sentence letter of reference: "Aihao Ding is the best student I have ever had. This is the shortest reference I will ever write." Thirty years later, Aihao retired as an independent professor with whom I had shared a lab. Her special gifts were the example of her personal fearlessness and the benefit of her unstinting criticism—two things on which a scientist depends.

To discover something unexpected in science is to be an outsider until others make room for it in their thinking. An advance that reinforces a familiar line of thought is warmly embraced; an insight that introduces an alternative to existing views encounters resistance. Perhaps that is why my sense of being an outsider persisted despite recruitments, promotions, elections, and prizes. Or perhaps it was the other way around—feeling like an outsider predisposed me to seek new ideas, and that attitude proved too useful to give up. Perhaps both.

To be comfortable with one's ideas in science is to have stopped thinking or to be thinking someone else's thoughts. A discovery scientist needs to position herself or himself at the edge of what is known. To work at the edge requires high tolerance for anxiety. The reward can be the greatest scientific privilege of all: to see something for the first time, and then to see it again.

Father

WHEN MY FATHER was five, he gave a piano concert in an Oakland, California, park that was reported in the local papers. At six, he played at the Presidio in San Francisco for soldiers wounded in World War I, which had ended the year before.

At forty-eight, while I was in high school, he was driving me to the train in Stamford so I could commute to my summer job at the lab at NYU. One morning, as men in suits lined the platform, a Black man who may have been drinking, judging from his gait, wended his way among them. The suits drew back, reforming their ranks as he passed. As the train approached, the man stumbled and fell from the platform onto the tracks. My father, and he alone, lay down on the platform, extended his hand, grabbed the man's arm at the wrist, and pulled him up. "Thank you," said the man. "You're welcome," said my father. No one else said anything. That's when I began to learn about racism. That's also when I began to grasp the idea of character. In her battles with sexism and cancer, my mother was teaching me about courage. In that moment, my father did as well.

At fifty-six, my widower father met Amy and me in Washington for a march against the Vietnam War. For several years he kept up his protest by refusing to pay federal taxes. The arrest he waited for never came.

In his mid-seventies, as our sons grew, he would sit at the piano and mesmerize us with his perfect pitch, on-the-fly improvisation, and love of stride.

At age ninety, widowed a second time, my father wrote:

> I sat up in bed,
> in the dimness glimpsed something
> that stood up from the covers.
> What is it?
> I stretched out my right hand
> and found myself holding my left
> . . . bony, dry, like
> a gnarled root beached
> on sun-baked sand.

Five months later, he wrote:

> **Round Trip**
>
> In the great hall of Death
> where no one knows your name
> we shuffle toward the gate
> the same through which we came.

For his ninety-third birthday, my brother's family and Amy and I took him to dinner at a restaurant where the owner, a courtly Spaniard, was quick to ready a ramp for the wheelchair. My sister, with whom we all were close, lived in California. She joined us in spirit, as she always did when she couldn't make the trip. As our table bubbled with catch-up talk—work, school, travel—the guest of honor picked at his paella. When he lifted a full-to-its-salted-brim margarita with a shaking hand, conversation froze as all eyes turned to the trembling glass. "I am here with you, but when I watch you talking, it's as if I'm gone," he announced. "I feel like I am already dead." The ensuing silence lasted long past his successful sip and his glass's safe landing.

When he was ninety-four and COVID lay thirteen years in the future, he reminisced about wearing a face mask in the influenza pandemic of 1918. He was five years old then and lived in Berkeley. He thought he may have developed his interest in music because he loved the sound of the bells of Cal's campanile. How different, I thought, than the sound of the bell of Memorial Church in Harvard Yard on November 22, 1963.

How much we shared in unexpected ways, in our separate times and places. We wore masks in pandemics a hundred years apart. Bells tolling on opposite coasts held such meaning that we carried their sounds the rest of our lives. When he said death's at the table, he echoed an awareness that shaped me since the day I lay on my back in the snow, hoping to breathe.

When he was ninety-six and extremely frail, we had the following conversation (when I got home, I wrote it down):

Father: I've been reading *Why Is There Something Rather than Nothing?* I enjoyed the book, but these chapters don't answer the question—it's a gyp.

Son: What do you think is the answer?

Father: I don't know. There might as well be something as nothing, but you can't prove it.

Son: Maybe it isn't either/or. Maybe somethingness and nothingness alternate. If there was nothing before there was something, why can't it happen again? Why can't it happen the other way around?

Our final conversation was this.

Son: How are you feeling?

Father: Somewhat skeptical.

After he died, on December 12, 2009, I wrote the following:

> *Cycles*
> He sent much of himself way in advance,
> as if on a de-installment plan.
> He became lighter to hold, floppy like a baby, nearly
>   as soft.
> Everything shrank but dignity,
> which then stood out more than
> haunches and ribs.
> Last rounds of breaths cycled
> silence (sampling death, gathering will?)
> with fast, hard huffs, like giving birth
> from the heart through the mouth,
> the final sigh commemorating
> drawing first air
> all that time ago.

Today, I'm often startled to see my father, and he is just as startled to see me (his image lives in mirrors.) When we were younger, our visages differed. With age they converged.

A Hand

THE QUAKER TEACHER stood in the stone chapel in the orange and yellow wood and spoke of the human hand.

Time and time again I have taken a patient's hand. Now I wonder who comforted whom.

Ann was a young technician in a lab near mine. I remember her wheaten hair, downcast eyes, and quiet, hard-working efficiency. After years of steady attendance, she stopped coming to work. Days passed. Calls to her apartment rang and rang. Concern mounted, but it seemed she was a cypher. She did not socialize with co-workers. She was not married. No one knew about her family, except that she was an only child. One of her lab mates told me he thought she took evening classes at NYU.

I called NYU and learned that Ann was enrolled in a PhD program in English. I called her thesis advisor. He told me she was a brilliant student but had been struggling for years with breast cancer. Now the disease was advanced. Recently she had entered Memorial Sloan Kettering Cancer Center, across the street from her lab. The professor said Ann had wanted to go home—she came from a small rural town—but her parents said they would not know how to care for her. She had asked them to come stay with her, but her mother said her father was frail, travel was hard, and they would be afraid to come to New York City. The professor said it was disappointing that Ann dropped out just before collecting her degree, and he was sorry he had no time to visit her.

I shared this news with Ann's lab head and suggested we go see her. He said, "Tomorrow." The next day, he said, "Tomorrow." I decided to wait no longer and invited a post-doctoral fellow in her lab to join me.

We found Ann propped on pillows, working to breathe. Her eyes were wet and red, flashing fear and pain. Her abdomen bulged with fluid. Her knees were bent, her swollen legs parted, modesty irrelevant. Nearing death, childless, she had the pose and pain of a woman laboring to launch a life.

I approached her bed and reached for her hand where it lay on the bedclothes. She pulled it away and glowered. With effort, she raised her hand, palm forward, made a pushing gesture, and let it fall back.

We lingered. Looking angry now, she gestured "push off" again. Then she went back to work, staring straight ahead but looking inward, trying to manage another breath.

We came back the next day. A nurse told us Ann had died the day before.

For several years I had seen Ann almost every day without thinking of her life. For the next forty years, I have thought almost daily of her death. Perhaps that is because she did not allow me the comfort of comforting her.

As a physician, as a scientist, as a human being, all I could give her has been to remember.

Why Death?

LIKE NATHAN the cat who gifted me dead prey, memory gifts me deaths and near deaths. I must be asking myself the timeless question, "Why do living things all die?"

Yes, there is predation, by organisms about our size, like lions and bears, and smaller, like viruses, bacteria, fungi, protozoa, and worms. There are envenomation, starvation, malnutrition, dehydration, drowning, suffocation, freezing, and fire. There is violence by accident, by crime, by self, and by war. There is disease of each body part and process. What I pondered is why people who manage to avoid all that all still die.

Seemingly, it could not be simpler. No process is perfect. Every part of a biological engine wears out. Mechanisms of repair are among those parts. Impaired capacity for repair makes aging more than the passage of time.

But that's not all. Aging is more than "running down." As they mature, some organisms, at least, take active biochemical steps to close down their capacity for repair. Biologists often use the tiny worm *C. elegans* as an experimental model for larger beings. Richard Morimoto and colleagues found that once these worms produce offspring, they suppress the expression of genes that encode the proteins that protect and repair their other proteins.

Why would evolution not only tolerate aging but promote it and its end-game, death? Because death turns the disadvantage of error-prone biology into an advantage—for the species, not the individual. This is just one aspect of nature making use of everything at hand, even what seems like waste.

Life speciates. Every species now living depends on others. The evolution of diverse species must be accompanied by the evolution of their responsiveness to the mutual impacts they have on one another, because all life on Earth draws directly or indirectly on the same resources. That interdependence connects everything living to every living thing. Once anything changes, anything else might, and something does. Genetic variation arising from imperfections in DNA replication and repair becomes an investment in approximating re-perfection—by adaptation to changed conditions.

Interdependency comes with costs. We would be over and done with without plants whose chlorophyll turns sunlight into food and oxygen. We depend on both: we use the oxygen to turn the food into power for our cells and minds. But oxygen "rusts" us, too, much as it turns iron red by oxidation. The oxygen on which we depend for life gives rise to reactive oxygen species that oxidize our DNA, proteins, and lipids, until some of these molecules can no longer fulfill their functions. For those and other reasons, mutations arise at the outset of new life and accumulate as we age, including in the founder cells of the next generation, ova and sperm.

For each person, life succeeds only if we take advantage of our mistakes. So too for life itself. Each species experiments when genes mutate in some of its individual members. The vast majority of genetic errors are non-adaptive—neutral. Some are maladaptive, causing disease. A very few are adaptive. With a larger number of experiments, there is a greater chance for a successful experiment—an individual whose mutations allow it and its descendants to better adapt to an altered environment.

Here's the rub: overpopulation of a niche, a specific environment, depletes the resources a species requires and becomes self-defeating. Death of individuals past reproductive age—even the healthy—solves the dilemma. Death does the math. Death makes room.

It's one of nature's many circles: death allows species to diversify so that diversification of species can sustain life in the face of changing environments, including changes caused by diversification of species.

That circle turns within us as well: As we develop from a fertilized egg to a few-cell mass to an embryo to a mature organism with distinct, interdependent parts, many cells die to make way for others more diverse.

Cells die in the normal course of development of an individual so an individual with interdependent parts can live as a member of its species.

Individuals die in the normal course of development of a species so interdependent species can live as members of an ecosystem.

Prescriptions

THAT DEATH OFTEN arises from the failure of self-repair does not exclude humans from repairing each other. Medical interventions will increasingly include repair, including the repair of faulty genes.

Yet our greatest *medical* need is for *societal* repair. We need major corrections to human interactions if people are to live their biologic spans.

In about a century we have consumed or destroyed resources that Earth took millennia to invent and amass. Now, environmental depletion, degradation, and invasion bring pandemic diseases of people and planetary diseases of skies, seas, soils, forests, wetlands, and aquifers, endangering most living things. If our environment differs too rapidly from what we evolved to thrive in, we cannot evolve our *genes* fast enough to adapt. Our only timely option is to adapt our *behavior*.

Nature makes use of its mistakes. We must make the right use of ours. First, we need to change environmental course. Many of us have chosen to do so. As more perish, we can only hope that more will follow.

The next choice is whether we take advantage of sharing grave dangers to move past the mentality of "us versus them." It seems that a fear of "others" and a penchant for tribal warfare became a heritable trait in the eras in our evolution when hominid families competed for resources before acquiring the skills and means to create and renew them. Over the last few millennia, as clans, then tribes, grew into large groups not defined by family ties, "tribal warfare" worsened. "Us versus them" became religious schism, casteism, colorism, racism, nationalism, imperialism. Now we have the most compelling reason in the history of life on Earth to enlarge our identity group until there are no "others," no "them." With Earth itself at risk, we must make use of our instinct for tribalism by grasping at last that we are all one tribe.

Yet it's fair to ask: Beyond self-interest, what difference does it make to struggle to postpone the end of human life on Earth, when we know the time will come that the Sun is done?

The answer comes from our deepest aspirations and their unfulfillment. Humankind's distinguishing feature is our drive for understanding, and we are far from learning answers to our most basic questions.

Physics is the bedrock of anything we know for sure. Physics has attained what seems like a perfect congruence of math with observation, from the subatomic to the intergalactic. But the bedrock is a cloud. The equations match, predict, and explain what we measure only if we postulate dark energy and dark matter, and we don't know what those are. We enthrone general relativity and quantum mechanics, while excusing their failure to explain gravity or time. We know when this universe began, but we do not know from what, how, for how long, or how often. We wonder how many universes there are. That means we do not know how to define one. Humankind needs far more time to understand the universe, our star and planet, other stars and planets, life, our origins, and our options. Yet our very ignorance leaves room for hope. We know so little of what is fundamental that what we can't imagine now but could learn in years to come might mean that life will thrive.

As individuals, we have a similar drive for understanding: of our personal universe, our own life, our family origins, our options that were, and those that remain. The tools are not those of mathematics, particle physics, and cosmology, but of memory, reflection, and contemplation. In place of proof by the match of theory to observation, we seek understandings that enable further understanding.

> Physicists insist
> the light from our star
> bounces through our shell
> of air to belie with blue
> the vast black spaces,
> careens off scenes
> my eyes to fill,
> incites rhodopsin—
> second only to chlorophyll
> in catching light—
> the one for sight,
> the other, sustenance.
> I know another option—
> imagination, too, is radiance.
> Dark pouring from my eyes
> paints the unseen places.
> Mine is the plaint
> that rays through deceiving blue
> to accuse the void of being true.

I have tried to illustrate one approach toward self-understanding, allowing one memory to lead to another and that to another. Sort them and see if they help answer questions like the ones I put to myself in the Preface, or your own.

Why make that effort, or put up with the pain of reflection? To thank. To forgive. To apologize. To quiet unresolved regrets. To appreciate the hand. To better take a hand and give a hand.

To see that how we live is shaped by how we think of death.

Here is how I've seen it since I was young: *Whenever I die, it will be soon.*

That is a liberating thought, a gift. It means that *now* is the time to love, to wonder, and to build.

Afterword

WHEN I WAS little and thrilled by the hill behind our house, I imagined my life-arrow flying high over the crest. My older self would be waiting on the other side to ask me how I'd fared.

My father was a writer. As I grew, my mother became a writer, too. I would be a writer, but first I would fill my life with stories to share.

My father began to stop writing to task when he retired and sold his business. He stopped completely when *Publishers' Weekly* terminated the column he had provided every week without fail for fifty-one years, not missing even the week of my mother's death. He was eighty when he broke free. He yoked experience to imagination and began publishing detective novels suffused with wry humor, gentle wisdom, and insight into societal issues. As I approached my seventies, that became my plan—to start writing at eighty. Of course, I was writing all along, but for scientists. At eighty I would write something for anyone.

Then came COVID-19. I have a list of risks. I am what our culture calls "old." Because biology is error-prone and I am one of its maladaptive experiments, my lymphocytes do not make secretory immunoglobulins, the antibodies that fortify the fluids lining the nose, lungs, and gut to restrict entry of infectious agents. Each day, I inhale immunosuppressive corticosteroids to suppress asthma. Multiple bouts of pneumonia have scarred my lungs, reducing their reserve.

Yet what drove me to compose these reflections during COVID-19 was not fear of death. It was the thought of not being there to receive the arrow from over the hill. I did not want to let young me down.

Glossary

Abscess: A pus-filled hole in a bodily tissue

Acute myelocytic leukemia: A rapidly advancing malignancy in which immature precursors of blood cells in the granulocyte series take over the bone marrow and crowd the blood, precluding the development of normal granulocytes, while failing to fulfill their function to protect the host from infection

Actin: An intracellular protein that can link together copies of itself to form cable-like filaments that help give a cell its shape and allow it to crawl

Active site: The space, often a cleft or pocket, within an enzyme where the enzyme uses the side chains of certain amino acid residues in its structure to catalyze a chemical change in its substrate, producing its product

Adaptive immunity: (Not to be confused with adopted immunity) The portion of the immune system contributed by B and T lymphocytes that allows for specific recognition of diverse antigens by individual lymphocyte clones and, upon the encounter of clones with their specific antigens, supports proliferation of those clones and the development of immunologic memory

Adenylyl cyclase: An intracellular enzyme that responds to an external signal received by a cell by removing two phosphates from ATP and hooking together the two remaining ends of the molecule, producing cyclic adenosine monophosphate, which participates in propagating the signal within the cell

Adopted immunity: (Not to be confused with adaptive immunity) A set of practices including sanitation (potable water, waste handling, shelter, hand washing, sterile surgical technique, etc.), nutrition, vaccination, and the development of antibiotics that societies began to employ recently in human history to compensate for the frequent failure of natural immunity to protect people from life-threatening infections

Allergen: An antigen against which the immune response provokes certain reactions that are troublesome to the host, such as wheezing, hives, rashes, and falling blood pressure

Autacoids: Small chemical compounds released by a cell that diffuse to neighboring cells and may alter their behavior—as distinct from cytokines, which are proteins that do so; and as distinct from neurotransmitters, which diffuse only to cells with which the producing cell has formed a private connection

AMR: Antimicrobial resistance, the acquired ability of bacteria to survive exposure to an antibiotic at a concentration that in the past had sufficed to kill bacteria of that type; a commonly used shorthand term for the global crisis of running out of effective antibiotics

Amyotrophic lateral sclerosis (ALS): A degenerative disease of nerve cells in the brain and spinal cord that progressively impairs a person's ability to use their muscles

Anaphylaxis: A sudden, severe allergic response in which airways and intestines may constrict and blood vessels may leak fluid into the tissues, causing hives, swelling of the lips and tongue, and a fall in blood pressure

Antibody: A glycoprotein of the immunoglobulin class, one part of which can bind specific antigens and another part of which can bind to receptors on immune cells, with such outcomes as neutralization of the antigen's function, ingestion of the cell bearing the antigen, or lysis of the antigen-bearing cell by complement

Antigen: A substance foreign to the body that elicits a specific immune response

Aortic stenosis: Calcification and stiffening of the valve between the chamber of the heart that pumps blood to most of the body and the artery that receives the blood, causing insufficient outflow

Atomic specificity: The propensity of a molecule to react chemically with only a few types of atoms in other molecules and only with certain atoms of that type, depending on their local environment

Atom: An element that is distinguished from other elements by its number of electrons, protons, and neutrons and that must join with other atoms to form a molecule

ATP: Adenosine triphosphate, the most abundant of a small number of chemical compounds within a cell that store energy in high-energy phosphate-phosphate bonds and use that energy to drive a wide range of enzymatic reactions

Autoantigen: A substance that is a normal component of the body but elicits a specific immune response

Bacillus anthracis: The bacterium that causes anthrax

B lymphocyte: A class of lymphocytes in the adaptive immune system that give rise to cells that secrete antibodies

BCG: Bacille Calmette-Guérin, an attenuated strain of *Mycobacterium bovis* used in many parts of the world as a vaccine against tuberculosis

Bronchodilators: Medicines, most of them related to epinephrine, that are used to fight asthma by relaxing the constriction of the airways

Calmodulin: A protein found in most non-bacterial cells that changes shape when there is an increase in the intracellular level of calcium ions, and, in its calcium-bound form, activates other proteins that carry out the cells' response to the signal that increased the calcium

Cancer: Used here in the lay sense to mean any malignant tumor, rather than in the technical sense of a malignant tumor of epithelial origin

Catalyst: A substance, such as an enzyme, that speeds up a chemical reaction without being irreversibly changed in the process

Chagas disease: South American trypanosomiasis, a disease caused by the parasite *Trypanosoma cruzi* and most often transmitted by biting insects, whose chronic form can cause heart failure and enlargement of the esophagus and colon

Chemokine: A type of cytokine that elicits chemotaxis and other responses in cells that bear a receptor for the chemokine

Chemotaxis: Migration of cells up a concentration gradient of a signal such as a chemokine and their immobilization at a place where the concentration reaches a certain level

Cheyne-Stokes respiration: A pattern of breathing characterized by cycles of slow, increasingly deep breaths followed by long pauses without breathing, associated with various metabolic disturbances and often seen in someone near death

Chromatography: A technique to separate molecules based on their size, charge, or other properties by the different times it takes them to percolate through fluid-filled channels surrounding tiny spheres with appropriate surface properties

Chronic granulomatous disease: A genetic disorder characterized by recurrent infections and persistent inflammation caused by loss of function in NOX2 (also called "phagocyte oxidase"), the major enzyme used by neutrophils and macrophages to make ROS when they encounter an infectious agent

Cilia: Small hair-like projections from a cell, such as cells lining the airways in the lung

Click chemistry: A set of methods for forming specific chemical compounds in one step and high yield under biologically tolerable conditions by joining together two other compounds

Clone (referring to a cell): As a noun, a cell that is distinguished from others in some way, such as by its unique antigen receptor, and that cell's genetically identical progeny; as a verb, the isolation of such a cell

Clone (referring to a gene): Molecular isolation of a segment of DNA comprising a gene or DNA complementary to the gene

Complement: An interacting group of enzymes in the blood and the tissues that can bind to cells, including bacteria, that have been tagged by antibodies, resulting in the cells' lysis or engulfment

Corticosteroids: Used here to refer to glucocorticoids, hormones that are chemical compounds of the steroid class having immunosuppressive and anti-inflammatory properties that are released by the cortex (outer layer) of the adrenal glands in response to stress, synthetic forms of which are used as medications

Cystic fibrosis: A genetic disorder affecting the function of a protein in cell membranes through which chloride ion is secreted, leading to excessively viscous mucus in the airways and gastrointestinal tract and associated respiratory, infectious, and nutritional difficulties

Cytokine: A protein released by cells that in very low concentrations can affect the growth, migration, gene expression, secretion, survival, or other behavior of cells bearing a receptor for the cytokine

Cytosol: The region within a cell that lies between its outer membrane and the membranes surrounding its nucleus, mitochondria, and other organelles

Cytotoxic: Causing death of mammalian cells

Dendritic cells: Cells in the immune system that take up antigen and use it to activate an immune response in previously antigen-inexperienced lymphocyte clones that display a receptor for the antigen

Dilaudid: A strong pain-killing medication related to morphine

Disseminated intravascular coagulation: A disorder in which the blood clots in diverse sites within the bloodstream, consuming clotting factors faster than the body can replace them, leading to bleeding at other sites

DNA: Deoxyribonucleic acid, a string-like molecule made of four different building blocks linked together in a sequence whose variation encodes the information that specifies a gene

Electrospray ionization mass spectrometry: A method to identify molecules after they are ionized out of a liquid by application of an electric field and fed into an instrument that reports the ratio of their accurate mass to their charge

Endothelial cells: Cells that line the inside of blood vessels and whose properties and actions help control whether white blood cells and platelets pass by or stick and whether underlying muscle cells relax or constrict

Endothelial NOS (NOS3): The form of nitric oxide synthase first cloned from the cells that line blood vessels, where its activation helps blood vessels relax and resist adhesion by platelets

Endotoxin: Also called lipopolysaccharide or LPS, a glycolipid from the cell wall of a major class of bacteria that is profoundly inflammatory and can contribute to septic shock during infections

Enzyme: A protein catalyst acting on certain substrates and producing certain products

Eosinophil: A white blood cell in the granulocyte family, distinguished by its large intracellular granules that stain with the dye eosin; it helps defend against parasites and worms but can also contribute to asthma and other allergic states

Epigenetic changes: Relatively long-lasting chemical modifications to DNA or histones that affect how readily a given gene can be expressed (transcribed) in the future

Epinephrine: Also called adrenalin, a small chemical compound secreted by the adrenal glands in an emergency that speeds the heart, counters anaphylaxis, and relaxes constricted airways; produced industrially as a medicine for injection

Epipen®: A syringe pre-filled with epinephrine and spring-loaded so that the touch of a button simultaneously releases a needle and ejects the contents of the syringe into the muscle of a person suffering from anaphylaxis

Eukaryotic cell: A cell with a "well" (eu) nucleus (karyon), including fungal, protozoal, animal, and plant cells, as distinguished from prokaryotic cells, which are bacteria and archaea

Extracellular matrix proteins: Proteins that fill spaces in the body between cells; they have fixed positions and affect the behavior of immune cells migrating through those spaces

Genome: Originally, all the genes that an individual inherits, now understood to refer variably to that genome (now called nuclear), the somatic genome (the nuclear genome as it changes in an individual's cells across their lifetime), the mitochondrial genome, and the microbiotal genome

Glutathione: An abundant intracellular peptide formed by the amino acids glycine, cysteine, and glutamic acid, in which the free sulfhydryl group on cysteine's side chain is readily oxidized, helping protect a cell from oxidative and nitrosative stress

Glycoprotein: A protein to which one or more sugar groups are attached

Granulocytes: White blood cells with named for their prominent granules (lysosomes), with neutrophils normally the most abundant, followed by eosinophils, whose granules take up a stain called eosin, and basophils, whose granules stain with an alkaline (basic) dye

Helicobacter pylori: A bacterium that infects the upper gastrointestinal tract and is the primary cause of gastric and duodenal ulcers

Hexose monophosphate shunt (HMPS): A pathway for metabolism of glucose that instead of producing ATP, produces NADPH from its oxidized form, NADP+, along with intermediates for synthesis of nucleic acids

Histones: Proteins in a cell's nucleus around which the DNA is wrapped

Homeostasis: The inter-cellular and intra-cellular signal-response processes and positive and negative feedback loops by which cells and the body maintain vital processes in a changing environment

Hypertension: Elevation of blood pressure above normal

Hypotension: Reduction of blood pressure below normal

Hydrogen peroxide: H_2O_2, a small molecule that acts as an oxidant, produced in abundance by neutrophils and activated macrophages when they engulf a pathogen

Hydroxyl radical: ·OH, a small molecule that is the most potent known oxidant formed in biological systems

Hypochlorite: ⁻OCl, the anion of hypochlorous acid (HOCl), a strong oxidant formed in the body by myeloperoxidase and produced industrially for bleaches

Immunoglobulin: The biochemical class of proteins to which antibodies belong

Immunoglobulin A (IgA): A class of antibodies that is secreted into the respiratory and gastrointestinal tracts

Immunoglobulin E (IgE): A class of antibodies that binds to receptors on eosinophils and mast cells before encountering antigen, and, upon encountering antigen, triggers those cells to release autacoids, cytokines, and enzymes

Immunoglobulin G (IgG): The most abundant class of antibodies in the bloodstream

Immunologic memory: Faster accumulation of antigen-reactive lymphocyte clones and their accumulation in greater numbers upon a second or further encounter with an antigen than upon the first encounter with the same antigen, often accompanied by emergence of clones with higher affinity for the antigen

Immuno-oncology: Treatment of a patient with cancer by increasing the ability of the immune system to kill tumor cells, often by inhibiting constraints on immune cell activation

Inducible nitric oxide synthase (iNOS, NOS2): The second form of nitric oxide synthase to be cloned, distinguished by its inducibility (condition-dependent transcriptional expression) and its independence of elevated levels of intracellular calcium ions for its activation

Inflammation: The body's earliest reaction to trauma and/or presence of foreign material, classically described in Latin by the four signs rubor (redness), calor (heat), tumor (swelling), and dolor (pain)

Inflammatory bowel disease: A set of disorders that include Crohn's disease and ulcerative colitis in which there is recurrent or persistent inflammation of the small and/or large intestines

Innate immunity: That portion of the immune system that does not depend on specific recognition of individual antigens by clonal lymphocytes, in which neutrophils, macrophages, and non-B, non-T lymphocytes play a prominent part

Inorganic: A chemical compound containing no atoms of carbon or hydrogen, a category once believed to exclude any products made by living organisms

Integrins: A family of proteins that bridge the outer membrane of certain cells, such that the integrins' outer portions engage extracellular matrix proteins and inner portions convey signals that affect the cells' migration, secretion, and other behaviors

Interleukin-10 (IL-10): A cytokine produced by monocytes and lymphocytes that inhibits macrophage activation and other aspects of inflammation

Intermediary metabolism: The set of enzymatic reactions that converts food into energy, reducing power and building blocks for proteins, nucleic acids, carbohydrates, and lipids

Interferon-gamma: A cytokine produced by lymphocytes that activates macrophages

Isoproterenol: A small chemical with properties similar to those of epinephrine, sometimes used in inhalers for rapid treatment of an asthma attack

Knockout mice: Mice whose heritable genome has been altered to selectively inactivate a given gene so as to enable assessment of that gene's function from the resulting impact on the phenotype of the mice

Leishmaniasis: A protozoal disease that involves infection of macrophages, which in different forms can cause isolated skin ulcers, disseminated infiltration of the skin and mucus membranes, or massive enlargement of the liver and spleen

Lepromatous leprosy: A form of infection by *Mycobacterium leprae* in which the person's T lymphocytes make insuf-

ficient interferon-gamma to activate their macrophages,
resulting in widespread infiltration of the skin with
infected macrophages

Leukotrienes: Small, bioactive lipids produced by neutrophils, eosinophils, basophils, mast cells, and monocytes
that can constrict airways in asthma and contribute to
inflammation

Lipopolysaccharide (LPS): Also called endotoxin, a glycolipid from the cell wall of a major class of bacteria that
is profoundly inflammatory and can contribute to septic
shock during infections

Lymphocytes: Cells of the immune system found in blood,
lymph nodes, spleen, tonsils, and other tissues

Lymphotoxin: A cytokine structurally related to TNF that
was originally identified as cytotoxic for certain kinds of
tumor cells and later found to play a key role in the development of the immune system's ability to aggregate lymphocytes in lymph nodes and the spleen in a way that
optimizes their function

Lysis: Digestion or disintegration, such as of a cell whose
membrane is disrupted

Lysosome: An intracellular organelle filled with diges-
tive enzymes, first called "granules" in white blood
cells

Macrophages: Long-lived, migratory or resident cells of the
immune system found in every mammalian organ from
local proliferation or through the immigration of monocytes from the blood; they engage in phagocytosis, cope
with a variety of bacterial and protozoal infections, help
heal wounds, and help control the function of tissues in
which they reside

Macrophage activation factor (MAF): A glycoprotein cytokine produced by antigen-reactive lymphocytes that augments the capacity of macrophages to fight infection, later

identified as interferon-gamma, although certain other
cytokines can also activate macrophages

Macrophage deactivation factor: An as-yet uncloned glycoprotein cytokine produced by tumor cells that prevents
and reverses macrophage activation; similar properties
were later ascribed to the cloned cytokines transforming
growth factor-beta and interleukin-10

Major histocompatibility complex: Proteins expressed
on the surface of most cells in the body, encoded by genes
diverse enough to distinguish most individuals from each
other, that display short stretches from proteins expressed
within the cell, allowing an individual's lymphocytes to
recognize the cell as normal-self, infected-self, or trans-
planted from another person

Malaria: An infectious disease caused by protozoal parasites
called *Plasmodia* that are transmitted by mosquitoes

Mast cells: A type of granulocyte that lies along the tissue side of airways and small blood vessels; its granules
can release autacoids during allergic reactions, including
anaphylaxis

Mastectomy: Removal of part or all of the breast to treat
breast cancer; in a radical mastectomy, underlying muscles and lymph nodes in the armpit are removed as well

Metagenome: The ensemble of an individual's nuclear,
somatic, mitochondrial, and microbiotal genomes

Microbiota: The collection of bacteria, bacteria-like archaea,
fungi, viruses, and other non-human life forms that
inhabit an individual's skin, gastrointestinal and urogeni-
tal tracts, and airways

Migration inhibitory factor (MIF): One of the first-discovered cytokines, characterized as a glycoprotein released by
antigen-stimulated lymphocytes that prevented macrophages from migrating away from each other when they
were packed together, but without harming them

Mitochondria: Intracellular organelles that generate most of
the ATP in a eukaryotic cell

Molecule: A substance composed of more than one atom
and distinguished from other molecules by the numbers and types of atoms it contains, the sequence in which
the atoms are connected, and the nature of the linkages
between them

Molecular specificity: The propensity of a molecule to bind
closely to and/or engage in a chemical reaction only with a
restricted set of other molecules

Monocytes: White blood cells that arise in the bone marrow,
patrol the blood vessels, and emigrate into inflamed tissues, where they can mature into macrophages

Mycobacterium bovis: The bacterium that causes tuberculosis in cows and many other animals, but rarely does so in
humans, now that cattle herds are checked for the infection and milk is pasteurized

Mycobacterium leprae: The bacterium that causes leprosy

Mycobacterium tuberculosis: The bacterium that causes the
vast majority of cases of tuberculosis in humans

Myeloperoxidase: An iron-containing enzyme, abundant in
the lysosomes of neutrophils and monocytes, that turns
hydrogen peroxide into bleach-like molecules, including
the active ingredient of Clorox®

NADPH: Nicotinamide adenine dinucleotide phosphate
(reduced form), a chemical compound that provides an electron (also called "reducing power") for numerous biochemical reactions, including the inactivation of oxidizing agents

Neuronal NOS (NOS1): The form of nitric oxide synthase
first cloned, which was from brain tissue

**Neurotransmitters (including gamma-aminobutyric
acid)**: Small chemical compounds released by neurons
into synapses with other neurons or with muscle cells,
which instruct the receiving cell to respond in some way

Neutrophils: The short-lived but numerically dominant type of white blood cells and the numerically dominant type of granulocytes in the blood, active in phagocytosis, loaded with degradative enzymes and antibacterial proteins, and capable of producing large amounts of reactive oxygen species

Nitric oxide: ·NO, an inorganic radical gas produced in the body by three types of nitric oxide synthase, giving rise to a family of reactive nitrogen species that can react with numerous other molecules with atomic specificity

Nitric oxide synthase (NOS): One of a family of three enzymes in mammals (nNOS or NOS1; iNOS or NOS2; eNOS or NOS3) that make nitric oxide from molecular oxygen, NADPH, and the amino acid L-arginine with the aid of tetrhydrobiopterin

Nitrogen dioxide: ·NO$_2$, one of the reactive nitrogen species arising from nitric oxide

NOS1, 2, and 3: Nitric oxide synthases 1 (also called nNOS), 2 (also called iNOS), or 3 (also called eNOS)

NOX: NADPH oxidases, a family of enzymes that make superoxide, whose first-discovered member, inappropriately named NOX2, used to be called "phagocyte oxidase" and is prominent in granulocytes and activated macrophages, where its deficiency causes chronic granulomatous disease

Nucleic acids: Strings (polymers) made up of four types of building blocks that are nitrogenous compounds ("bases") consisting of purines or pyrimidines, each of which is linked to a phosphorylated ribose in ribonucleic acids (RNA) or to a phosphorylated deoxyribose in deoxyribonucleic acids (DNA)

Nucleotides: The phosphorylated (deoxy)ribopurines or phosphorylated (deoxy)ribopyrimidines that are the building blocks of nucleic acids

Oncogene: A gene that when mutated or over-expressed can cause a cell to become cancerous

Organelle: A membrane-bound structure within a cell other than its nucleus and having a specialized function

Pathogen: An infectious agent; the term is usually used to refer to a bacterium or protozoan

Peroxynitrite: ($OONO^-$), a compound arising from the interaction of nitric oxide and superoxide, belonging to both the reactive oxygen species and the reactive nitrogen species and giving rise to another member of the reactive oxygen species (hydroxyl radical or $^{\bullet}OH$) and another member of the reactive nitrogen species (nitrogen dioxide radical or $^{\bullet}NO_2$)

Phage (also called bacteriophage): A virus that can infect a bacterium

Phagocyte: A cell that is proficient in engulfing particles such as bacteria

Phagocyte oxidase: The original name of a superoxide-producing enzyme expressed in granulocytes, monocytes, and macrophages that is now called NOX2

Phagocytosis: The act by which a cell engulfs a particle into a membrane-bound vesicle

Phenotype: The constellation of an organism's observable properties in a given environment or under a given set of conditions, as distinct from its genotype, its heritable genetic sequences

Phosphatase: An enzyme that removes a phosphate residue from its substrate

Platelet: A type of tiny cell without a nucleus that arises by breaking off from a larger cell in the bone marrow to circulate in the blood, where it sticks to the endothelial cells at sites of injury

Pneumonic plague: A contagious, potentially lethal respiratory disease caused when the bacterium *Yersinia pestis* is

inhaled, as opposed to bubonic plague, which arises when
the same bacterium is transmitted by the bite of a flea

Pus: A collection of dead cells, mostly neutrophils, whose
green tint comes from the iron in myeloperoxidase

Radical: A molecule with an unpaired electron, such as
superoxide ($O_2^{\cdot-}$) or nitric oxide ($\cdot NO$)

Reactive nitrogen intermediates: Enzymatically produced
nitric oxide ($\cdot NO$) and its spontaneously arising products
that are chemically reactive, namely, HNO, $\cdot NO_2$, N_2O_3,
N_2O_5, and NO_2^-

Reactive oxygen intermediates: Enzymatically produced
superoxide (O_2^-), its spontaneously arising products that
are chemically reactive, namely, H_2O_2, $\cdot OH$, and $^1O_2$, and
by convention, the enzymatically catalyzed products of
H_2O_2 with chloride, iodide, and bromide, namely, HOCl,
HOI, and HOBr

Recombinant protein: A protein expressed in a cell (which
may be bacterial, yeast or mammalian) from DNA that is
foreign to that cell and/or artificially contains sequences
from more than one gene

Respiratory burst: The sudden production of reactive oxygen species by granulocytes, monocytes or macrophages
when they ingest a particle or are otherwise triggered,
such as when neutrophils with engaged integrins are
exposed to tumor necrosis factor

Rheumatoid arthritis: An autoimmune disease marked by
progressively destructive chronic inflammation in the
joints

RNA: A polymer (string) of ribonucleic acids whose sequence
is determined by the DNA that an enzyme called RNA
polymerase copies as it synthesizes the RNA

Septic shock: A life-threatening fall in blood pressure accom-
panying a body-wide inflammatory response to infection

Stevens-Johnson syndrome: A potentially life-threatening reaction to an infection or a medication in which the outer layer of the skin and mucus membranes may blister, die, and fall away

Substrate: A molecule on which an enzyme acts

Superoxide: $O_2{}^{\cdot-}$, an inorganic radical gas produced by NOX2 (phagocyte oxidase) and mitochondria that gives rise to additional reactive oxygen species

T cells: A class of lymphocytes in the adaptive immune system that can kill infected host cells, help B cells make antibodies, and release cytokines that activate macrophages, among many other effects

Tetrahydrobiopterin: A chemical compound that serves as a cofactor for nitric oxide synthases

Toxins: Products secreted by bacteria that contribute to disease

Toxoplasma gondii: A protozoan parasite most often transmitted from feces of cats that infects macrophages in vulnerable individuals, particularly those who are pregnant or immunocompromised

Trained immunity: The ability of cells in the innate immune system to respond more vigorously to an infection or other inflammatory stimulus a second or subsequent time than they could on the host's first encounter with the same pathogen or stimulus, because of epigenetic changes in the immune cells or their precursors, which, unlike immunologic memory, does not involve reactivation and expansion of antigen-specific clones

Transforming growth factor-beta: A cytokine that deactivates macrophages, suppresses T cell activation, promotes fibrosis, and has diverse other effects

Transcription: Expression of a gene by synthesis of the RNA encoded by the gene's DNA

Trypanosoma cruzi: The protozoan parasite that causes
  Chagas disease

Trypanosomiasis: Infectious diseases caused by protozoal
  parasites of the trypanosome family; in South America,
  Trypanosoma cruzi infects macrophages, gastrointestinal
  muscle cells, and heart muscle cells, causing Chagas disease, while in Africa, *Trypanosoma brucei* infects blood,
  lymph, and brain, causing "sleeping sickness"

Tryptic peptides: Fragments of a protein after it is par-
  tially digested by the enzyme trypsin, often for the purpose of subjecting the fragments to electrospray ionization
  mass spectrometry to identify the protein from which
  they came

Tuberculosis: A chronic disease most often caused in people by *Mycobacterium tuberculosis* and sometimes by other
  mycobacteria, that can affect any organ or combination of
  organs, usually including the lungs

Tumor necrosis factor (TNF): A cytokine whose multiple
  effects range from activation of neutrophils to collapse of
  the vasculature of some tumors to loss of muscle mass in
  individuals with cancers or chronic infections

Urushiol: The lipid from poison ivy that causes a rash and
  hives in people who are sensitive to it

Ventricular tachycardia: A life-threatening heart rhythm
  in which the pumping chambers of the heart (the ven-
  tricles) constrict too many times per minute (tachy, from
  the Greek for speed) to allow adequate circulation of well-
  oxygenated blood

White blood cells: The granulocytes (neutrophils, eosinophils, and basophils), monocytes, and lymphocytes in the
  blood, as distinguished from the red blood cells, which
  owe their conspicuous color to their large content of iron
  bound to the protein hemoglobin

References

These references are in National Library of Medicine format.

1. Nathan C. Cooperative development of antimicrobials: looking back to look ahead. Nat Rev Microbiol. 2015;13(10):651–7. doi: 10.1038/nrmicro3523. PubMed PMID: 26373373.
2. Boyden S. The chemotactic effect of mixtures of antibody and antigen on polymorphonuclear leucocytes. J Exp Med. 1962;115:453–66. doi: 10.1084/jem.115.3.453. PubMed PMID: 13872176; PMCID: PMC2137509.
3. Nathan C. Points of control in inflammation. Nature. 2002;420(6917):846–52. doi: 10.1038/nature01320. PubMed PMID: 12490957.
4. Nathan C. Nonresolving inflammation redux. Immunity. 2022;55(4):592–605. doi: 10.1016/j.immuni.2022.03.016. PubMed PMID: 35417674; PMCID: PMC9003810.
5. Nathan C, Ding A. Nonresolving inflammation. Cell. 2010;140(6):871–82. doi: 10.1016/j.cell.2010.02.029. PubMed PMID: 20303877.
6. Nathan C. Plague Prevention and Politics in Manchuria, 1910–1931. Cambridge, MA: Harvard University Press; 1967. 106 pp.
7. Nathan C. Antibiotics at the crossroads. Nature. 2004;431(7011):899–902. doi: 10.1038/431899a. PubMed PMID: 15496893.
8. Nathan CF. Neutrophil activation on biological surfaces. Massive secretion of hydrogen peroxide in response to products of macrophages and lymphocytes. J Clin Invest. 1987;80(6):1550–60. doi: 10.1172/JCI113241. PubMed PMID: 2445780; PMCID: PMC442423.

9. Bryk R, Gold B, Venugopal A, Singh J, Samy R, Pupek K, Cao H, Popescu C, Gurney M, Hotha S, Cherian J, Rhee K, Ly L, Converse PJ, Ehrt S, Vandal O, Jiang X, Schneider J, Lin G, Nathan C. Selective killing of nonreplicating mycobacteria. Cell Host Microbe. 2008;3(3):137–45. doi: 10.1016/j.chom.2008.02.003. PubMed PMID: 18329613; PMCID: PMC2423947.

10. Bryk R, Griffin P, Nathan C. Peroxynitrite reductase activity of bacterial peroxiredoxins. Nature. 2000;407(6801):211–5. doi: 10.1038/35025109. PubMed PMID: 11001062.

11. Bryk R, Lima CD, Erdjument-Bromage H, Tempst P, Nathan C. Metabolic enzymes of mycobacteria linked to antioxidant defense by a thioredoxin-like protein. Science. 2002;295(5557):1073–7. Epub 20020117. doi: 10.1126/science.1067798. PubMed PMID: 11799204.

12. Darwin KH, Ehrt S, Gutierrez-Ramos JC, Weich N, Nathan CF. The proteasome of Mycobacterium tuberculosis is required for resistance to nitric oxide. Science. 2003;302(5652):1963–6. doi: 10.1126/science.1091176. PubMed PMID: 14671303.

13. Lin G, Li D, de Carvalho LP, Deng H, Tao H, Vogt G, Wu K, Schneider J, Chidawanyika T, Warren JD, Li H, Nathan C. Inhibitors selective for mycobacterial versus human proteasomes. Nature. 2009;461(7264):621–6. Epub 20090916. doi: 10.1038/nature08357. PubMed PMID: 19759536; PMCID: PMC3172082.

14. Vandal OH, Pierini LM, Schnappinger D, Nathan CF, Ehrt S. A membrane protein preserves intrabacterial pH in intraphagosomal Mycobacterium tuberculosis. Nat Med. 2008;14(8):849–54. Epub 20080720. doi: 10.1038/nm.1795. PubMed PMID: 18641659; PMCID: PMC2538620.

15. Vaubourgeix J, Lin G, Dhar N, Chenouard N, Jiang X, Botella H, Lupoli T, Mariani O, Yang G, Ouerfelli O, Unser M, Schnappinger D, McKinney J, Nathan C. Stressed mycobacteria use the chaperone ClpB to sequester irreversibly oxidized proteins asymmetrically within and between cells. Cell Host Microbe. 2015;17(2):178–90. Epub 20150122.

doi: 10.1016/j.chom.2014.12.008. PubMed PMID: 25620549;
PMCID: PMC5707119.

16. Venugopal A, Bryk R, Shi S, Rhee K, Rath P, Schnappinger D,
Ehrt S, Nathan C. Virulence of Mycobacterium tuberculosis depends on lipoamide dehydrogenase, a member of three
multienzyme complexes. Cell Host Microbe. 2011;9(1):21–31.
doi: 10.1016/j.chom.2010.12.004. PubMed PMID: 21238944;
PMCID: PMC3040420.

17. Nathan C. Nitric oxide as a secretory product of mammalian
cells. FASEB J. 1992;6(12):3051–64. PubMed PMID: 1381691.

18. Nathan C, Shiloh MU. Reactive oxygen and nitrogen
intermediates in the relationship between mammalian
hosts and microbial pathogens. Proc Natl Acad Sci U S A.
2000;97(16):8841–8. doi: 10.1073/pnas.97.16.8841. PubMed
PMID: 10922044; PMCID: PMC34021.

19. Nathan C, Ding A. SnapShot: Reactive Oxygen Intermediates
(ROI). Cell. 2010;140(6):951–e2. doi: 10.1016/j.cell.2010.03.008.
PubMed PMID: 20303882.

20. Nathan CF, Murray HW, Wiebe ME, Rubin BY. Identification
of interferon-gamma as the lymphokine that activates human
macrophage oxidative metabolism and antimicrobial activity. J Exp Med. 1983;158(3):670–89. doi: 10.1084/jem.158.3.670.
PubMed PMID: 6411853; PMCID: PMC2187114.

21. Nathan CF, Kaplan G, Levis WR, Nusrat A, Witmer MD,
Sherwin SA, Job CK, Horowitz CR, Steinman RM, Cohn ZA.
Local and systemic effects of intradermal recombinant inter-
feron-gamma in patients with lepromatous leprosy. N Engl
J Med. 1986;315(1):6–15. doi: 10.1056/NEJM198607033150102.
PubMed PMID: 3086725.

22. Ezekowitz RA, Dinauer MC, Jaffe HS, Orkin SH, Newburger
PE. Partial correction of the phagocyte defect in patients
with X-linked chronic granulomatous disease by subcutane-
ous interferon gamma. N Engl J Med. 1988;319(3):146–51. doi:
10.1056/NEJM198807213190305. PubMed PMID: 2838754.

23. Muhlebach TJ, Gabay J, Nathan CF, Erny C, Dopfer G, Schro-
ten H, Wahn V, Seger RA. Treatment of patients with chronic
granulomatous disease with recombinant human inter-

feron-gamma does not improve neutrophil oxidative metabolism, cytochrome b558 content or levels of four anti-microbial proteins. Clin Exp Immunol. 1992;88(2):203–6. doi: 10.1111/j.1365-2249.1992.tb03062.x. PubMed PMID: 1572085; PMCID: PMC1554300.

24. Nathan C. Specificity of a third kind: reactive oxygen and nitrogen intermediates in cell signaling. J Clin Invest. 2003;111(6):769–78. doi: 10.1172/JCI18174. PubMed PMID: 12639979; PMCID: PMC153776.

25. Nathan C, Cunningham-Bussel A. Beyond oxidative stress: an immunologist's guide to reactive oxygen species. Nat Rev Immunol. 2013;13(5):349–61. doi: 10.1038/nri3423. PubMed PMID: 23618831; PMCID: PMC4250048.

26. Mackaness GB. Cellular resistance to infection. J Exp Med. 1962;116:381–406. doi: 10.1084/jem.116.3.381. PubMed PMID: 14467923; PMCID: PMC2137547.

27. Mackaness GB. The Immunological Basis of Acquired Cellular Resistance. J Exp Med. 1964;120:105–20. doi: 10.1084/jem.120.1.105. PubMed PMID: 14194388; PMCID: PMC2137723.

28. Mackaness GB, Blanden RV. Cellular immunity. Prog Allergy. 1967;11:89–140. PubMed PMID: 4860381.

29. David JR. Delayed hypersensitivity in vitro: its mediation by cell-free substances formed by lymphoid cell-antigen interaction. Proc Natl Acad Sci U S A. 1966;56(1):72–7. doi: 10.1073/pnas.56.1.72. PubMed PMID: 5229858; PMCID: PMC285677.

30. Bloom BR, Bennett B. Mechanism of a reaction in vitro associated with delayed-type hypersensitivity. Science. 1966;153(3731):80–2. doi: 10.1126/science.153.3731.80. PubMed PMID: 5938421.

31. Ward PA, Remold HG, David JR. Leukotactic factor produced by sensitized lymphocytes. Science. 1969;163(3871):1079–81. doi: 10.1126/science.163.3871.1079. PubMed PMID: 5764874.

32. Granger GA, Shacks SJ, Williams TW, Kolb WP. Lymphocyte in vitro cytotoxicity: specific release of lymphotoxin-like materials from tuberculin-sensitive lymphoid cells. Nature. 1969;221(5186):1155–7. doi: 10.1038/2211155a0. PubMed PMID: 4975283.

33. Baehner RL, Gilman N, Karnovsky ML. Respiration and glucose oxidation in human and guinea pig leukocytes: comparative studies. J Clin Invest. 1970;49(4):692–700. doi: 10.1172/JCI106281. PubMed PMID: 4392648; PMCID: PMC322524.

34. Noseworthy J, Jr., Karnovsky ML. Role of peroxide in the stimulation of the hexose monophosphate shunt during phagocytosis by polymorphonuclear leukocytes. Enzyme. 1972;13(1):110–31. doi: 10.1159/000459652. PubMed PMID: 5075803.

35. Nathan C, Rosenberg S, Karnovsky ML, David JR, editors. Effects of MIF-rich supernatants on macrophages. Proceedings of the Fifth Leukocyte Culture Conference; 1969.

36. Nathan CF, Karnovsky ML, David JR. Alterations of macrophage functions by mediators from lymphocytes. J Exp Med. 1971;133(6):1356–76. doi: 10.1084/jem.133.6.1356. PubMed PMID: 5576335; PMCID: PMC2138934.

37. Nathan CF, Remold HG, David JR. Characterization of a lymphocyte factor which alters macrophage functions. J Exp Med. 1973;137(2):275–90. doi: 10.1084/jem.137.2.275. PubMed PMID: 4119587; PMCID: PMC2139484.

38. Fowles RE, Fajardo IM, Leibowitch JL, David JR. The enhancement of macrophage bacteriostasis by products of activated lymphocytes. J Exp Med. 1973;138(4):952–64. doi: 10.1084/jem.138.4.952. PubMed PMID: 4200649; PMCID: PMC2180559.

39. Nathan CF, Root RK. Hydrogen peroxide release from mouse peritoneal macrophages: dependence on sequential activation and triggering. J Exp Med. 1977;146(6):1648–62. doi: 10.1084/jem.146.6.1648. PubMed PMID: 925614; PMCID: PMC2181906.

40. Nathan C. Ralph Steinman, 1943–2011. Nature Immunology. 2011;12:1129.

41. Griffin FM, Jr., Griffin JA, Leider JE, Silverstein SC. Studies on the mechanism of phagocytosis. I. Requirements for circumferential attachment of particle-bound ligands to specific receptors on the macrophage plasma membrane. J Exp Med. 1975;142(5):1263–82. doi: 10.1084/jem.142.5.1263. PubMed PMID: 1194852; PMCID: PMC2189973.

42. Luster AD, Unkeless JC, Ravetch JV. Gamma-interferon transcriptionally regulates an early-response gene containing homology to platelet proteins. Nature. 1985;315(6021):672–6. doi: 10.1038/315672a0. PubMed PMID: 3925348.

43. Murray HW, Rubin BY, Rothermel CD. Killing of intracellular Leishmania donovani by lymphokine-stimulated human mononuclear phagocytes. Evidence that interferon-gamma is the activating lymphokine. J Clin Invest. 1983;72(4):1506–10. doi: 10.1172/JCI111107. PubMed PMID: 6415111; PMCID: PMC370435.

44. Van Voorhis WC, Kaplan G, Sarno EN, Horwitz MA, Steinman RM, Levis WR, Nogueira N, Hair LS, Gattass CR, Arrick BA, Cohn ZA. The cutaneous infiltrates of leprosy: cellular characteristics and the predominant T-cell phenotypes. N Engl J Med. 1982;307(26):1593–7. doi: 10.1056/NEJM198212233072601. PubMed PMID: 6216407.

45. Nathan C, Squires K, Griffo W, Levis W, Varghese M, Job CK, Nusrat AR, Sherwin S, Rappoport S, Sanchez E, et al. Widespread intradermal accumulation of mononuclear leukocytes in lepromatous leprosy patients treated systemically with recombinant interferon gamma. J Exp Med. 1990;172(5):1509–12. doi: 10.1084/jem.172.5.1509. PubMed PMID: 2121891; PMCID: PMC2188674.

46. Nathan CF, Horowitz CR, de la Harpe J, Vadhan-Raj S, Sherwin SA, Oettgen HF, Krown SE. Administration of recombinant interferon gamma to cancer patients enhances monocyte secretion of hydrogen peroxide. Proc Natl Acad Sci U S A. 1985;82(24):8686–90. doi: 10.1073/pnas.82.24.8686. PubMed PMID: 3936042; PMCID: PMC391501.

47. Badaro R, Falcoff E, Badaro FS, Carvalho EM, Pedral-Sampaio D, Barral A, Carvalho JS, Barral-Netto M, Brandely M, Silva L, et al. Treatment of visceral leishmaniasis with pentavalent antimony and interferon gamma. N Engl J Med. 1990;322(1):16–21. doi: 10.1056/NEJM199001043220104. PubMed PMID: 2104665.

48. Murray HW, Spitalny GL, Nathan CF. Activation of mouse peritoneal macrophages in vitro and in vivo by interferon-

gamma. J Immunol. 1985;134(3):1619–22. PubMed PMID: 3918107.

49. Kamijo R, Le J, Shapiro D, Havell EA, Huang S, Aguet M, Bosland M, Vilcek J. Mice that lack the interferon-gamma receptor have profoundly altered responses to infection with Bacillus Calmette-Guerin and subsequent challenge with lipopolysaccharide. J Exp Med. 1993;178(4):1435–40. doi: 10.1084/jem.178.4.1435. PubMed PMID: 8376946; PMCID: PMC2191201.

50. Jouanguy E, Altare F, Lamhamedi S, Revy P, Emile JF, Newport M, Levin M, Blanche S, Seboun E, Fischer A, Casanova JL. Interferon-gamma-receptor deficiency in an infant with fatal bacille Calmette-Guerin infection. N Engl J Med. 1996;335(26):1956–61. doi: 10.1056/NEJM199612263352604. PubMed PMID: 8960475.

51. Arrick BA, Nathan CF, Cohn ZA. Inhibition of glutathione synthesis augments lysis of murine tumor cells by sulfhydryl-reactive antineoplastics. J Clin Invest. 1983;71(2):258–67. doi: 10.1172/jci110766. PubMed PMID: 6401768; PMCID: PMC436864.

52. Nathan C, Brukner L, Kaplan G, Unkeless J, Cohn Z. Role of activated macrophages in antibody-dependent lysis of tumor cells. J Exp Med. 1980;152(1):183–97. doi: 10.1084/jem.152.1.183. PubMed PMID: 6995552; PMCID: PMC2185907.

53. Nathan C, Cohn Z. Role of oxygen-dependent mechanisms in antibody-induced lysis of tumor cells by activated macrophages. J Exp Med. 1980;152(1):198–208. doi: 10.1084/jem.152.1.198. PubMed PMID: 6995553; PMCID: PMC2185894.

54. Nathan CF, Arrick BA, Murray HW, DeSantis NM, Cohn ZA. Tumor cell anti-oxidant defenses. Inhibition of the glutathione redox cycle enhances macrophage-mediated cytolysis. J Exp Med. 1981;153(4):766–82. doi: 10.1084/jem.153.4.766. PubMed PMID: 7252413; PMCID: PMC2186135.

55. Nathan CF, Brukner LH, Silverstein SC, Cohn ZA. Extracellular cytolysis by activated macrophages and granulocytes. I. Pharmacologic triggering of effector cells and the release of hydrogen peroxide. J Exp Med. 1979;149(1):84–99.

doi: 10.1084/jem.149.1.84. PubMed PMID: 368287; PMCID: PMC2184749.

56. Nathan CF, Cohn ZA. Antitumor effects of hydrogen peroxide in vivo. J Exp Med. 1981;154(5):1539–53. doi: 10.1084/jem.154.5.1539. PubMed PMID: 7299347; PMCID: PMC2186528.

57. Nathan CF, Klebanoff SJ. Augmentation of spontaneous macrophage-mediated cytolysis by eosinophil peroxidase. J Exp Med. 1982;155(5):1291–308. doi: 10.1084/jem.155.5.1291. PubMed PMID: 6802924; PMCID: PMC2186678.

58. Nathan CF, Silverstein SC, Brukner LH, Cohn ZA. Extracellular cytolysis by activated macrophages and granulocytes. II. Hydrogen peroxide as a mediator of cytotoxicity. J Exp Med. 1979;149(1):100–13. doi: 10.1084/jem.149.1.100. PubMed PMID: 216763; PMCID: PMC2184732.

59. Szuro-Sudol A, Nathan CF. Suppression of macrophage oxidative metabolism by products of malignant and nonmalignant cells. J Exp Med. 1982;156(4):945–61. doi: 10.1084/jem.156.4.945. PubMed PMID: 7153714; PMCID: PMC2186804.

60. Srimal S, Nathan C. Purification of macrophage deactivating factor. J Exp Med. 1990;171(4):1347–61. doi: 10.1084/jem.171.4.1347. PubMed PMID: 2109038; PMCID: PMC2187851.

61. Tsunawaki S, Sporn M, Ding A, Nathan C. Deactivation of macrophages by transforming growth factor-beta. Nature. 1988;334(6179):260–2. doi: 10.1038/334260a0. PubMed PMID: 3041283.

62. Bogdan C, Vodovotz Y, Nathan C. Macrophage deactivation by interleukin 10. J Exp Med. 1991;174(6):1549–55. doi: 10.1084/jem.174.6.1549. PubMed PMID: 1744584; PMCID: PMC2119047.

63. O'Donnell-Tormey J, DeBoer CJ, Nathan CF. Resistance of human tumor cells in vitro to oxidative cytolysis. J Clin Invest. 1985;76(1):80–6. doi: 10.1172/JCI111981. PubMed PMID: 2991343; PMCID: PMC423713.

64. Szatrowski TP, Nathan CF. Production of large amounts of hydrogen peroxide by human tumor cells. Cancer Res. 1991;51(3):794–8. PubMed PMID: 1846317.

65. Shen C, Nathan C. Nonredundant antioxidant defense by multiple two-cysteine peroxiredoxins in human prostate cancer cells. Mol Med. 2002;8(2):95–102. PubMed PMID: 12080185; PMCID: PMC2039972.

66. Hibbs JB, Jr., Taintor RR, Vavrin Z. Macrophage cytotoxicity: role for L-arginine deiminase and imino nitrogen oxidation to nitrite. Science. 1987;235(4787):473–6. doi: 10.1126/science.2432665. PubMed PMID: 2432665.

67. Stuehr DJ, Kwon NS, Gross SS, Thiel BA, Levi R, Nathan CF. Synthesis of nitrogen oxides from L-arginine by macrophage cytosol: requirement for inducible and constitutive components. Biochem Biophys Res Commun. 1989;161(2): 420–6. doi: 10.1016/0006-291x(89)92615-6. PubMed PMID: 2735902.

68. Kwon NS, Nathan CF, Stuehr DJ. Reduced biopterin as a cofactor in the generation of nitrogen oxides by murine macrophages. J Biol Chem. 1989;264(34):20496–501. PubMed PMID: 2584226.

69. Tayeh MA, Marletta MA. Macrophage oxidation of L-arginine to nitric oxide, nitrite, and nitrate. Tetrahydrobiopterin is required as a cofactor. J Biol Chem. 1989;264(33):19654–8. PubMed PMID: 2584186.

70. Stuehr DJ, Cho HJ, Kwon NS, Weise MF, Nathan CF. Purification and characterization of the cytokine-induced macrophage nitric oxide synthase: an FAD- and FMN-containing flavoprotein. Proc Natl Acad Sci U S A. 1991;88(17):7773–7. doi: 10.1073/pnas.88.17.7773. PubMed PMID: 1715579; PMCID: PMC52385.

71. Xie QW, Cho HJ, Calaycay J, Mumford RA, Swiderek KM, Lee TD, Ding A, Troso T, Nathan C. Cloning and characterization of inducible nitric oxide synthase from mouse macrophages. Science. 1992;256(5054):225–8. doi: 10.1126/science.1373522. PubMed PMID: 1373522.

72. Xie QW, Kashiwabara Y, Nathan C. Role of transcription factor NF-kappa B/Rel in induction of nitric oxide synthase. J Biol Chem. 1994;269(7):4705–8. PubMed PMID: 7508926.

73. Xie QW, Nathan C. Promoter of the mouse gene encoding calcium-independent nitric oxide synthase confers inducibility by interferon-gamma and bacterial lipopolysaccharide. Trans Assoc Am Physicians. 1993;106:1–12. PubMed PMID: 7518621.

74. Bredt DS, Hwang PM, Glatt CE, Lowenstein C, Reed RR, Snyder SH. Cloned and expressed nitric oxide synthase structurally resembles cytochrome P-450 reductase. Nature. 1991;351(6329):714–8. doi: 10.1038/351714a0. PubMed PMID: 1712077.

75. Kwon NS, Stuehr DJ, Nathan CF. Inhibition of tumor cell ribonucleotide reductase by macrophage-derived nitric oxide. J Exp Med. 1991;174(4):761–7. doi: 10.1084/jem.174.4.761. PubMed PMID: 1717630; PMCID: PMC2118959.

76. Nathan C, Xie QW. Nitric oxide synthases: roles, tolls, and controls. Cell. 1994;78(6):915–8. doi: 10.1016/0092-8674(94)90266-6. PubMed PMID: 7522969.

77. Stuehr DJ, Gross SS, Sakuma I, Levi R, Nathan CF. Activated murine macrophages secrete a metabolite of arginine with the bioactivity of endothelium-derived relaxing factor and the chemical reactivity of nitric oxide. J Exp Med. 1989;169(3):1011–20. doi: 10.1084/jem.169.3.1011. PubMed PMID: 2784476; PMCID: PMC2189276.

78. Stuehr DJ, Nathan CF. Nitric oxide. A macrophage product responsible for cytostasis and respiratory inhibition in tumor target cells. J Exp Med. 1989;169(5):1543–55. doi: 10.1084/jem.169.5.1543. PubMed PMID: 2497225; PMCID: PMC2189318.

79. Cho HJ, Xie QW, Calaycay J, Mumford RA, Swiderek KM, Lee TD, Nathan C. Calmodulin is a subunit of nitric oxide synthase from macrophages. J Exp Med. 1992;176(2):599–604. doi: 10.1084/jem.176.2.599. PubMed PMID: 1380065; PMCID: PMC2119310.

80. Ruan J, Xie Q, Hutchinson N, Cho H, Wolfe GC, Nathan C. Inducible nitric oxide synthase requires both the canoni-

cal calmodulin-binding domain and additional sequences in order to bind calmodulin and produce nitric oxide in the absence of free Ca2+. J Biol Chem. 1996;271(37):22679–86. doi: 10.1074/jbc.271.37.22679. PubMed PMID: 8798440.

81. Shen Y, Zhukovskaya NL, Guo Q, Florian J, Tang WJ. Calcium-independent calmodulin binding and two-metal-ion catalytic mechanism of anthrax edema factor. EMBO J. 2005;24(5):929–41. Epub 20050217. doi: 10.1038/sj.emboj.7600574. PubMed PMID: 15719022; PMCID: PMC554124.

82. Bush LM, Abrams BH, Beall A, Johnson CC. Index case of fatal inhalational anthrax due to bioterrorism in the United States. N Engl J Med. 2001;345(22):1607–10. Epub 20011108. doi: 10.1056/NEJMoa012948. PubMed PMID: 11704685.

83. MacMicking JD, Nathan C, Hom G, Chartrain N, Fletcher DS, Trumbauer M, Stevens K, Xie QW, Sokol K, Hutchinson N, et al. Altered responses to bacterial infection and endotoxic shock in mice lacking inducible nitric oxide synthase. Cell. 1995;81(4):641–50. doi: 10.1016/0092-8674(95)90085-3. PubMed PMID: 7538909.

84. Laubach VE, Shesely EG, Smithies O, Sherman PA. Mice lacking inducible nitric oxide synthase are not resistant to lipopolysaccharide-induced death. Proc Natl Acad Sci U S A. 1995;92(23):10688–92. doi: 10.1073/pnas.92.23.10688. PubMed PMID: 7479866; PMCID: PMC40677.

85. MacMicking JD, North RJ, LaCourse R, Mudgett JS, Shah SK, Nathan CF. Identification of nitric oxide synthase as a protective locus against tuberculosis. Proc Natl Acad Sci U S A. 1997;94(10):5243–8. doi: 10.1073/pnas.94.10.5243. PubMed PMID: 9144222; PMCID: PMC24663.

86. Karupiah G, Xie QW, Buller RM, Nathan C, Duarte C, MacMicking JD. Inhibition of viral replication by interferon-gamma-induced nitric oxide synthase. Science. 1993;261(5127):1445–8. doi: 10.1126/science.7690156. PubMed PMID: 7690156.

87. Nathan C, Calingasan N, Nezezon J, Ding A, Lucia MS, La Perle K, Fuortes M, Lin M, Ehrt S, Kwon NS, Chen J, Vodo-

votz Y, Kipiani K, Beal MF. Protection from Alzheimer's-like disease in the mouse by genetic ablation of inducible nitric oxide synthase. J Exp Med. 2005;202(9):1163–9. Epub 20051031. doi: 10.1084/jem.20051529. PubMed PMID: 16260491; PMCID: PMC2213235.

88. Perreault M, Marette A. Targeted disruption of inducible nitric oxide synthase protects against obesity-linked insulin resistance in muscle. Nat Med. 2001;7(10):1138–43. doi: 10.1038/nm1001-1138. PubMed PMID: 11590438.

89. Nathan C. Is iNOS beginning to smoke? Cell. 2011;147(2): 257–8. doi: 10.1016/j.cell.2011.09.031. PubMed PMID: 22000003.

90. Seimetz M, Parajuli N, Pichl A, Veit F, Kwapiszewska G, Weisel FC, Milger K, Egemnazarov B, Turowska A, Fuchs B, Nikam S, Roth M, Sydykov A, Medebach T, Klepetko W, Jaksch P, Dumitrascu R, Garn H, Voswinckel R, Kostin S, Seeger W, Schermuly RT, Grimminger F, Ghofrani HA, Weissmann N. Inducible NOS inhibition reverses tobacco-smoke-induced emphysema and pulmonary hypertension in mice. Cell. 2011;147(2):293–305. doi: 10.1016/j.cell.2011.08.035. PubMed PMID: 22000010.

91. Shiloh MU, MacMicking JD, Nicholson S, Brause JE, Potter S, Marino M, Fang F, Dinauer M, Nathan C. Phenotype of mice and macrophages deficient in both phagocyte oxidase and inducible nitric oxide synthase. Immunity. 1999;10(1):29–38. doi: 10.1016/s1074-7613(00)80004-7. PubMed PMID: 10023768.

92. Drutman SB, Mansouri D, Mahdaviani SA, Neehus AL, Hum D, Bryk R, Hernandez N, Belkaya S, Rapaport F, Bigio B, Fisch R, Rahman M, Khan T, Al Ali F, Marjani M, Mansouri N, Lorenzo-Diaz L, Emile JF, Marr N, Jouanguy E, Bustamante J, Abel L, Boisson-Dupuis S, Beziat V, Nathan C, Casanova JL. Fatal Cytomegalovirus Infection in an Adult with Inherited NOS2 Deficiency. N Engl J Med. 2020;382(5):437–45. doi: 10.1056/NEJMoa1910640. PubMed PMID: 31995689; PMCID: PMC7063989.

93. Chung AW, Anand K, Anselme AC, Chan AA, Gupta N, Venta LA, Schwartz MR, Qian W, Xu Y, Zhang L, Kuhn J,

Patel T, Rodriguez AA, Belcheva A, Darcourt J, Ensor J, Bernicker E, Pan PY, Chen SH, Lee DJ, Niravath PA, Chang JC. A phase 1/2 clinical trial of the nitric oxide synthase inhibitor L-NMMA and taxane for treating chemoresistant triple-negative breast cancer. Sci Transl Med. 2021;13(624):eabj5070. Epub 20211215. doi: 10.1126/scitranslmed.abj5070. PubMed PMID: 34910551.

94. Bronte V, Kasic T, Gri G, Gallana K, Borsellino G, Marigo I, Battistini L, Iafrate M, Prayer-Galetti T, Pagano F, Viola A. Boosting antitumor responses of T lymphocytes infiltrating human prostate cancers. J Exp Med. 2005;201(8):1257–68. Epub 20050411. doi: 10.1084/jem.20042028. PubMed PMID: 15824085; PMCID: PMC2213151.

95. Nathan C. Kunkel Lecture: Fundamental immunodeficiency and its correction. J Exp Med. 2017;214(8):2175–91. Epub 20170712. doi: 10.1084/jem.20170637. PubMed PMID: 28701368; PMCID: PMC5551579.

96. Calderon F, Fairlamb AH, Strange M, Williams P, Nathan CF. Surmounting structural barriers to tackle endemic infectious diseases. J Exp Med. 2021;218(9). Epub 20210819. doi: 10.1084/jem.20211418. PubMed PMID: 34410327; PMCID: PMC8383816.

97. Nathan C. Aligning pharmaceutical innovation with medical need. Nat Med. 2007;13(3):304–8. doi: 10.1038/nm0307-304. PubMed PMID: 17342145.

98. Nathan C. Taming tuberculosis: a challenge for science and society. Cell Host Microbe. 2009;5(3):220–4. doi: 10.1016/j.chom.2009.02.004. PubMed PMID: 19286131.

99. Nathan C. Making space for anti-infective drug discovery. Cell Host Microbe. 2011;9(5):343–8. doi: 10.1016/j.chom.2011.04.013. PubMed PMID: 21575903.

100. Nathan C. Fresh approaches to anti-infective therapies. Sci Transl Med. 2012;4(140):140sr2. doi: 10.1126/scitranslmed.3003081. PubMed PMID: 22745440; PMCID: PMC3712344.

101. Nathan C. Resisting antimicrobial resistance. Nat Rev Microbiol. 2020;18(5):259–60. doi: 10.1038/s41579-020-0348-5. PubMed PMID: 32300248.

102. Nathan C, corresponding author. Authors listed alphabetically. Aldridge BB, Barros-Aguirre D, Barry CE, 3rd, Bates RH, Berthel SJ, Boshoff HI, Chibale K, Chu XJ, Cooper CB, Dartois V, Duncan K, Fotouhi N, Gusovsky F, Hipskind PA, Kempf DJ, Lelievre J, Lenaerts AJ, McNamara CW, Mizrahi V, Nathan C, Olsen DB, Parish T, Petrassi HM, Pym A, Rhee KY, Robertson GT, Rock JM, Rubin EJ, Russell B, Russell DG, Sacchettini JC, Schnappinger D, Schrimpf M, Upton AM, Warner P, Wyatt PG, Yuan Y. The Tuberculosis Drug Accelerator at year 10: what have we learned? Nat Med. 2021;27(8):1333-7. doi: 10.1038/s41591-021-01442-2. PubMed PMID: 34226736.

103. Nathan C, Cars O. Antibiotic resistance—problems, progress, and prospects. N Engl J Med. 2014;371(19):1761-3. Epub 20141001. doi: 10.1056/NEJMp1408040. PubMed PMID: 25271470.

104. Nathan C, Goldberg FM. Outlook: the profit problem in antibiotic R&D. Nat Rev Drug Discov. 2005;4(11):887-91. doi: 10.1038/nrd1878. PubMed PMID: 16247440.

105. Schrader SM, Vaubourgeix J, Nathan C. Biology of antimicrobial resistance and approaches to combat it. Sci Transl Med. 2020;12(549). doi: 10.1126/scitranslmed.aaz6992. PubMed PMID: 32581135; PMCID: PMC8177555.

106. Ding AH, Porteu F, Sanchez E, Nathan CF. Shared actions of endotoxin and taxol on TNF receptors and TNF release. Science. 1990;248(4953):370-2. doi: 10.1126/science.1970196. PubMed PMID: 1970196.

Carl Nathan, MD, has been chair of the Department of Microbiology and Immunology at Weill Cornell Medicine for twenty-five years. He graduated from Harvard Medical School and trained in internal medicine and oncology at Massachusetts General Hospital, the National Cancer Institute, and Yale. He joined the faculty at Rockefeller University before moving to Weill Cornell Medicine as Stanton Griffis Distinguished Professor of Medicine, where he is now the R. A. Rees Pritchett Professor of Microbiology. He is a director of the Tres Cantos Open Lab Foundation and the Sanders Tri-Institutional Therapeutics Discovery Institute, co-chairs the editorial board of the *Journal of Experimental Medicine*, and serves on the boards of the *Proceedings of the National Academy of Sciences* and *Science Translational Medicine*. He received the Robert Koch Prize and the Sanofi-Institut Pasteur Senior International Scientist Award and has been elected to the American Academy of Microbiology, the American Academy of Arts and Sciences, the National Academy of Medicine, and the National Academy of Sciences. *An Arrow's Arc* is his first book for a general audience. He lives in Larchmont, New York.